Exiled *to* Motown

A Community History of
Japanese Americans in Detroit

Detroit JACL History Project Committee

Exiled to Motown

©2003-2023
Detroit JACL History Project Committee

Distributed by University of Washington Press
Fourth Printing, January 2024

Editors: Mary Kamidoi, Scott Kurashige, Toshi Shimoura
Design & typesetting: Ian Tadashi Moore
Calligraphy [p. 11]: Michael Nagara

Some of the photos were originally organized for the purpose of a photo show "From Manzanar to Motor City" coordinated by Valerie Yoshimura & Bill Shay in 1995. The photos were collected by the following families and individuals:

- From the Chapter's files [JACL, ChapterAct, President, & JACLAct]
- The Miyao family [Miyao]
- The Ishino family [Ishino]
- The Fujioka family [Fujioka]
- The Takemoto family [Takemoto]
- The Okubo family [Okubo]
- The Yamazaki family [Yamazaki]
- The Bassett family [Bassett]
- The Yamamoto family [Yamamoto]
- The Shimoura family [Shimoura]
- The Hirozawas [Hirozawa]
- American Citizens of Justice [ACJ]
- Mary Kamidoi [Kamidoi]
- Maryann Mahaffey [Mahaffey]
- Valerie Yoshimura [Yoshimura]
- Grace Hedemann (p.31)

This book is being published

in respect and admiration

of the Issei who

endured struggles and hardships

with determination to make a

better life for their children

6

Editor's Introduction

Scott Kurashige

This book comprises the most sustained effort to document and publish the history of Japanese Americans in the Detroit area. It is the collective product of a community of people who came together to tell their stories and to preserve this history for future generations. Working on it has been a labor of love, driven primarily by many volunteer hours of thought and labor from the members of the Detroit JACL History Project Committee. While creating this book was not easy or quick, its meandering path into existence could be seen as a reflection of the long and difficult journey it seeks to tell about. It was made possible by the efforts of JACL leaders and others, who have served as guardians of their personal, family, and community histories for many decades. I was fortunate to meet many of these folks after moving from California to Michigan in 2000 and attending annual JACL picnics and luncheons.

From my scholarly research, I knew that there had not been any books specifically focused on Japanese American history in Detroit, and I was grateful to learn as much as I could by hearing elders talk story. These conversations led to the formation of a project committee that included Mary Ishino, Mary Kamidoi, Emily Lawsin, Miyo and Ann O'Neill, Asae Shichi, Nob Shimokochi, Toshi Shimoura, Soh Suzuki, and myself. We generally met at the O'Neill or Shimoura residences, where Ann and Toshi frequently nourished us with delicious refreshments. Through our gatherings, we discussed potential interview subjects and themes, examined archival photographs and documents, and conducted workshops so that all committee members—regardless of their age, occupation, or educational background—could participate in the process of interviewing and research. Sadly, two of our original committee members are no longer with us: Iwao Ishino, whose story appears in this book; and Maryann Mahaffey, a long-time Detroit JACL board member for whom a short tribute has been provided by Hy Dooha. Unfortunately, we were unable to conduct an interview with Mahaffey, but her illustrious career as a social worker and member/president of the Detroit City Council has been well chronicled. We were also saddened by the loss of interview subjects Walter Haruo Miyao, Miyoko Inouye Bassett, Nob Shimokochi, Art Morey, James Okubo, Eiko Takemoto, Max Koga, Frank Kuwahara, and Frank Ebisuya *(Mr. Kado)*.

By late February 2015, we had completed all substantial elements of the book and were finalizing the design and layout. However, our joy at the prospect of finally seeing this longstanding project fruition came to an abrupt halt when we were stunned and devastated by the passing of Toshi Shimoura. Toshi was a pillar of our history project, the Detroit JACL chapter, and the local Japanese American community. She received well-deserved honors from local groups and the Government of Japan. At the same time, Toshi worked tirelessly beyond the spotlight to advocate for justice, promote education, and spread cultural awareness through her community organizing, ikebana practice, and commitment to maintain the archives of the Detroit JACL and many other entities. While the unique role she played in documenting and preserving Japanese American history in Detroit becomes immediately apparent in the chapters bearing her name, her fingerprints can be found throughout the entirety of the manuscript.

I feel blessed to have garnered so many new insights through my participation in this project. This was critical as I sought to adapt to living in a new place but particularly so as I began teaching Asian American history courses at the University of Michigan. At that time, I could only incorporate snippets of local history here and there. We should always be aware, however, that history is far more than what has been recorded in books. Just because peoples' stories and experiences cannot be found on the written page does not mean that they are not an important part of history. Indeed, the "winners" in history often times have a vested self-interest in sanitizing history to make those with power and wealth look favorable while marginalizing or rendering invisible those who struggled, sacrificed, and suffered.

Recovering the histories of those on the margins is essential to developing a full understanding of our past and how we got to this present. Moreover, we vitally need the perspectives of those who have confronted racism and oppression to enhance American democracy. From our firsthand experience and our reflections on that of others, Japanese Americans know the imperfections of American democracy and know that it is only through constant vigilance that the pursuit of democracy can be sustained.

Since Asian American Studies arose during the social movements of the late 1960s, scholars and students in the field have recognized the tremendous value of oral histories. The movements for ethnic studies erupted to redress the distortions and omissions prevalent within textbooks and curricula. Within mainstream education and public discourse, scant reference was made to the experience of Japanese or any Asians in America, except perhaps a couple sentences about Chinese Americans building the railroads. (Sadly, many college students tell me today this was still largely the case for them growing up.) If Japanese American internment was mentioned, it was most likely to be portrayed—if not as a justified act of military necessity—as an unfortunate incident rather than the product of decades of systematic discrimination and

Below the surface stereotyping of the Motor City... lies a rich history that is too often overlooked.

racial prejudice ingrained within the fabric of American economics, politics, and culture. In the aftermath of World War II, Nisei and Sansei were expected to be grateful that they could now live in relative freedom within American society, so long as they accepted the role of "model minority."

Oral histories helped to break this silence and reveal the depths of Japanese and Asian American history. As more of these stories surfaced, the entire self-image of the Japanese American community began to change. In turn, the public's view of Japanese American history began to change, as well. Testimonies of no longer silent Nisei became central to the redress and reparations movement, creating a new sense of empowerment while establishing a public record of a shameful period of official, state-sanctioned racism and deprivation. Not only did the voices for redress prod the federal government to issue a formal admission of wrongdoing and apology, they helped to set a new standard for civil liberties in the United States by popularizing the notion of "never again" to mass internment.

For the *Sansei* and *Yonsei* generations, oral histories became part of a broader mission to rediscover the past. Many of us—in large measure because of language and generational barriers—never came close to learning the histories of our immigrant ancestors. While there were some outspoken *Nisei* making waves, most of us grew up learning very little about the concentration camp experiences, failing to appreciate how much the government had terrorized, imprisoned, and threatened our parents and grandparents. State repression effectively threw a blanket of silence over much of the Japanese American community for a generation after World War II. Like many of my peers growing up, I heard a brief reference here and there to my mother being in "camp" many years ago but never understood why what I presumed to be a summer camp experience lasted several years or more. In the absence of learning the truth about history, the study of history was a dry, meaningless exercise. This might sound strange, given that I now work as a history professor. But these two phenomena are not unrelated. Like many Japanese Americans, I was indoctrinated to believe that our ancestors never did anything important enough to count as history. Discovering the significance of their histories and understanding the political implications of their silencing drove me to learn more about and eventually research and write about the histories of Japanese Americans and other people of color.

As a place, Detroit has also been much maligned and marginalized. Below the surface stereotyping of the Motor City, however, lies a rich history that is too often overlooked. Asian American Studies encompasses two perspectives that are especially vital to consider in Detroit. First, whereas it is easy to feel as if one is alone in Detroit and faced with a uniquely grim predicament, Asian American Studies pushes us to think about the global and international dimensions of the Japanese and Asian American experience, which encompass war, migration, and the quests for citizenship and belonging. Second, whereas Detroit history is often linked to the intractable problems of black/white segregation and inequality, Asian American Studies has by necessity pushed us to see our experiences within a multiracial frame of analysis. Thus, the histories in this book speak to audiences beyond those specifically interested in Japanese Americans.

At the same time, we should appreciate why Detroit is crucial to Asian American Studies. Though there are more Asians within the metropolitan region, only a fraction of these are ethnic Japanese. However, these figures should prompt us not to dismiss Detroit as being of little relevance because numbers alone never dictate significance in history. Otherwise, why would we ever devote such a disproportionately large emphasis in U.S. history to that small group of Europeans who lived in Jamestown or Plymouth and comprised but a microscopic proportion of the North American population of the early 1600s? I see our ventures into history as efforts to make sense of an evolutionary process, one that is connected to a present reality that we are trying to comprehend and to a future ideal that we are trying to create.

As such, the stories in this book provide new insights into the past, present, and future of Japanese Americans, Detroit, and America. They reflect a diverse range of experiences, primarily revolving around *Nisei* who resettled to the Detroit area during and after World War II but also incorporating histories of those who settled in Detroit before the war and shin *Issei* who migrated from Japan after the war. The personal narratives recounted in this book provide a sense of what it was like to be detained by the U.S. government during World War II, as well as what it was like to grow up overseas in Japan and its occupied territories during that same period. In all cases, we get a sense of the trials and tribulations, the opportunities and hardships as our subjects—usually in the early years of adulthood—embarked on new careers and new lives in Detroit and surrounding areas as distant as Ann Arbor and East Lansing. These histories provide an important counterpoint to the existing literature on Japanese Americans that has been centered on Hawaii and the West Coast.

For instance, there may be no better place than Detroit to examine how and why Japanese Americans encountered and embraced the modern industrial world. From interviewing Toshi Shimoura, I learned how her Issei father-in-law in the early 1910s knocked on the door of Henry Ford's house in Highland Park and became the first Issei to work in the Detroit auto industry. Imagine the chutzpah of this immigrant pioneer to believe that a Japanese might have something to contribute to the making of cars. Though he was not the first Issei in Detroit,

Detroit again emerged as a beacon of Japanese American progress, this time for the most educated and ambitious Nisei, those who insisted they had a contribution to make to American culture.

Mr. Shimoura set off a mini-chain migration of Issei who came here to be a part of what was considered by many to be one of humanity's most exciting developments, a new technological system and organizational structure whose potential seemed limitless. If you look closely in the Detroit Institute of the Arts at Diego Rivera's landmark mural of the Ford assembly line (or just buy the poster), you can see Issei engineer James Hirata standing within a sea of mostly white, black, and Mexican auto workers.

The majority of our subjects were part of the Nisei migration from the West Coast to the Midwest, directly or indirectly prompted by the mass uprooting of the Japanese American community during the war. During the period of exclusion from the West Coast, Detroit again emerged as a beacon of Japanese American progress, this time for the most educated and ambitious Nisei, those who insisted they had a contribution to make to American culture. Many prominent Nisei stayed for just a brief period, including Fred Korematsu and John Okada, whose novel *No-No Boy* was written in postwar Detroit, at a time when the city was at the forefront of shaping patterns of urban racial integration in the United States. But the seven-decade endurance of the Detroit JACL is testimony to those who stayed and were part of a broader Japanese American community that has left its mark upon the region. The most prominent evidence of this in built form is what I jokingly call Detroit's *Little Tokyo*, the intersection of Woodward and Jefferson in the heart of Downtown Detroit, where a Minoru Yamasaki skyscraper faces an Isamu Noguchi plaza and sculpture. Noguchi came as an invited guest of the Cranbrook Institute's Eero Saarinen, but Yamasaki made his home and established his architectural firm in metro Detroit. It was in his local office, of course, where much of the plans were drawn for the World Trade Center, a building he created to symbolize the twin ideals of "global trade and global peace." That this contradictory unity has unwound so tragically should only make studying the dialectics of Nisei modernism in Detroit even more intriguing.

Of course, almost every student of Asian American history has learned something about Detroit because of the prevalence of the Justice for Vincent Chin movement. Most know how the movement originating from Detroit helped spur a second wave of pan-Asian identification and activism; how it almost single-handedly put concepts like "Japan-bashing" and "anti-Asian violence" into our vocabulary; and also, in my opinion, how it helped give rise to the type of thinking about law and justice that came to be known as critical race theory. We can also see how

the Vincent Chin case represented the Chinese notion of crisis as both danger and opportunity. De-industrialization and economic decline killed a sense of community and stability that was tied to the factory system, thus heightening fear, xenophobia, and racial scapegoating. But it also brought Japanese Americans together with other Asians and other communities of color to form coalitions for empowerment and social justice. While some of our interviews address this critical historical moment, there is still much to be learned about how the Vincent Chin case served as a defining moment for the Sansei generation. Demonstrating the intergenerational links within history, Jim Shimoura, grandson of the Issei pioneer who knocked on Henry Ford's door, was a leading attorney and activist in the Justice for Vincent Chin movement. This should give us just a small sense of how important it will be for a future project to record Sansei histories in the region.

As we ponder the future of Japanese Americans in Detroit, it is hard to ignore the fact that we are releasing this book at a time when the Japanese American community in this part of the country is small and scattered. To our knowledge, our small JACL chapter is the last organized grouping of Nisei, Sansei, or Yonsei in metropolitan Detroit. In part, this can be traced back to the concerted efforts of the War Relocation Authority and the federal government to promote the systematic dispersal of Japanese Americans into midwestern communities. This was an imperative shaped both by a concern that whites would more readily accept Nisei in isolation from their ethnic cohort and by a paternalistic desire to assimilate Nisei into the mainstream white American culture the authorities considered superior. But it is also the product of the efforts by Japanese Americans and their allies to overcome discrimination and achieve a new level of acceptance in American society. American-born Japanese now live all across the region, some identifying with new clusters of Japanese immigrants and businesses in places like Novi but most going on living primarily among non-Japanese persons. Many Sansei and Yonsei have moved to suburban areas or further away, and they have often intermarried—in most cases with members of the white majority but some living within Detroit found partners within the city's majority African-American community. While Detroit's Japanese America community may feel less cohesive, it is also more diverse geographically, generationally, and ethnically. In this way, the significance of this book is heightened by the fact that Japanese American history is now part of the fabric of more communities and part of the heritage of many more families, including those of children born at the intersection of multiple ethnicities and nationalities.

We can rest assured that while we cannot foresee exactly what the future holds for Japanese Americans in Detroit, we know that the lessons of Japanese American history must be shared with all. We hope you will treasure the stories collected in this volume. They are the product of our collective efforts, though we do not claim that they tell a complete history and encourage others to go beyond what we have been able to accomplish.

In the end, these are not stories of victimhood; they are testament to survival and resilience. As such, we hope and expect that they will continue to be remembered and passed on for many generations to come.

The Detroit JACL

Fifty Plus Years of History

The history of the JACL in Detroit began in the early 1940's when over 50 Japanese Americans relocated here from the War Relocation Camps of Manzanar, Heart Mountain, Topaz, Minidoka, Rohwer, Jerome, Tule Lake, Poston, Amache, and Gila River. These new arrivals felt strongly that they must create a local JACL chapter to fulfill their unique needs as a small, displaced group in a new community. The Detroit JACL officially became a chapter on June 17, 1946 with Peter Fujioka as its first President. Meetings and activities were held at the old International Institute located in a YWCA building on East Grand Boulevard in Detroit. It should be noted that the International Institute has befriended Detroit JACL on many occasions throughout our history.

To fulfill the needs of the early post-war community and to increase the chapter's membership, a multitude of social and informational activities were held. These included picnics, dinners, dances, lectures, other special programs, and monthly newsletters. Japanese movies were shown at the International Institute to entertain the Issei (first generation Japanese Americans). The early Detroit JACLers worked hard in support of the National JACL organization, especially in its efforts to gain fair play and equal rights for Americans of Japanese ancestry.

Early Years

In the early 1950's, Detroit JACL embarked on a spirited letter writing campaign to Congress urging passage of the Walter-McCarran Omnibus Immigration and Naturalization

Bill. Thanks in part, to the support of JACLers everywhere, this landmark bill was passed, enabling many Issei to become U.S. citizens, many in their sixties and seventies. As a reward for their determined efforts to gain U.S. citizenship, the chapter sponsored a tour of the Nation's Capital. The chapter celebrated its tenth Anniversary in 1956, with former National JACL President Dr. Thomas Yatabe as speaker, and Governor Williams and Senator Potter as honored guests. Other important chapter events in the 1950's included presentation of the National JACL Distinguished Achievement Award to Detroit architect and JACLer Minoru Yamasaki; *ondo* and *judo* demonstrations at the Michigan State Fair; cooperation with the Anti-Defamation League of the B'nai B'rith and other groups to improve community relations; hosting Kei-Ro-Kai to honor the Issei; and extensive participation in the Detroit-Windsor International Freedom Festival.

In addition, the Detroit chapter became beneficiary of a $10,000 Educational Loan Fund from the estate of Detroit JACLer Taizo Kokubo. A second fund of $20,000 was used later to build the Japanese Room at Wayne State University. The Loan Fund is still a source of loans and scholarships for college students today.

The crowning achievement of Detroit JACL

in the 1960's was its work in hosting the 18th Biennial National JACL Convention in Detroit in 1964. Other important events included hosting the MDYC-MDC Convention in 1968; conducting the convention's oratorical contest for young adults ("What Evacuation Means to Me"), with winner Karen Mayeda of Detroit; co-sponsoring, with the International Institute, the six part cultural series "Aspects of Contemporary Japanese Culture"; starting the Detroit JACL Blood Bank; forming the JAY's Club; working on the *Issei History Project.*

The early 1970's found Detroit JACL extensively involved in the Detroit Far Eastern Festivals. Working with other ethnic groups, the Detroit chapter played a major role in the formation and operation of these festivals for nearly ten years. The chapter gained many friends from its close association with the other far eastern ethnic groups in the festival, laying the groundwork for later multi-ethnic associations such as the American Citizens for Justice. Other events of the 1970's included hosting Japanese cooking and language classes; sponsoring a Japan trip; hosting the EDC-MDC Convention; presentation of a Detroit JACL Friendship Plaque to Toyota City by Frank Kuwahara; formation of an education committee and a building committee; starting a bowling league; and start of discussions concerning

We wish to pay tribute to all of our dedicated JACL members and friends, many now deceased, whose dedication to the JACL ideals and dream of creating "Better Americans in a Greater America" have bequeathed to us such a rich and inspiring legacy for the future.

Redress. Plans for a Japanese Room at Wayne State University were also initiated in the late 1970's.

The early 1980's saw the completion of the Japanese Room at WSU. Manoogian Hall (Detroit JACLer Hideo Fujii was the architect) at a cost of $42,750 — with most of the money provided by the Kokubo Fund. The Japanese Room was used often in the 1980's for JACL functions. Also in the 1980's, the Detroit chapter became heavily involved in the formation and support of the American Citizens for Justice, a multi-ethnic group originally formed to fight for justice in the case involving the murder of Vincent Chin. Today, the ACJ still fights racial discrimination on behalf of Asian-Americans. For his work in making the National JACL Organization and the Asian American communities throughout the United States aware of the need for vigilance in the area of racial justice, Jim Shimoura received the 1984 JACLer of the Biennium Award in Hawaii. Redress was another area of extensive JACL involvement and the Redress Commission hearing in Chicago was well attended by Detroit JACLers; several of our members testified at the hearing. Other important events of the 1980's included our participation in the Old World Market; hosting a Redress Fund Raiser Recognitions Dinner; supporting Detroit JACLer Dr. Kaz Mayeda in his successful bid for National JACL V.P. in charge of Public Affairs; and hosting a reception for the Muromachi Period Ink Paintings Exhibition at the Detroit Institute of Arts.

In the early 1990's, following a long and arduous struggle by the National JACL and other organizations, Civil Liberties Act of 1988 was passed, authorizing $20,000 redress payments to former internees of the WWII War Relocation Centers. The Detroit JACL then embarked on a letterwriting campaign to members of Congress requesting support for the full and timely distribution of the funds necessary for the redress payments. An exciting event of a different nature was Detroit JACL's co-sponsorship of the very successful Executive Order 9066 Exhibit with the Central Methodist Church of Detroit. Also in the early 1990's, Detroit JACLer Ernie Otani created the Speakers' Bureau, providing a forum for educating school and church groups about the WWII internment experiences of Japanese-Americans.

Notable Achievements

Other significant chapter events in the 1990's include participation in the U.S. Veterans 50th Anniversary Pearl Harbor flag raising ceremony in Frankenmuth, Michigan; the honoring of Japanese-American WWII veterans at the 1994 Installation Dinner; the Kobe-Osaka Earthquake Fund and MDC Flood Relief fund drives; the achievement of 100% of our assigned National JACL Legacy Fund Drive quota (donations totaling $85,620); the arrival of Mr. Enoki, Detroit's first Japanese Consul General; the selection of Lansing, Michigan resident and JACLer Herbert Yamanishi as the National Director of JACL; the illustrious Installation Dinner guest speakers of the 1990's — Ken Kashiwahara, Karen Narasaki, Capt. Bruce Yamashita, and George Takei; and the securing of a $2500 Legacy Fund grant by Detroit JACL to help fund Detroit JACL's Fiftieth Anniversary Historic Exhibition.

In 1996, our efforts were concentrated on the events marking the 50th Anniversary of the Detroit JACL Chapter, especially the exhibit of JACL's historic photos and artifacts entitled "From Manzanar to Motor city. A History of Michigan's Japanese American Community." This exhibit premiered Feb. 9, 1996 at the Detroit Historical Museum, accompanied by a Japanese cultural program including *ikebana*, *shodo*, *koto*, tea ceremony, and films. Concluding the 50th Anniversary Celebration will be our Installation Dinner Dance featuring George Takei of *Star Trek* fame as guest speaker.

During the 2000's, the Detroit Chapter continued on with the Speakers Bureau. We participated in the rights of any Civil Rights problems and have supported any bills that were processed by other chapters as well as the National JACL.

The Chapter hosted the Midwest District Council Meeting on October 10, 11 & 12, 2003 and participated in the Day of Remembrance at the University of Michigan in Ann Arbor, Michigan in February, 2004.

We wish to pay tribute to all of our dedicated JACL members and friends, many now deceased, whose dedication to the JACL ideals and dream of creating "Better Americans in a Greater America" have bequeathed to us such a rich and inspiring legacy for the future.

Detroit JACL Past Presidents

Founded June 7, 1946

1946-48	Peter Fujioka		**1980**	Toshi Shimoura
1949	Roy Kaneko		**1981**	Elaine Prout
1950	Mark Kondo		**1982**	Ron Yee
1951	Wallace Kagawa		**1983**	Elaine Prout
1952	Shig Ouchi		**1984**	Kaz Mayeda
1953	Minoru Togasaki		**1985**	Gerry Shimoura
1954	Kenneth Miyoshi		**1986**	Elaine Prout
1955	Sadao Kimoto		**1987**	Dave Maxon
1956	Miyo O'Neill		**1988**	Lisa Archer (Young)
1957	Yoshio Kasai		**1989-90**	Scott Yamazaki
1958	Charles Yata		**1991**	Kaz Mayeda
1959	Walter Miyao		**1992-93**	Ernie Otani
1960	Frank Watanabe		**1994-95**	John Takemoto
1961	Peter Fujioka		**1996-98**	Valerie Yoshimura Shay
1962	Wallace Kagawa		**1999-**	
1963	Minoru Togasaki		**2001**	Scott Yamazaki
1964	Jim Shimoura		**2002**	—
1965	Walter Miyao		**2003-04**	Toshi Shimoura
1966	William Adair			
1967	Art Morey			
1968	Mary Kamidoi			
1969	George Ishimaru			
1970	Kaz Mayeda			
1971	William Okamoto			
1972	Scott Yamazaki			
1973	Elaine Akagi			
1974	Minoru Togasaki *			
1975-76	Sadao Kimoto *			
1977	Jan Ishii			
1978	Kaz Mayeda			
1979	Kaz Mayeda / Elaine Prout			

After **2004**, there were no future elections, and the the Detroit JACL was carried on by Mary Kamidoi and Toshi Shimoura.

Detroit Jays

Junior JACL Past Presidents

1957	Jan Ishii	**1967**	JoAnn Shimamura Myers
1958	Carolee Matsumoto	**1968**	Constance Abe Parsons
1959	Shirley Satoh Shimamura	**1969**	Susanne Morey
1960	Elaine Takemoto Yang	**1970**	Gerald Shimoura
1961	Geraldine Ouchi Miyoshi	**1971**	Gerald Shimoura
1962	Marilyn Nagano Schlief	**1972**	Nancy Nakayama
1963	Gary Otsuji	**1973**	Art Teshima
1964	Gary Otsuji	**1974**	Paul Teshima
1965	Elaine Akagi Prout	**1975**	Keri Fujii — Karen Yoshikawa
1966	Elaine Akagi Prout	**1976**	Susan Tagami Matsui

Detroit Bowling League

In the early 1940's when the Japanese Americans came to Detroit, the younger men felt that there was a need for sports activities. They had baseball teams with members from Detroit and Ann Arbor. The Detroiters formed a bowling league and as the years went by, they moved on with life and married and they felt that they needed to assume their responsibilities as parents and the league was dissolved.

Then, in the late 1970's and part of the 1980's, the Detroit JACL started a bowling league with ten teams. This league was not only for Japanese Americans but anyone who wanted to join us, mostly friends of the JACL'ers.

Again, as the bowlers felt they had family responsibilities, they wanted to spend more time with their children and grand-children. As the years went by, the league gradually lost more and more bowlers causing the league to be dissolved.

JACL sponsored Bowling League, 1972
[ChaptAct]

Detroit Buddhist Church

During World War II many thousands of Japanese relocated to Detroit, a large metropolitan area that had no previous Japanese community, church, or anything Japanese. Reverend Shawshew Sakow, then at Poston Relocation Center, felt that there was a great need for a Buddhist Church in Detroit. In April of 1945, he arrived in Detroit with his family.

The first Sakow home in Detroit was an apartment on East Vernor Avenue owned by Suejiro Kosai formerly of Tacoma, Washington. After months of hunting, he found a three-story commercial building at 3915 Trumbull which he leased. The first floor had at one time served as a funeral parlor so there was a large room appropriate for Buddhist gatherings. The upper floors contained rooms which the family used for living quarters. Unused space was rented out to augment the family income.

In June, 1945, under the chairmanship of Toshio Yoshida, Reverend Sakow and the nucleus group: James Kubota, Mrs. Yoshiko Tanaka, Hideko Harada, Mitsuko Tanaka, Masajiro Ishioka, Mrs. Sakamoto, Suekichi Koga, Suejiro Kosai and the following whose first names are not available: Ito, Haneda and Butsumyo, met to organize the Detroit Buddhist Church. The first service of the was held on July 1, 1945. About 60 persons were in attendance.

In 1948, the lease had expired on the Trumbull address and Reverend Sakow found another place where the group could meet. This time it was a large house at 1604 Putnam Street. By this time, the size of the group had diminished due to members returning to the West Coast, making it necessary for Reverend Sakow to seek employment to support his family. He worked in a bakery by night and served as a minister during the day until 1958 when he was assigned to the Salinas Buddhist Church.

Mrs. Sakow and daughter maintained residence at the Putnam address for a time, and the church services were continued by Reverend Masami Nakagaki, a student at the University of Michigan in Ann Arbor, a college town approximately thirty five miles west of Detroit. When Mrs. Sakow and family vacated the Putnam address in 1959, the services were held in the home of Isao Sunamoto at 5191 Lumley Street.

Reverend Nakagaki was instrumental in getting the group of twenty families to elect a president and to start assessing membership dues so the Church would have an operating fund. Edward Shiroma was elected president and remained in this capacity until his untimely death in September 1965. Harry Kadoguchi was elected to fill the vacancy, but in January 1967, he too suddenly passed away. He was the last elected leader. Mrs. Masa Kosai, senior advisor, and Isao Sunamoto, treasurer, had been arranging the monthly services and acting as liaison to the Buddhist Churches of America Headquarters in San Francisco, California.

In 1959, after completing a year of study, Reverend Nakagaki was called to a new post in California, leaving Detroit without a minster. Reverend Gyodo Kono of the Midwest Buddhist Temple of Chicago was contacted to serve the needs of the Church, and he conducted services regularly until the end of 1967. At the request of Reverend Kono, the Cleveland Buddhist Church was contacted and with their assistance and Reverend Kono, the Church as able to continue regular services.

Reverend Zuikei Taniguchi of the Cleveland Buddhist Church commuted regularly once a month from 1968 until he left to fill a position at the Church in Oakland, California in 1971. Reverend Kyogyo Miura, while serving the group in Cleveland, came to conduct services whenever requested. Eventually, like all the others, he was transferred to another location. Since the departure of Reverend Miura, we were assigned to the new incoming minister Reverend Koshin Ogui of the Cleveland Church until he was transferred to the Midwest Buddhist Temple in Chicago. After his departure, Reverend Yukei Ashikaga of the Chicago Buddhist Temple came to serve our church.

In the late 1970s, under the leadership of president Tom Tagami, the Buddhist Church decided to participate in the Detroit Festivals at the various shopping centers. A group of Far Eastern countries decided to join forces with the Detroit JACL and became the Far Eastern Festivals of Detroit. After the Detroit JACL decided not to participate any longer, the Buddhist Church, though small in number, felt this would be a good fundraiser for the Church and not depend solely on membership dues to finance our Church. After years of participating, we felt that if the City of Detroit was going to dictate to the participants regarding the companies that had to be hired for security, insurance, etc. we would no longer be a part of the Far Eastern Festivals.

In the early 1980s, The Far Eastern Festivals came to a close for the Buddhist Church as well as all the other countries due to the high costs that were imposed on us before entering the Festivals.

From the 1990s, Reverend Yukei Ashikaga served the Detroit Buddhist Church until the middle of 2004. With members passing on, relocating and the members becoming older and not able to attend the services we were forced to dissolve the church. All church funds were donated to the Chicago Buddhist Temple with Reverend Ashikaga stating he will be available for any services requested by the Detroit church members.

For the remaining members, it was a sad closure, since they all felt that there is no gift as great as the gift of Dharma.

The Motor City Golf Club

Art Matsumura

The Motor City Gold Club was formed in October 1947 at Warren Valley Golf Course. Some early members were very prominent in our community; Peter Fujioka, Roy Kaneko, George Kubo, James Shimoura, Sr., and Minoru Togasaki. The membership consisted of over fifty at its height to the present number of sixteen. The golfing season starts in April and the last tournament is held in the last week in September or the first Sunday in October. The Club plays approximately three Sundays a month or sixteen to eighteen tournaments a year. Each tournament required eight or nine tee-off times to the present three or four.

The format of each tournament is *Stroke Play:* the player with the lowest net score being the winner of that tournament. *Match Play* was incorporated with the weekly tournament. Thirty-two players qualified during the three or four early rounds. Each player eliminated one another until one remaining player becomes the champion. At the end of the season, a major tournament is held. This consists of two rounds of golf (thirty six holes) played in one day. This format was revised due to scheduling difficulties—the first change was eighteen holes on two successive Sundays to three best rounds played on five successive Sundays. In the formative years of the Motor City Golf Club, Detroiters met friends in Cleveland and Clevelanders traveled to Detroit for a friendly game of golf. This led to the formulation of the Inter-City Tournament. This consisted of a team (twelve players) who qualified on two designated tournaments to represent the Club.

Lloyd and Paul Joichi talked to their brother Roland and his club member in Chicago to form the Tri-City Tournament (Cleveland, Chicago and Detroit). This consisted of a team (ten players) who qualified on four designated tournaments to represent the Club. The Inter-City was held in June and the Tri-City was held on Labor Day weekend. Each Tournament was held at a different city on a rotating basis. In each tournament one member from each club met head to head. A point was given to the winning player and the team with the most points was the winning team.

In the mid-70s, an event was created to meet and golf with the Japanese Nationals who were here on job-related assignments. Kaz Mayeda handled this tournament. This was an individual stroke play format. Sadly the special events, Inter-City, Tri-City, and Japan Society Tournaments were dissolved when the entire club had difficulty fielding a team. Today, the weekly tournament combined with Match Play and major tournaments are held with sixteen members. Also, on Labor Day weekend a special two-day club tournament is held.

Maryann Mahaffey
Photo © Grace Hedemann

Maryann Mahaffey

Significant Contributor to the
Japanese American Community

Hy Dooha

Maryann and Kids
at the Barrack, c. 1943
[Mahaffey]

Maryann Mahaffey is a champion of civil liberties and human rights, particularly as it relates to the Japanese American and Asian Pacific American communities. From her position as the long-standing President of the Detroit City Council, she has been able to exert considerable influence in supporting causes and issues concerning minorities and the disenfranchised. Her special interest and concern for Japanese Americans stems from the time she spent in the Poston Relocation Center as a college student, as a social worker.

Maryann was shocked by the imprisonment of men, women, and children, never even accused of wrongdoing but simply due to their Japanese ancestry, in what she called "concentration camps." She formed life-long friendships with girls she met there. Her first boyfriend was a Japanese American soldier who was visiting family in the camp. She joined the JACL and was a member since the 1940s and an active Board member of the Detroit Chapter.

She was a great supporter of the JACL. She first joined JACL in 1946 by becoming a member of the Seattle Chapter, and later became involved with the Detroit Chapter when she moved to Michigan. The following is a partial list of the activities that Maryann Mahaffey has been involved in over the years that have impacted upon the JACL, the Japanese American and Asian Pacific American communities in Detroit, as well as nationally.

- Where there was a Congressional hearing on redress, she testified in a Chicago hearing in support of redress.

- Social worker at the Poston Relocation Camp

- Long time member of the Detroit JACL

- Board member for the JACL Chapter, and Chair of the Human Rights and Community Advocacy Committee

- Outspoken advocate in support of the Redress campaign

- Appeared before the Commission on Wartime Relocation and Internment of Civilians, giving testimony in Chicago.

- Authored numerous resolutions on behalf of JACL and the Asian Pacific American community before the Detroit City Council

- Gave countless number of speeches and lectures to public groups and in the classroom to recount her experiences and to tell the Evacuation story.

- Spoke on numerous occasions to the Peace Center Group in Detroit.

- Advocate and supporter of the Vincent Chin case.

- Passionate believer in nuclear disarmament, giving public addresses on the Hiroshima/Nagasaki anniversary every year.

- Provided invaluable assistance in providing the support of the City of Detroit for the Far Eastern Festival annually.

- Founding member of the National Women's Political Caucus.

- Former national officer of the National Association of Social Workers.

- Gave great public support of ethnic intimidation laws, including the Michigan Ethnic Intimidation statute.

- At great political risk to her career, she criticized the UAW and the automobile companies for Japan-bashing in the 1980's.

View of Temple
[Miyao]

Scott Yamazaki

Biography and Ancestral History
April 14, 2003

My history begins with my grandparents on my father's side, who came to the United States from Tokyo, Japan in 1906, by way of Hawaii. My grandfather, Zenzi (Thomas) Yamazaki, was recruited to work the pineapple fields in Hawaii in 1904, and my grandmother (Fuyu Yamazaki) accompanied him. They left Hawaii in 1906 for farm work in Fresno, California, which seemed to be more promising, financially. In 1910 they moved to Helper, Utah to work in the coal mines, which, again, seemed to offer better pay. Their first child, Tosuke (my dad), was born in 1912 in Denver, Colorado, where they took their first vacation in their married life. Two subsequent children, Sanzo and Yuta, were born in Price, Utah. While working the coal mines, my grandmother began to earn money by supplying lunches for the miners. From this venture they saved enough money to buy an old restaurant in an abandoned building in Price, Utah, turning it into the Utah Café. Through years of hard work they earned enough to convert the remainder of the building into a small hotel, the Utah Hotel. They ran the Utah Café and Hotel up until the time of my grandfather's death in 1961. My grandmother lived with her daughter, Yuta, before moving into a nursing home shortly before her death in 1970. Because they were living in Price, Utah at the time of Pearl Harbor, my grandparents were not put into internment camps, although my grandfather (Zenzi Yamazaki) was imprisoned for 3 months at Missoula, Montana because he was suspected of being a Japanese collaborator because he was a regular contributor the *Rafu Shimpo* newspaper.

My grandparents on my mother's side, Saburo Tsuda and his wife, Etsuko, came to the United States in 1902 to work the farms around Sacramento, California. My mother, Lorraine Nobuko Tsuda, was the second of four children and was born in 1910 in Sacramento.

In 1920, they opened a small grocery and dry goods store in Dos Palos, California, which they operated until Saburo Tsuda's death in 1936. My grandmother, Etsuko, and two of her children (excluding my mother, Lorraine), as well as her grandchildren, were interned at Jerome and Rohwer Relocation Camps in Arkansas during WWII. Following the war, my grandmother lived alternately with us and with her other daughter, Flora Tsuda, until her death in 1959, in Washington, D.C.

My father, Tosuke Yamazaki, was born in Denver, Colorado in 1912 and spent his boyhood in Price, Utah, where his father and mother operated the Utah Café and Utah Hotel. He entered the School of Journalism at the University of Missouri in 1929 and graduated in 1933. After graduation, he worked as a reporter for the *Rafu Shimpo* Newspaper until moving to Tokyo, Japan in 1936, to become a reporter and feature writer for the Domei News Service.

My mother, Lorraine Tsuda, was born in Sacramento, California in 1910 and grew up in Dos Palos, California on a small farm. After graduation from high school, she worked at her father's dry goods store in Dos Palos until 1934 when she moved to Japan to take a job as secretary for the Stanley Steamship Company's branch office in Tokyo. She met my father at the American Club in Tokyo in 1936 and they married in 1937. I was born in Tokyo (their first child) in November, 1938.

As a reporter in Japan for the Domei News Service, my father was sent to China in 1937 to cover the Japanese invasion of the south coast of China. After reporting on the war in China from 1937 to 1939, he became discouraged by the brutal nature of the war, especially with the atrocities committed by Japanese soldiers against the Chinese population, and he requested reassignment back to Japan. Life in Tokyo, however, was just as discouraging to him because of the rise of militarism in Japan and the increased anti-western sentiment. He strongly believed that Japan's policies would directly lead to a fatal war with the United States and that it would be extremely dangerous to continue living in Japan. Therefore, he requested a transfer out of Japan to the New York bureau of the Domei News Service, which was granted in late 1940. We arrived in New York City in January, 1941 and lived in a small apartment in Manhattan until January, 1942, when we were told by FBI that we must leave the East Coast and relocate to the interior of the United States. The New York bureau of the Domei News Service was shut down shortly after Pearl Harbor in December 1941.

In January 1942 we moved to Price, Utah and lived for four months with my grandparents in the living quarters above the Utah Café, where my dad worked in the kitchen and waited tables. Shortly after arriving in Utah, my sister, Ellen, was born in Price, in late January 1942. In June 1942 my dad was hired as a picker and farm hand by an Italian-American farm owner named Rafael Sheretta, who operated a large strawberry, chicken and sheep farm in Utah, just south of Salt Lake City. We lived in a converted chicken coop, which my mother decorated on the inside with wallpaper. After the farming season ended, my father found work at a coal mine just north of Helper, Utah in the Was atch mountain range, where he worked as a coal miner until March 1943.

In early 1943, the U.S. Government and the U.S. Military began to selectively offer jobs to Japanese Americans who they believed could help the United States in its war effort against the Axis powers. In March, 1943 my mother and father were offered jobs by the F.B.I.S. (Federal Bureau of Investigative Services). a branch of the Office of War Information, to work as language translators of Japanese shortwave radio broadcasts emanating from Tokyo. So, from Utah, we moved to Denver, Colorado in March, 1943, where my parents attended a foreign language training school and indoctrination center for three months. Following Japanese language school, we moved to Washington, D.C. where my parents worked for the FBI as Japanese language translators. In August 1945, at the end of WWII, my dad went to

Life in Tokyo, however, was just as discouraging to him because of the rise of militarism in Japan and the increased anti-western sentiment.

Tokyo, Japan to work as a foreign language interpreter and reporter for General MacArthur's administration during the Japanese war crimes trials. At the conclusion of the war crimes trials in the spring of 1947, my dad returned to Washington, D.C. and both he and my mother went to work for Mike Masaoka, the National Director of JACL. Lorraine was employed as Mike's secretary, and Tosuke was the dispatch writer for information that Mike took with him every day to Capitol Hill. Their work for Mike is mentioned in Mike's autobiography entitled *They Call Me Moses Masaoka*.

In 1950, my mother left her JACL job and became the first

social secretary of the Japanese Embassy when it reopened following WWII. My dad also left his job with Mike Masaoka and opened SpeeDee-Que Duplicating Services, a high-speed mimeograph and multilith office, with George Kushida as his partner. He worked at SpeeDee-Que until 1967, when he sold his half of the business to Melvin Smith, a longtime employee, and moved to Gardena, California. My mother retired from the Japanese Embassy at the same time and moved with my dad to Gardena. In California, they soon grew tired of retirement and both of my parents hired into Security Pacific Bank in Los Angeles, where they continued to work for another ten years, my mother as a secretary and my dad in the duplicating service department. Soon after their second retirement, my mother died of a heart attack in 1983. Two years later, my dad married June Fujita, a woman who had worked with him at the FBI in Washington, D.C. during WWII, and they settled on her farm in Fresno, California. My dad went into a nursing home in 1989 suffering from Parkinson's disease and diabetes and died from associated complications in 1990.

Although born in Tokyo in November, 1938, I have no memories of Japan. My earliest memories are of the time I spent on the Sheretta's farm and at the cabin and creek next to the coal mine in Utah. My formal education began in kindergarten in 1944 in Washington, D.C., at Benjamin Stoddard Elementary School. Soon after arriving in Washington, we moved into the U.S. Government Housing Project at Tunlaw Terrace in Washington, D.C. My aunt and uncle, Flora and Barry Tsuda, and their two children were released early from Rohwer Relocation Camp in Arkansas in 1944 and moved to Washington where they obtained jobs with the United States Printing Office. As soon as they obtained housing at Tunlaw Terrace, they notified Lorraine (Flora's sister) and we were able to rent the housing unit next door to theirs. Upon finishing 9th grade at Gordon Junior High School, we moved from Tunlaw Terrace to Chevy Chase, in the northwest section of Washington, in 1953, and I graduated from Woodrow Wilson High School there in 1956. As a boy, I was active in many activities, but was only an average student academically. I joined Boy Scout Troop 3 in Georgetown when I was eleven and was awarded my Eagle Scout Badge when I was sixteen.

Most of my extracurricular time was spent in scouting, fishing, and playing baseball, although I also sang in the choir at Georgetown Presbyterian Church for several years and played the cornet in my high school's marching band and orchestra. After graduating from Woodrow Wilson in 1956, I went to Gardena, California for six months to work at Kobata Brothers Plant Nursery and then to Price, Utah for six months to work for my grandparents at the Utah Café. Upon returning home to Washington, D.C. in 1957, I entered Georgetown University and graduated in 1961 with a B.S. degree in biology. After working at Microbiological Institutes in Bethesda, Maryland for two years, I moved to Detroit, Michigan to pursue a master's degree in genetics. This turned out to be more of a challenge than I could master, and I left the program at Wayne State University in 1964 and went to work for Ford Motor Company as a automobile parts scheduling analyst in May, 1964. While singing in the choir at St. Martha's Episcopal Church in Detroit, I met Barbara Goodison and we were married September 5, 1964. We have three grown children now. Mark, the oldest, was born in 1965 and works for Ford Motor Company as a research engineer. He is married to the former Tracy Harry and they live in Canton, Michigan. Our second child, Gordon, was born in 1972 and works for Jacques Whitford Environmental Company in Fredericton, New Brunswick, where he is employed as a geologist. He is married to the former Katy Haralampides, who teaches civil engineering at the University of New Brunswick in Fredericton, and they live just south of Fredericton.

Our third child, Jennifer, was born in 1974 and works for Conrad Insurance Agency in Canton. She lives in Westland, but will soon be living in Kalamazoo, Michigan and entering the master's degree program in anthropology at Western Michigan University.

My wife, Barbara, was born in Detroit, Michigan. Her parents were born in England and came to the United States in 1918. Barbara graduated from Fordson High School in Dearborn and worked at Manufacturer's Bank in Detroit, at K-Mart and at United Home Health Services before retiring in 1999. I worked at Ford Motor Company for thirty-five years in several departments, the last job serving as an assembly plant production scheduling analyst in Dearborn, and I retired in 1999. For the first ten years of our marriage we lived in Detroit and Dearborn, but moved to Canton in 1977 and have lived in Canton ever since. Although we met at St. Martha's Episcopal Church in Detroit and sang in the choir there for twenty-five years, we left there in 1995 to become members of Rosedale Gardens Presbyterian Church, where we also sing in the choir. We also are members of the Plymouth Community Chorus and have been singing with the Chorus since 1977. We became Master Gardeners after we retired and are on the Landscape Committee at our church. We are members of the Detroit Chapter JACL, and I have served as chapter president for three terms.

Since retiring, our long-range plans are to do more traveling, and to that end we have been on three Caribbean cruises and a trip to England, and next summer we plan to buy a travel trailer and explore the western part of the United States.

Scott Yamazaki & Family
[Yamazaki]

Calendar Club Picnic, c. 1968
[JACL]

Art Morey

My father was born in 1869 in Kokawa, Wakayamaken, Japan and my mother was born in 1886 in Arame, Japan which was the next town south of Kokawa. My father Saburo was the last of six children of Bungaro and Fujiino Mori.

My parents were farmers in Japan and when they passed away, the eldest son usually came into all the holdings of the family. Since the other siblings would not receive anything, they moved on to another life. One such option was to marry as a *yoshi* (marrying into a family with no sons) to carry on their name to avoid giving it back to the government or would be inducted into the army.

My father left Japan in the 1880's to the Pacific Northwest. While passing through immigration, he protested the way the customs man was writing his name and was told not to tell him how to do his job and this is the reason my name has an odd spelling instead of *Mori*. Dad did any type of work available, lumberjacking, farming, etc. Worked his way South to Los Angeles and decided to open a General Store on Alameda street.

After getting on his feet, he thought he was successful enough to return to Japan to find a bride. My mom remembers arriving and taking a train to California, stopping in Oakland—across from San Francisco that was in ruins from the earthquake of 1906. After arriving in Los Angeles they feared a [tuberculosis] scare and moved to Monrovia. My sister Shizue was born in 1908. Kiyo was born in 1911 in South Pasadena. George was born in 1913 in Los Angeles. Roy died at infancy around 1916, Miyo was born in 1918, and I was born in 1921.

My parents rented a bungalow in 1928 on Halldale which had two bedrooms downstairs and one bedroom upstairs, kitchen, living room and a porch. The water closet was near the ceiling and flushed by pulling a chain. All of the kids attended Vermont Avenue Grammar School and then [went on] to James A. Foshay Junior High and high school at Los Angeles High School. Shizue attended University of California and graduated in 1928; Kiyo graduated in 1931 from UCLA at Westwood; George attended UCLA for two years and transferred to University of California graduating in 1934 in Foreign Trade. Miyo attended University of California and graduated in 1940, and I attended UCLA in pre-engineering for two years in 1940, and transferred to Cal Berkeley. After attending high school, attending UCLA was much more harder due to the competition and also being we were all commuting to and from. The atmosphere was different for the Japanese students because we were from all different parts of California. All in all, college life on the campus was fun although studying was intense. Social life on campus was meager because most of it was done during lunch hours. I played football though 1 was of small stature in high school. This life came to a sudden end on December 7, 1941 around 10:00 A.M.

Japanese town was about one-half mile away with Fujisaka Drugs, Furuya Market, Yasaki Cleaners, a restaurant jeweler, and other small shops. Our social center was the Methodist church. We all had a very busy schedule; going to school, Japanese school, Boy Scout meetings, as well as *kendo* classes. Through all of these activities I have met friends stretching nearly sixty years. Our only means of transportation was to bicycle where we went. I recall only one incident during our bicycling days that was nothing crucial and kept going. We pedaled to airports and [a] mine field, which is now Los Angeles International. Many plants were located in and around the area producing war planes. I enjoyed watching all the activities, but it was not a safe thing to do.

1940. President Roosevelt embargoes oil and scrap iron shipments to Japan.

1941. A so-called "peace mission" was sent to Washington to negotiate with the Secretary of State stating a deadline of December 6, 1941 at 11:30 P.M. and sent to President Roosevelt, and his response was this means war. *December 7th* Japan attacks Pearl Harbor.

I returned home the night before curfew was declared and stayed home until evacuation, taking only what we can carry. I had my suitcase and my mother's suitcase. We boarded buses and were transported to Santa Anita Assembly Center where we were fingerprinted and assigned our living quarters. The parking lot was covered with rows of dark tarpaper covered barracks. All facilities for the internees were communal type: showers, mess halls, lavatory stall, washing facilities, etc.

I got a job at the mess hall as a time-keeper which was a simple job. My shift was from 5 A.M. to 5 P.M. and this was to check the cooks in and out. All timekeepers had to take turns on the night shift from 9 P.M. to 5 A.M. Cooks would cook themselves other dishes that were not served to the internees and it was great, since we were able to be in on the deal.

Eventually, we were shipped to Amache Relocation Center in Colorado. We boarded old trains. For the older Issei the seats were not the ideal setup. Upon arrival we were unloaded and transported into camp. I lived in camp about a week and some of my friends and I decided to leave camp to work on sugar beet farms, topping sugar beet.

Later with the shortage of labor, the government allowed farmers to pick up intern-ees to do the harvesting of their crops, and five of us went. We were transported by trucks to Vineland: that was ten miles east of Pueblo. Our job was to pull the sugar beets out of the ground and put the beets into stacks with the help of a tractor that edged the ground loose to make it easier to pull beets out of the ground. We spent Thanksgiving in Pueblo and went back to camp. After returning to camp I joined a motor pool run by a man that was five by five and didn't get along too well.

Next, we went to the railroads for coal shoveling used for heating purposes in camp. Three loads were expected in the morning from each crew. We roomed together and decided to load six loads at once into hoppers

and then boxcars. Truck loads of coal were shipped to the mess halls, etc. Regardless of what we had to do, we felt the air was much fresher on the outside.

Eventually, in the spring of 1943, we were given clearance to leave camp for school or to work. I was relocated to attend school at Washington University, which brought me to St. Louis, Missouri.

Met a man named Mr. Taylor who was a stockbroker with Paul Brown Company who employed me as a houseboy and chauffeur. Also, I worked for his father-in-law who was living with them and was a former Vice President of the Missouri Pacific Railroad. It was great getting to drive and have use of all of his cars.

Met Yo Matsumoto who was attending Washington University and after graduating decided to come to Detroit and stayed. Yo got a job at the Detroit Water Department and finally worked for Mercury Engineering Company; that was not connected to the Ford Motor Company. Being at the bottom of the scale, I finally progressed to the upper part of the scale and worked with Tom Tanase. I tried to help Tom, who was an architect with the Mechanical Engineering process. Another job was subcontracted to Chrysler working with bits and pieces for the Atomic Energy Plant for about a year and went into an architec-tural firm.

I Married Kay Ouchi at Central Methodist Church. Lived in a duplex on the east Side of Detroit and Jeff was born in 1946; Carol in 1949 and Susan in 1951.

During this time the Mr. and Mrs. Club was formed, and we became involved with some of the early settlers. Eventually, when the children became older we joined the Detroit JACL. June

Otsuji introduced us to the fundraisers that were being held by the JACL Old World Market with the Detroit International Institute selling wares of different types and Japanese food on the open riverfront. After participating for several years, the International Institute decided they wanted a larger margin of profits and so the JACL decided to go to shopping centers, such as Northland, Westland and Southgate, selling our Japanese wares. Soon after, the City of Detroit decided to build booths underground at the Hart Plaza for all nationalities to rent booths and have continuous festivals. Our festival was called the *Far Eastern Festival,* and as the years went by, the city started to raise the price of booths and insurance was outrageous so the Detroit JACL decided they could no longer participate. The Detroit Buddhist Church decided to take the slot from the JACL and after participating for three years, the city decided that we must hire all security wards from the city, [so] the Church no longer was able to participate because of the high costs.

After joining the Detroit JACL as a member, I was nominated as Vice President and then to President of the chapter. At this time, we decided that a Junior JACL was needed since the children were all in their teens. My wife Kay volunteered to become an advisor along with other parents with children ready for a Junior JACL.

In 1945, I went to work for Giffels &. Rossetti, an architectural firm in Detroit. Worked alongside of Karl Nomura and Toki Aoki. When the war ended we were out into the mechanical division for two years, mostly doing work for Ford Motor Company. Three years later, I went to M & S Engineering mainly doing work on bumpers and specifications for smoke stacks near the UN Building. Then, I went on to work for Savior & Grivas doing structural jobs—smoke stacks and worked with various types of individuals until 1989. In 1989 I switched companies to work for a friend of mine, John Halmstrom for a few years and then moved on to Colasanti, Inc., and retired in 2001.

All three children attended elementary schools in Detroit. Jeff attended McKenzie High and Wayne State University and received his BA. Volunteered for the Air Force for three years and was sent to Korea for two years. Upon returning home, he was sent to K.l. Sawyer base in upper Michigan until his discharge.

Carol graduated from Michigan State University and worked for Governor John Engler when he was a representative in the Legislature. Served first term as secretary of the Michigan Senate. Carol is married to James Viventi who has a private practice in Okemos. MI.

Susan attended Michigan State University and decided she would like to go to Arcosanti in Arizona where they were building arches with earthforms at nearby Cortis Junction. Relocated to Alaska returned to Eugene, Oregon and Colorado Spring, Colorado and back to Michigan. She is married to Gordon Melms whose father was in advertising for the Jacobson Company.

Opposite, left to right:
Nob Shimokochi, Ann O'Neill, Miyo O'Neill, Asae Shichi,
Toshi Shimoura, Mary Kamidoi

Reflections of
Detroit JACL Leaders

*interviewed by Scott Kurashige & Emily Lawsin
in Dearborn, Michigan.
July 13, 2003*

The following is a conversation with Mary Kamidoi, Miyo O'Neill, and Toshi Shimoura, three current and former leaders of the Detroit chapter of the Japanese American Citizens League.

SK: *Could you start by introducing yourselves?*

TS: My name is Toshi Shimoura.

MK: And I'm Mary Kamidoi. A long, long time JACLer.

MO: And I'm Miyo O'Neill and I am a long, long, long, long, time JACL member.

SK: *How did you come to live in the Detroit area.*

TS: My initial introduction to Michigan was going to the university here, Michigan State, from camp. I was in Topaz and Michigan State was the only college in Michigan that was open to people from the camps. I moved to East Lansing in 1944 to attend Michigan State University. When the war ended my family in Topaz, Utah moved back to California to their former home. I continued at MSU for 2 years and moved to Berkeley, CA to continue at the University of California getting a BA in Microbiology. My first job was Director of a Public Health laboratory covering Sutter and Yuba county in California. I moved back to Berkeley & worked at the UC Laboratory. In 1952 I married James Shimoura whom I had met at Michigan State University. James was a native Detroiter, so we moved back to Michigan.

MK: Oh, I am here in the Detroit area because when the camp let out in rural Arkansas, my parents couldn't go back to California because we had no home left there. So we went to Missouri first. After Missouri, we moved out to Flint because my brothers had some very good friends from the service that lived in Flint and they said they would take care of us when we came to Flint. While I was going to business school in Flint, I was recruited to work at Ford Motor Company by a Ford human resources people that came to the school and recruited me. And that's how I ended out in Detroit.

MO: I was a follower. My brother had gone to Washington University in St. Louis. And I followed him out there while he was finishing his bachelor's degree. Then he came to Michigan to go to Cranbrook School of Architecture. And he got his master's degree there and I followed him over here. Then in June, 1946…

MK: You were at Wayne State.

MO: I was at Wayne State, and as I was working there, I started as a secretary at the graduate school at Wayne State University. Then, by the time I stopped working, I was an assistant to the dean at the graduate school. In the meantime, I was going to the graduate school at Wayne State also.

MK: Then you met Bill.

MO: Oh yes! See how old I am? At my sister-in-law's wedding. Bill was the best man. And I was the bridesmaid. Then he called me and we started going out. And we had so much in common. It was really something. Then there went my schooling. And in 1956 was the first President and I don't remember after that who was president. Yo Kasai. That was 1957.

MK: And I did that one year. (1968)

SK: *How did you all first get involved in the Detroit JACL?*

MK: Well I got involved because when I first hit the town of Detroit, I don't know how this lady got my name, but she called and she did tell me who she was calling for. And I owed it to the Detroit Chapter to join and be a member when I told her, "I have to think about it and I have to call you back." When I hung up, I said to myself, *Who in the world is this woman calling me, telling me what I have to do?* That is how I joined [the] JACL. *[group laughing]* It was Mary O' Neill.

SK: *When was that?*

MK: 1953.

TS: We started the group when Mike Masaoka—and who was the other person that came? Were you there? I remember, Misako. They came and they wanted to start a chapter here in Detroit. And a lot of us were enthusiastic, but there was some people who didn't like JACL. We had a little problem then, but somehow we got organized thanks to the International Institute and the director of the International Institute. They were very helpful and we started our chapter at the International Institute on West Grand Boulevard, and it went on from there.

TS: And that time, I think both my sister-in-law, Helen Teshima and Katherine Sugimoto, were very active in JACL.

MK: They were on the board. They're the ones that introduced me to JACL at the time. That's when I met Katie.

TS: Miyo mentioned that some people were afraid to form a group because we were told to disperse as we left the camp. And to form an organization was something we were kind of leery about. Then there were

Japanese Americans who were anti-JACL because they felt that JACL sold them down the river. That they did not put up enough of an argument against the evacuation.

MK: We have some here in Detroit that I know of.

TS: When I first started working in Marysville—that was in the Sacramento valley when I first got out of school—there were a number of those valley people that were against [the] JACL. They said, "JACL didn't do anything for us when the war started. They sold us down the river and we have nothing to do with them."

MO: So the bad rap still exists. Which is very unfortunate. That's right. If it hadn't been for Mike Masaoka and Mas Satow and George Inagaki who were—

MK: They were in their late 20s. What were they doing to these people who criticized? They have no room to criticize unless they came up with something definite.

TS: My family. My older brother was just seventeen at the time. My parents had no citizenship rights because they couldn't get their citizenship. My older brother was not of voting age. So we really didn't have any leg to stand on to oppose evacuation. So my parents accepted it as something that was inevitable.

MO: JACL was the only organization that the government knew that was organized. Unfortunately, they were all very young. When Mike Masaoka said, if the government comes to you and says, "We are going to evacuate you and if you are not going to go, we will do it with the bayonet and the gun." And they said, "What are you gonna do to my people?" You either go or you will be forced to go. I don't think many people knew what they were up against.

MK: I have that question asked all the time when I go speak at colleges. "Why didn't you people stop the evacuation?" So it's like we really didn't have a leg to stand on because we didn't have enough resources and people that were really educated to do anything about it. But if you speak to these students, they are really shocked to hear that we did not stop it. I said in those days, there wasn't much we can do about it. If the government says "you're going," you're going.

TS: We were teenagers. The average age of the Nisei was something like eighteen, and they were not of voting age and also their parents were not citizens. They felt they didn't have anything to stand on citizenship-wise.

MK: I had a friend of mine, from the condo. She saw some documentary on TV and she had got around to ask me if I knew anything about it because she knew I was Japanese American. And I said, "Yes, I do." She said, "Well, that's terrible." She said, "From what I saw on TV, why did you let the government do this to you?" I said, "If the government came and told you to jump off that ledge, I'd think you would jump off that ledge, right?" She said, "Well, yeah, I guess I would. I can't fight the government, you know." And I said that was our situation. There's nothing you could do to stop it. So she felt very bad about it, knowing me—Japanese American. She was very apologetic to me. She said, "I wasn't alive in those days, but I want to apologize about the people that caused it." I said I appreciated it, but you know it's really something that really stays with you. Because she often asks me—she said, "When you go out in public, do you have any people say anything?" And I said, "Well, we had a man who lived here who constantly called me a foreigner, so I straightened him out one day." So I said, "I get that all the time. Of course a lot of people when they are approached by people who want to be nasty, they usually just walk away." I said, "I am not that type of person." Unless you explain to them and give them the story, they are never educated about what happened. That's the reason I go the schools and I speak because these kids, especially the middle school kids, are very grateful.

TS: It's not the kids. It's the teachers too. They are unaware. I think it was Mercy. There were seven history teachers, and they asked me to come and speak, so I did. And when I started to talk about the evacuation, one teacher said, "What country are we talking about?" So there really was no knowledge of evacuation. I think the press also suppressed a lot of it. The only press whom I think I am most grateful for are the Quakers. They made it a point to discuss evacuation and also take a stand on it. There was the Friends group that helped evacuees like myself in camp get out and go to different colleges. They're the ones that really helped us get into colleges. So I have great respect for the Friends group.

MK: All our gifts came from the Quakers, they always had the children's names on the packages, so I made three real nice pen pals. Unfortunately three of them are gone now. But for long time, I was pen pals with them because I appreciated getting a little gift even if it was a pencil when you are in camp. They are the ones that sent us the gifts for Christmas and Easter. And all the kids there, you know, they enjoyed all the gifts, but I guess none of them felt like they wanted to write to the people that gave the gifts because they always put their name and address in there. So when I started writing to them, we became long-time friends through correspondence until they passed on.

TS: I had a pen pal from Ohio and she would never say—she was Amish—she was one or the other. That was a good experience for me in camp.

SK: *So I know all three of you had lived on the West Coast prior to the war. Could you say what your experience was coming to Detroit in that era of 1940s compared to what you experienced before?*

TS: When evacuation warnings came out, we were told we couldn't leave the house after a certain hour. We were held at stay-in. We couldn't travel more than typically five miles beyond our house and so forth. This was actually before the evacuation. This was after Pearl Harbor. I was, believe it or not, I was embarrassed. I was ashamed that I was not like everybody else. It's hard to mention it now, but at that time I was embarrassed. But once the evacuation orders came out, we were told not to go to school anymore: "Stay home until you are told where to assemble." So we quit going to school, and we waited until the ordinance came so they can tell us what to take and where to assemble and how to conduct ourselves. So that was a very demoralizing experience for a young high school child I was. The fact that you are cut off from all your friends. Nowadays, you pick up the cell phone and you can chitchat back and forth. In those days, we didn't have that privilege. We felt really cut out.

When we first assembled in south of San Francisco, a very good friend of ours came to visit us. He was on one side of the fence, and we were on the other side of the fence and all we could do was stick our fingers through and say hello to shake hands. I'll never forget that. This gentleman stood there and he was about to cry. He just couldn't imagine that this was America. I remember that very, very vividly.

MK: Well my story is just about the same as Toshi's. Before the war or after the war broke out, we were on curfew also. And one incidence I had never forgotten is two of my brothers had gone into town to go to a movie, and when they came out of the movie, one of my brothers was kidnapped. This is why when I hear about children being kidnapped, it really hits home to me. For about three nights, we all stayed up waiting for him to come home. We didn't dare leave our homes. We waited and on the fourth day, these Filipinos had pulled into our driveway and left him. We had always asked him what had happened in the three days, but he would never even talk about it. So being I'm the most inquisitive in the family, every now and then we'd be talking about something else, I'd drop it to him and he would never mention what happened. So even to this day, my sisters and brothers wonder what had happened to him that he had never told us about. And I said, "More than likely they had threatened him not to say anything." But

it seemed as though he had changed. His characteristic had changed a little. So my mother used to always say to us when she'd hear us asking him, "Don't ask him any more because something has happened and he doesn't want to talk about it." So he took it to his grave. He would never tell us anything about it. So every time I read or hear about children being kidnapped or adult being abducted I do feel that. I feel for them because I have gone through that. And I can remember while we were waiting for him, I never shook so much in my life. I'm surprised I even stop shaking. Back then we were so scared. So I just sat around shaking. I can remember myself: I was just scared to death. I can remember how I shook. Sometimes, even today my older sister will remind me how she used to do this, "Stop shaking! Stop Shaking!" Then I'd stop for a minute but then I was just scared. So I have never forgotten that.

TS: The thing that scared us as a family was when the FBI came in to go through the house. My father had burned—everything that had been written in Japanese—he burned, the dictionary even. He said, "We have to protect ourselves." He burnt every thing that was written in Japanese. He used to write music. To this day, I regret. I wished I had kept some of that. But the FBI came in and they went through every book and that was it. They didn't come back or say call back or anything like that. So we didn't know what—I guess they found nothing of value in the house, that's why.

MO: Let's see, Before the war came, I was in Sacramento College and they start talking about evacuating us. My brother was at the University of California, so I was the only one and my sister had tuberculosis so I was the only one that was left. So I had to quit school to try to clean up everything for the evacuation. The thing I remember most is, on the day we were supposed to leave for the evacuation camp, we were going out the front door. And I happened to look back and my mother had tears coming down her face and that's really hard. And we went to the assembly center and I remember when we walked in there was grass growing from our floor because it had just built it over a field. And mother looked at that and she said, you know, "My goodness." But we made it through, and we ended up at Tule Lake, which became a no-no camp after we left.

TS: My mother was like that too. She was very stark. She never cried, but the first time I ever saw her cry was in Tanforan, where were given a bag to stuff our mattress with straw. She saw my little sister who was about eight or nine, and she had asthma and she's sneezing and coughing and she was stuffing the mattress and my mother started crying. I never saw her break down like that. I don't think the Isseis did ever have a breakdown.

MK: They were very straight. They were very strong people. They never showed any weakness, but there were a few times when she did break down.

TS: I think it was harder on us looking at our parents.

MO: Exactly! And their reaction. Yeah! How they reacted to the situation.

EL: *How long did you stay in Tule Lake?*

MO: Hmm. Let me see. When did that "yes-yes, no-no" come out? It was soon after we had taken that questionnaire, and then we went out and joined my brother when he went to Washington University. He had educational—what do you call it?—deferment. He wasn't drafted, and he was lucky he went to school to finish his master's degree.

SK: *What kind of process did you have to go through in order to leave camp?*

MO: For one thing, we had that questionnaire and which twenty-seven and twenty-eight had to be "yes-yes" instead of "no-no." That's why they called it "no-no." When you served in the United States Army, you were called and you said yes.

MO: The hardest thing to answer was when you give up your allegiance to the emperor of Japan, you would look like a person without a country. The U.S. wouldn't accept you, and you were supposed to give up allegiance all the way around. That was very difficult to produce an answer.

I think a lot of the people that said "no-no" really didn't understand the question. They really didn't because I've read different cases of people that have been to Tule Lake and people that had been sent to Japan and back. And they had made the statement in their write-ups that they did not understand the question. Our families too. Some said "yes"—the other said "no." So then they split. I think from fear, they really didn't know what was going on. So they really couldn't read the question properly and read it and answer properly.

EL: *So what were you saying about leaving? How did you get to leave? What was the process that you went through?*

MO: I was going out to join my brother in St. Louis, Missouri, and I went to apply to a business school there. I was accepted and I was there until my brother moved over to Cranbrook School of Architecture to get his master's degree and then I followed him here. At that time, my father was a "no-no" person, so my mother and the rest of the family were in Minidoka, and they came out and joined us in Michigan. And my father, we didn't know for a long time where he was, but he was very influenced by the *Kibei* who were very much against, you know—but somehow he must have said he's willing to stay here because he ended up in California. When we found out he was out there, a family friend said to us that our father was out there, "Why don't you come after him because he's all alone?" So I went out there, and I brought him home.

SK: *So your father was in Tule Lake while you went to Minidoka with the rest of the family?*

MO: Yes, what a stubborn man! *[laughs]* I think he was very influenced by these other people who said, "Why should we do anything for this country when they throw us in the concentration camp?" I think that influenced a lot of people, oh yes!

EL: *So can you describe to us, what was your first day like in Michigan?*

MO: We went to the relocation office which was owned by—who was it? Then they sent me to stay at the hostel run by Reverend Satow, who is a minister, and his wife. I found a room there. Of course my brother was here, and he came to pick me up at the railroad station where we came. So you know, I found a place for my parents to stay, and they all came out and we stayed in Detroit. Then Mother bought a home in Northwest Detroit. We were there for the longest time until I got married. Everyone else got married, you know, after I. And then I lived in Birmingham most of my life.

EL: *What was the area that you were living in like when you first arrived?*

MO: When we first arrived the area was all white. I don't remember it being you know—I remember there were, I was just lucky for one thing. My mother used to tell me I was a Yankee. I was the Yankee of the family. I was just that way. I don't know why, but I did things differently from my brother and sister. My sister was very Japanese and she was very demure. We both had to learn tea ceremony. That's when we were in junior high school. I remember my mother said that was what the ladies are supposed to learn how to do. We learn to keep our man. And my brother was like a Ken doll and, you know, manly things. We had a strange family. Then we bought a house in Northwest Detroit, and we moved out there. When we were moving out there, the real estate people went around asking if it was all right for a Japanese family to live in your area and evidently they said "it's fine" because we moved there.

EL: *Where did you live in Northwest?*

MO: On Braille Street. Evergreen and Five Mile.

TS: In Southfield, it started to build there. There was a man who was a farmer, who had that whole area, and he went to the neighbors and asked if it was alright if the Japanese family came and stayed. He was very much aware of Japanese because he had the Checker Cab Company in Detroit, and there were lot of Japanese who were working the Checker Cab Company. And he used the word "Nisei," and I said, "How did you learn that word?" He said, "Oh I got a number of Japanese working at my shop repairing cars."

TS: They were drivers! There were Checker Cab drivers and Gilbert Kurihara was a mechanic. He was a mechanic there. That's why it was very interesting to see, you know, this farmer out in Southfield *[laughs]* who knew about a Nisei. That was a big plus for us, you know.

MK: When I came to Detroit — since I lived in the Rouge area — I really wanted to buy a home, and because I had to take two buses to get to work. So my parents said, "Why don't you just buy a home?" I thought that was great! They're gonna buy me a home. *[group laughs]* So I went to Dearborn, and I went to a real estate office. And I inquired about homes that were for sale, and this gentleman said to me, "I can sell you a home, but," he said, "you'll be on your own." Of course, at that time, I was young. I wasn't much afraid of anybody at that time. So I didn't know what he meant, and I said, "What do you mean on my own? I am going to pay for it." He said, "I don't mean that." He said, "If you have any problems, if you buy the house." Well, I said, "The house should have been inspected. I shouldn't be having any problems." Well that wasn't what he was saying because Dearborn didn't allow

Japanese. So this was what he was trying to tell me, and I said, "In other words if you are telling me, if my neighbors or anybody discriminate against the Japanese, you wouldn't be able to help me?" And he said, "That's what I'm trying to say because you know…" He had nodded around about it, and the bottom line was the Japanese were not allowed in Dearborn. So I asked him, "Well just right down the street, there's a Chinese family that own a laundry." He said, "Well they were here before Dearborn was built up, so they were allowed to stay there in their business." Shortly after that I had friends of mine that lived in West Dearborn, and their landlady asked them to move out. So they had to go into Detroit. So at that time, I wouldn't have been safe buying a home because if the neighbors came and threw rocks or burned it down, I wouldn't get help from the mayor or the city police. So when I got to know Mayor Hubbard through a friend of mine, I brought it up, and I asked him about it. Of course, he was a little embarrassed, and he started hee-hawing around about it, but he did say, "We had never had Orientals living in Dearborn, and that's just one of the rules that we had." And I said, "Well, I don't think that's fair because," I said, "I'm going to pay for a house just like everybody else." And I did bring the fact that this Chinese family had a laundry right down the street. He said, "They were here long before Dearborn was built so we didn't have any choice. We couldn't make them move, but now," he said, "now we have that law." I said, "Well, I don't think that's fair." He said, "Well that's what our laws are." He didn't sympathize with me either.

EL: *Isn't that horrible?*

TS: Min Togasaki, who was president of JACL several times. He had the same experience in Dearborn. He was putting money down in Dearborn and the realtor says, "You really shouldn't do that. You're gonna get trouble here." So that's why they bought East Outer Drive, way out there on the Eastside [of Detroit]. When we were buying in Southfield, we couldn't buy in Lathrup. Because Lathrup was run by this woman named Louise Kelley and it was her ruling: no foreigners could buy into that place. I was talking to the Italian lady in my subdivision some time and we talked about Lathrup, and she said, "It's not just you. With my Italian name, I couldn't buy there either. So Lathrup Village is very, very tightly" controlled by the realtors there.

EL: *What year was this?*

TS: Nineteen—around '60, '61.

EL: *Is that so? Wow!*

TS: Now, of course, it's all open.

EL: *What year for you Mary, did your family move to Northwest Detroit?*

MK: 1960.

EL: *So we see this progression.*

SK: *I'm curious to know, Toshi and Mary—all three of you have been friends for so long—but starting with you two, can you tell us how you met and what your first impressions were? And how you came to be involved in the JACL?*

TS: Member of the JACL board of the early '50s so that's how I got to know Mary.

And also, we worked on the Far Eastern Festival on the day it started. In fact, she and I were one of the people that started it with the other group. We worked the festival until we were forced to get out of it because the city wanted to charge us too much money for booths. Then the city started saying we had to have liability insurance and we had to go to a certain insurance that Coleman Young had, you know, gotten himself with—probably his insurance company—but the insurance rates were so bad. It was so high that we couldn't even afford it. We said, we could somehow or another come up with a booth, but we can't afford the liability plus the security that they wanted us to hire, which was another company that he… Unfortunately, as we dropped out, other festivals started dropping out and the festivals just went down the drain. Hart Plaza was built purposely for the festivals, and now it's just going to waste.

EL: *Let's go back a little bit. Tell us the first day you all met each other.*

TS: The first time I met Mary was on the JACL board, and I said, "That's Mary."

EL: *What did you think of Mary? [laughs]*

TS: At that time with four youngsters like that, I wasn't that concerned about personalities or anything like that. *[background laughing]* I think JACL was the organization that brought us all together.

EL: *Mary?*

MK: When I met Miyo? When I met Miyo, I was like, "Now that's the lady that called." Like Toshi said, we met down at the festival, working in the kitchen and outdoors. At first our booth was on the Riverfront and outside.

TS: It was a rustic recruit setup.

MK: We worked closely together with the festivals and we've been friends since.

MO: I guess I met Toshi when she arrived to marry Jim because I knew Jim and I knew his two sisters. And I don't remember how I met Mary. At the JACL gathering? I think it was a dance or something. I was looking around, looking around and I asked somebody who was close by to me, "By the way, who is the president of the JACL?" And he pointed you out and I never forgot you. You had this white hat on and in those days everybody wore a hat and white gloves. She had this white little hat on with this feather sticking out. JACL was going great. We used to have dances. We used to invite dignitaries to our affairs and so forth. They were big affairs.

MO: Yeah and Book-Cadillac.

MK: Just recently one of the Sanseis wanted to know why we didn't have installation where we can hire a band and all that. But, you know, they don't know how expensive it was to hire a band in those days. It was so expensive when we used to hired them and we lost money every time we hired a band because not enough people came out. And also when we did charge, we didn't charge that much to make up for expenses. So when she had approached—I think you had called this restaurant, and this Sansei girl said, "Why don't you have it here?" If you had dances and stuff, she would come out. How many Sanseis could she bring out to make it worth our while

to go to this expensive restaurant for lunch, which I don't think half of the Nisei that attended the dances would have gone. Because it's way out and also even if we had a dance, we would lose a lot of money. The Nisei would not come out, and the Sansei— the ones I know of, I could tell which ones would come out, and it would just be a handful. So, you know, I think that's sort of turned the Sanseis off on JACL because we're not having anything that attracts them, but we can't just have it for a handful because of the expenses. I really believe that's the reason a lot of Sanseis don't want to join JACL or want to be active.

SK: *What do you think got through to people to join JACL in the Forties and the Fifties?*

EL: *What do you think drew people to join the organization in the early years?*

TS: A lot of people were young then and a lot of people weren't married, so as a result when we did have a social dance, there were a lot of people who came out. So I think the fact they needed a social group to affiliate with because they are freshly out of camp and assessed a certain insecurity. And this was a group that they could impress each other and know each other real well.

MK: I think we had just about every activity you could think of in those days, and it's too bad when you think back that we don't have any of that now.

EL: *So what were some of those activities and where would they be held? What were the kinds of things you would do?*

MO: Oh goodness! We used to go to Book-Cadillac [Hotel], Sheraton-Cadillac—Where was that? Washington and Woodward?

TS: International Institute. Yeah, we used to have a lot of things at the International Institute. Talent show at the International Institute. Some of those girls that did the *can-can. [background laughter]* Yes, long time ago.

MK: It's amazing what people were into in those days.

EL: *So you had talent shows, dinners, what else?*

TS: I remember when the 442nd boys came home, we had a get-together, and that was just great. We were in the newspapers. In fact, I just found that program recently.

EL: *Did you?*

TS: Yeah. In 1952, when the Issei were able to get their citizenship, JACL sponsored classes on American citizenship. That was a good thing that JACL did.

EL: *And how were those classes run?*

MO: A lot of Issei parents came out to be citizens. Even my mother, she was determined to become a citizen. One of the things she said, "My children are all Americans and I'd like to have the same privilege as they have." So she went to English classes and she became a citizen.

MK: I remember my dad used to attend the citizenship classes, and he had to come in from Flint. So either I had to drive him in if I was home, or my brother had to drive him in. So I used to ask him, "Why are you so determined?" And he said, "Because I am going to own something in my lifetime before I die." Because everything was in my brother's name or sister's names. So he just made up his mind, "Before I die, I am going to own while I am living right now," and sure enough he became a citizen. He had all that changed over to his name. My brother said, "You must think I was gonna take over this farm," and I said, "Well, you might." *[laughter]* I always stood up for my dad. Very seriously, he said, "Are you crazy?" "Well no," I said. "You know he's going to struggle through the class." And he used to bring home these tests, and he would ask us all the questions and we'd have to turn our back to think our way through the answers to all of them. My sister would say to me, "I know that's not right." I said, "I'm not going to tell him." Every time he got on our backs about anything, he'd say, "Is this what I'm sending you kids to school for?" I didn't want him to tell us again, so I just told him anything because I didn't want him to think I was stupid sending me to school, you know. And he did pass it. He passed it with flying colors. He was so proud of himself.

SK: *So you just said that your father had a farm in Flint. Could you tell us more about what they were doing there?*

MK: When we came to Michigan, he started out with this spearmint and peppermint farm. Do people know what spearmint and peppermint plants are? One year we had such a bad rainstorm, and his farm was flooded. It was like a lake, and I could remember Mariko Tsutsui. Do you know who she is? Her and her mother came to visit us and she went to the back porch and she said to me, "Mary, how nice, you live right next to a lake!" *[laughter]* "I don't want to hear you say that." She said, "Why?" She was so serious. I said, "Because that's his farm. Half of his plants are probably underwater. They're probably rotten." She said, "Oh my gosh, I'm glad he wasn't here to hear me." Because he could understand English, and my mother could too, you know. "Don't you let any one of them hear you because they're so upset about the rain because he's losing all his spearmint and peppermint plants." So she said, "Don't let them ever hear I said that." I said, "No I won't." Afterwards they moved to Capac because he wanted a larger tract of land and he had to give up the peppermint and spearmint. Because if they rot, you can't buy that root anywhere because there's very few people that have it. So he couldn't get into that again when he moved to Capac, which is near Imlay City, he started growing sugar beets and parsnips. Then after that he started growing carrots. and when he retired from farming and my brother wasn't farming anymore, they just leased the grounds out. But just recently he sold the whole farm. So when my dad retired from farming, he had just made up his mind that he didn't want to work in the fields anymore. Of course, he was in his eighties, but he was very healthy. He was able to do it, but he just said it was time to just sit around the house. My brother said he didn't really care to farm anymore. But they had this really rich soil—this muck, they call it. You don't find too many farms like that. So my brother didn't want to get rid of it because he thought if somebody bought it down the road, they would just plant corn. That would've been a waste of that land. So he

finally sold it to a company that raises sugar beets and so that's what's happening on the farm now.

EL: *So when your father had the farm, who worked the farm?*

MK: Oh immigration at the time used to ask farmers to please get help from Mexico because they needed work. So my dad and my brother would go to Port Huron. That was their immigration office there, and he would have to put his name in and ask for so many help from Mexico. So all the help on the farm was from Mexico. They were sort of interesting people. When I went home, I would mingle with them. Finally, my mom got acquainted with the younger ladies, and so one day I went home and, my goodness, they had a mass production making tacos. I was standing in front of the stairs like, "What is going on?" My mother is laughing, and she says, "Oh, these are the girls that live here on the farm." She said, "They are making tacos for us." I think that was the first time I started eating tacos.

EL: *That's interesting.*

MK: It looked so good. So after that, I guess every weekend they wanted to go to my mother's house to use her kitchen and make something Mexican for them. Which was great. So when I went home, I would always get to eat something Mexican.

TS: Hayashi farm—was that near you?

MK: Yeah.

TS: Because I went to Eastern Market one time. There was this truck with a Japanese name on it. There was another Yoshi—

MK: Yoshihara.

TS: Yoshihara and I thought, gee, Japanese farmers from that Capac area. I think Shebo Hayashi said he was growing carrots. He was selling carrots to Kroger's and Farmer Jack on a big scale. That was kind of interesting to see Japanese people come to Eastern Market with those big trucks.

MK: If you shopped at Wrigley's for carrots, you would have found my father's carrots packaged in plastic bags.

EL: *What year was this when the Japanese Americans had these farms?*

MK: Oh, my dad went back from the time when we came out here from camp, and then my brother sold it about five years ago to a company that said they would come and raise sugar beets. He knew of this company. Otherwise he would not have sold it to just anybody because he didn't want everybody to just ruin the farm. Because it takes years to have this land to be what it was, so he sold it. He was having health problems too. He really shouldn't have been on the farm.

SK: *So Mary, why did you decide to move from Flint to Detroit?*

MK: Well, because I was going to business school there, and Ford sent out recruiters to these business schools for accountants. So they recruited me from the school to work at Ford Motor Company. That's how I ended out at Ford's. Then the man I came to talk to, he was very nice and he said, "If you girls don't have a place to live, just take your time." Well, dumb-dumb me, we went home and we goofed around at home, and my younger sister said, "When are we going to work?" I said, "He said take your time." *[laughter]* So we were home about two-and-a-half weeks, and one day it dawned on me, "You know what, I think we gotta go back to Detroit and find out if we still have a job." My mother said, "Why were you sitting here so long?" And I said, "The man said take your time." We hadn't even budged from home to look for an apartment here. So when we came here, we went into Ford's, and I asked Mr. Phelps. "By the way, are

A Band on the Stage, 1981
[Kamidoi]

62

our jobs still here?" He said, "Yes ma'am. I am holding it for you." So I said, "Okay, we will be into work next week." Because this is like a Thursday, and we didn't have anywhere to stay. So we knew Mr. and Mrs. Ambo, so I went over there and I said, "Mrs. Ambo, do you think we could stay here for a while until we find an apartment?" She said, "Sure you can live here forever." So we moved in, but Mr. and Mrs. Ambo worked at Devin Gables, and they didn't come home until late. Also, you know, I started feeling guilty because they came home late. You know, neither one of ourselves had even fixed dinner because we didn't know what to do. And later, you know, after feeling so bad that she had to make dinner after she came home, I finally said to my sister, "We are gonna move out of here because we gotta go somewhere else. I feel bad we don't have dinner ready for them." Well, she said, "She didn't ask us to make dinner." So we moved out and we lived on the Boulevard—West Grand Boulevard. That's why I had to take two buses to get to work at the Rouge. But you know in those days, very few people drove. They all took buses, so I really didn't mind. They were also safe then. If you told me to take the bus today. I wouldn't even know how to get on the bus or how much it cost.

SK: *What was it like working at Ford?*

TS: You mention Ambo and Mr. and Mrs. Ambo are a very interesting couple. She was an opera singer that toured Europe. Mr. Ambo was a very learned man. He was a calligrapher. Beautiful calligraphy—in fact, he was the one that did all the calligraphy programs for us for the cultural program at the International Institute. He was a very learned person. He did fine carpentry work too. Just amazing. He made a couple of screens—Japanese folding screens—for me. In fact, the one that you got here—Mr. Ambo made that for me. He was very good. It's too bad they are not around because they would be an interesting couple.

EL: *They were older Nisei?*

MK: She was put into a nursing home because she was hit by a car. Her son Dennis was a teacher at Macomb College, and his wife was also. So she decided she didn't want to live with her son and the wife because they were going to adopt two boys. So she rented her own apartment. She was living in Utica in her own apartment and a busy intersection when she was crossing, and some young kid ran a light and hit her. She was injured quite bad, but she did heal up and she was on her own again. But as the years went by, Dennis just felt like she shouldn't be by herself, so they decided they would put her in this Casa Maria home, which is like retirement nursing homes. But it had three different grades, and she had a different apartment. She was very alert, and from there, eventually, she started losing her mind, so they put her into the next level. Dennis decided he wanted to go to Florida because he retired from teaching, and they took her down to Florida. And I really have to believe she is gone today because she is close to one hundred now.

TS: I remember visiting her in the nursing home. We went up to Utica, Michigan.

EL: *Utica.*

MK: We went to that dedication of the museum and on the way home we went to see her.

EL: *Frank Murphy museum?*

63

MK: Yeah, Frank Murphy museum.

EL: *Harbor Beach?*

TS: Harbor Beach! That's it! We went up there for the dedication because it was quite a—they had brought in a speaker and so forth. On the way home, I told Mary, I said, "Let's stop and see Mrs. Ambo." She said, "The last time I ever saw her, I had stopped in Utica to say hello to her."

MK: I've been to see her later, but she was losing it and I could see that. She was an interesting lady. I still remember her when she came home, she would be showering and she'd be practicing singing. And you know my sister and I were like twenty-one, twenty-two, and we laughed like crazy. They had a little boy in the later years, you know, and Dennis would always bang on the door telling, "Mom! Mom! Stop singing!" We used to laugh all the time. And they had this home that was duplex, so this other Japanese family lived there [Yamada] and they could hear her because the shower was next to the wall. I guess the kids often told Dennis about it, so every time she started singing, he would bang on the door and say "Stop singing mom." I said, "That's okay; she's got to practice more," and he said, "She could practice to and from work, Mary. She's with my dad you know. They could just sing in the car." I said, "No that would distract your dad from driving." We used to laugh about it. Her oldest son, still lives in L.A., and her other son by another marriage lives in Chicago.

SK: *Do you know how they ended up in Detroit?*

MK: Yes. You know what? They were our neighbors in Flint.

EL: *Oh!*

MK: They knew somebody, and I think it was through Mrs. Ambo because she knew a lot of people from her singing opera days, you know, and someone had suggested she come out this way after the camps. That's how I got to know her, and she became very good friends with my parents. That's why I was able to barge in on her and say, "Can I stay here for a while until we find an apartment?" It's funny you know from the day 'til I retired, this man was still working—the man that hired us in. He would always say to me, "Well did you find a place yet?" I would say, "Keith, I had found a place, and it's gone already." But he never forgot that, and when he got to know me he did say, "Did you have a problem finding a place?" He thought because of discrimination we couldn't find a place. I said, "What do you mean a problem?" He said, "Well, it took you girls so long. We thought you were having problems, you know." I said, "Well the problem was—I don't know why—we just sat at home fooling around. I don't know why I did it, but I am grateful to this day that you held the job open for both of us." He said, "Well, I remember that day when you came in and said, 'Well, I am ready to work now.'" He never let me forget that. But I really don't know what ever made us fool around like that.

EL: *We have just maybe one or two questions for you. One of them is you've been mentioning a lot about the families that were here in the area, and I wanted any of you talk a little bit about what were some of the family activities or children's activities that you helped through JACL.*

MK: We had a Christmas party.

TS: We organized the Junior JACL.

EL: *What was that?*

TS: It was the youth group and it was on the national scale too, but we have organized one locally. It was a great way to get to know other Sanseis because they not only got to know those within the Detroit area, but they used to have conferences with other cities. So to this day, my oldest son, Jimmy, has done quite a bit of traveling. He said, "If it wasn't for Junior JACL, I would not know all the Japanese Americans in the different cities. I can go to New York, and I'll find someone I know. I can go to Houston and find somebody I know or San Francisco or Los Angeles." And it's all through the Junior JACL connections that he's gotten to know, so he's very grateful for that.

EL: *Others?*

TS: Well, they have a lot of activities for the children. There's probably a lot of pictures in that box.

TS: When they were little we used to take it to them Christmas parties, and what other parties were there?

MO: The Halloween party.

TS: Doll day?

MK: Girl's day.

SK: *Could you talk about what were the important issues the JACL worked on in the Forties or Fifties? Even the Sixties?*

MO: Well the Americanization of our parents. I think that was important to us.

EL: *What types of things would you do around that issue?*

TS: Writing to our congress people to pass legislation. A lot of that was done. Getting to know for the first time how to work with Washington, D.C. to get things done. That was the first introduction to the local people to tie in with the legislators in Washington. Then I think the other big thing is all the festivals.

MK: Yeah, festivals.

TS: We were really active... and ACJ.

EL: *What role did JACL play in that?*

TS: They played a major role.

MK: Because Jim Shimoura and her son was one of the main leaders.

TS: When it happened, I don't think the Chinese people were immediately aware that this was a racially motivated incident and it has national repercussions. I guess Jimmy had, you know, law school and that bit, so he was a little bit more aware. And so he and Helen Zia and Harold Leon—

MK: Roland?

TS: We got together, and we said, "We got to educate the Chinese community on this." So I remembered there was a period there, every Saturday they used to get together with some of the Chinese leaders at a restaurant in Ferndale. I can't remember the name of the restaurant. It's still there I think, and they used to have an

Testimonial Dinner, May 15, 1955 [JACL]

educational session where they talked about the history of Chinese in this country, all the discrimination we had gone through. Because these were all the second and third and fourth generations, Chinese weren't aware of some of this because they had never experienced or had the opportunity to run into situations like this. So that was a training session, sort of. So that's when JACL really worked with the other Asian groups. Well, unfortunately, ACJ is going downhill, I think.

MK: Yeah, I think they are thinking of reviving it.

TS: They are down to very few members.

EL: *What were some other issues? Any other issues that you think were major issues?*

SK: *How about when you were President Miyo? What were your main activities or goals?*

MO: Oh my gosh, that was a long time ago. Oh yeah, that's right. Citizenship. Citizenship probably was the — we were awfully busy and active.

TS: There were a lot of social activities in those days.

MK: Yeah.

TS: The other time when JACL really got involved was the Legacy Fund. It's connected with the Civil Liberties Act, you know?

EL: *What was the Legacy Fund?*

MK: We had many, many letter writing sessions, and we'd get together in someone's home and wrote letters and licked stamps, and all that to mail and so forth. At that time, Lisa Archer was really active.

MK: We had Lisa Archer as President at that time, and she really worked hard. She had stayed up until three o'clock in the morning doing all this work with us. We also had Dave Maxon, the Jewish fellow. I guess he's not well today, and Lisa Archer is busy with her father's law firm because her father just passed away and she's taking over the firm. We don't see either one of them anymore.

MO: Oh, that's too bad. I think we should invite them sometimes too.

MK: Well, I am still in touch with Lisa. They get flyers, you know, that we send to all the members. But, you know, she has two kids, you know, that she has to look after. Well, I think she's busy.

MK: She's adopted a Chinese girl.

EL: *What would Japanese Americans say about the camp experience back in the later '40s, in the '50s, and the '60s?*

TS: A lot of them didn't even want to talk about it. They had really—even today. They want to put it behind them. I never forget the time I talked about my camp experience. Jimmy, my oldest son, said he thought I was going to summer camp. *[laughter]*

TS: That's when I thought we really have to talk about this at home. We started talking

about it, and they got interested. The Nisei even today, they don't want to talk about it.

EL: *Miyo, what was your experience?*

MO: You know, I was just trying to think after my children got older. I remember my son going to school, and someone called him a "Jap." And he came home, and he said to his father, he is called a "Jap." So my husband said to him, "So what? You are an American." After that he hasn't had any trouble with any other people. And then Ann was lucky because my son was very husky. If anyone tried to boss my daughter, they'll say, "Hey, hey! Don't you know who her brother is?" *[laughter]* I told him never to pick on girls and never to pick on boys who are smaller than your stature. And he never did. Everyone knew that the only time he came home with a black eye was when two of his playmates—they were the same size—they were going to fight it out. Well, the boy was fighting with my son's friend. His brother came along and took my son's friend and pulled him so his brother could hit him. My son said, "They all shouted leave him alone. It's a fair fight, but he wouldn't do that." So guess who went and charged the big brother? My son. He just went in and pounded on the fellow until he came home with a black eye. I didn't punish him for that.

EL: *Did you ask him how the other kids looked?*

MO: He was a big brother so he must have been fine.

TS: I think they have—all the Sansei children have their share of experiences like that. My oldest son too, he's like your oldest son. He was the one who opened the road for the rest of the family. Jimmy had his share.

67

I'll never forget when he was waiting for the bus outside. He came home once, he said, "If they call me that again one more time, they are going to get it from me!" Well, I was looking out the window, and here he is and he is a big fellow. There's a Catholic family down the street. They had fourteen children, and they used to gang up together and wait for the bus there. I never forget that because I looked out the window, and I said, "Oh my goodness! What is Jimmy doing?" He had taken the older boy—you know we had ditches in our neighborhoods, but you know if it rains and filled with water. He had this big fellow in the ditch, and he was shaking him up and down. I said, "What in the world did you do?" The younger sister came to the door and said, "Mrs. Shimoura, your boy is hurting my brother." *[laughter]* So I really called Jimmy, "Son, what in the world went on?" He said, "They're not going to call me names anymore. They are going to quit throwing green apples." They used to have a bag full of green apples that they picked from somebody's yard, and they were throwing it at him. So, he said, "They are not going to do that," and they never did. They became friends after that.

SK: *What types of things would the three of you have said or thought about the camp experience back in those—prior to the redress era, back in the '30s, '40s, '50s, '60s?*

TS: I just felt like anything that happens you just have to have a certain degree of reconciliation, and I think you do think about it and you look inside of different things. Some of the action that JACL has taken has helped us come to certain conclusions, such as pushing Asian education in the public universities and

so forth. Things like that I think have helped us decide that yes, it was a bad thing, but we must go on.

MK: Well for me, the thing that really did help was my mother's attitude. Her attitude from the day she left camp to the day she died: "You know, it's happened. There's no use crying about it. Just forget about it. Let's go on." That was the attitude my whole family had. It hurts, but she made it clear, "You are not gonna get anywhere just crying about it. Let's go on. Let's go on."

TS: I think all Issei felt that way because my mom was very strong about that. She always told us, "You know life has to go on. This has happened and it was something that was shameful, but we survived so you just have to keep going on." So I think most of the Isseis felt that way. It is something you just couldn't do anything about.

TS: So you have to think you weren't so strong, and yet they were so strong about everything, and I think that translated into our era too.

EL: *Miyo?*

MO: My mother just said, "You are an American citizen, and you do what's right for your country." By then, she was an American citizen too. I don't think she had any regrets, or she didn't say. She did regret that she didn't have enough money for us to finish college because she ran out of money, so most of us had to work our way through. But she had never said—I don't remember her saying anything against the government or...

Children's Christmas Party, 1957 [ChaptAct]

MO: I remember Pearl Harbor.

MO: It is a regretful thing that Japan has done. And my mother said [it was] crazy to even think [of attacking] the United States. I think she decided some time ago when she took us back to Japan for a trip, she said, "Once we got to Japan, you kids would say let's go home." And home was the United States. And home has always been that way, and my mom always took it that way.

MK: I think all the Issei were like that. They were all a different breed.

TS: I give them so much credit for them being so strong and their stamina and convictions. They have very strong convictions.

EL: *So we talked a lot about the span of history from you coming here, mostly from California, settling here, and working. What is your most memorable moment here in Michigan? Either in JACL or in your personal lives? What would be your most memorable moment?*

TS: Mine would be when all the kidswere out of college. *[laughter]*

MK: Well, I am just glad I got hired by Ford, and I am retired now and I am getting a pension check every month. I thought of quitting twenty million times in my thirty-seven years, believe me, but I am glad I stuck by. It was only because my dad used to hear me complaining when I used to go home, "I don't like my job. I want to come home to my old job." And I worked at Buick and Pontiac dealership as a bookkeeper, and he was holding the job for me. I'd go and see him, and he would say, "I'm still holding it. When are you coming in?" So I'd go home and I'd complain, and finally one day, my dad said, "I want to talk to you for a minute. Just sit down." You know, my dad was a man of very few words. But when he said six words, it was like twenty words—the meaning of it. So I sat down, and he was having a drink. And my brother is laughing from the other room, and he said, "You better not just even open your mouth. You better listen to him." I said, "Okay." We

JACL Dinner Party. Miyo O'Neill

didn't say anything to my dad when he says "sit down." So he just came out and said, "I hear you girls complaining all the time about your job. If you think you are going to quit your job and come home and live under my roof, you are mistaken." So anyway, I thought, "Okay, I just can't come home, so I might as well stick it out at Ford's," and I stayed thirty-seven years. A long time, but I have to thank him for that because I would have quit many, many times over when I got fed up with my job. Today, I wouldn't even get a pension from anybody, so I was glad he was that stern about us quitting. He said, "I have ten kids, and I never raised a quitter." And I could remember him telling my younger brother when he got

mad on his job and came home early. We were sitting around the table playing monopoly, and he looked up and he said to my brother, "Are you sick or something?" My brother says, "No!" and he started on about why he quit the job because he didn't like his boss and his boss said this and that. So my dad said very quietly, while he was rolling the dice, "Tomorrow you are going to look for an apartment, okay?" *[laughter]* And it stuck with me. So you know, if I didn't hear him tell my brother, that I wouldn't have believed what he said. So my brother said, "Yeah, I'll look for an apartment." He got up bright and early and went into town looking for an apartment, and he came home really furious. And I said, "Now what's your problem." And he said, "You know what? When you rent an apartment, you have to furnish it." I said, "What did you expect?" He said, "Well, I didn't know that. I guess I have to go back to work because I can't afford to furnish an apartment." And I said, "Don't look around this house, because we don't have any spare things for you to take." So he went back to work and luckily his boss knew he had a temper, so he kept his job open for him. I remember him doing that before I even got a job, and I thought he really means business when he says, "You are not living under my roof." So I said to my mother, "Did you hear what Dad said. He said we can't come home and live under this roof." She said, "He's the boss in this house. I have nothing to say." I said, "Well, I just can't come home and live here anymore." She said, "Well, you just have to ask your dad. I don't care if you do, but you have to ask your dad." I knew better than to question my father.

EL: *Miyo? The most memorable moment?*

MO: The most memorable? Well, I remember raising my children, and I told them that whatever they do to go into a field that they really love and that they really like. I am really glad that my son has become an attorney and my nice little daughter became a physicist. That's what they want to do, and they are both happy in their work. And I am so glad that, you know, their father before he died said, "We have two good kids. They know what they want, and they'll do what they want and they'll do it well." That was my nicest part.

EL: *That's great. Now let's me go back and so what's your most memorable moment in JACL? We'll start with Toshi over there and*

maybe the two of you might want to...

TS: I guess we worked so hard for that redress, and when that passed, that was really a landmark in JACL here. Because we did work hard for that.

EL: *How did you work on it? What did you do?*

TS: Well, most of it was letter writing and letting the people in the community know what it is all about. But you know in the past, there was lots of talk about it and nothing was done, and it finally got done. That's why.

EL: *Mary?*

MK: Well, mine was really working with all the different ethnic groups in the festivals. I really enjoyed those days, especially when we were outdoors. You know, I made a lot of friends through the festivals, and I am still friends with them, which I really enjoyed being friends with. So I think when we had to back out of the festivals, I went to a meeting and I had to tell a friend who was with me, "Do we really want to back out of the festivals because I think we're both going to miss it." He said, "Well, I'll miss it too." But he said, "Well, I am not going to have the rest of the groups talking to me in that tone." You know, he handled the booths and some of the groups had accused JACL of taking more than our share. So because of that, we decided to back out of the group and when we backed out the whole Far Eastern Festival closed up. The sad part of it is the treasurer at the time—every year the treasurer always holds back an *x* amount of dollars to start with because you always had fees for everything before you even got in. It belonged to all the different nationality groups, but this young fella took the books over and he just sat on it. One day I went in his office to talk to him about everything and nothing because I was working at the ACJ office and he was just across the street. And I asked him about the money. He didn't know a thing about it. Unfortunately, the other groups didn't remember that we always hold back about five thousand dollars. I guess nobody questioned him, and I was the only one who questioned him, "What happened to the money?" He laughed it off, and he said he didn't know where the checkbook went. He asked his wife. She didn't know anything about it, and so all that money went down the drain—for his business really. But I think that was what I really enjoyed, JACL festivals. It was really a fun time.

SK: *When did they start?*

MK: I think it started like in the 60s. Filipino lady—Felipa Bantugan. She started it. She was with the board of education, and she knew the man Ed Gajac that was on the city board. They got to thinking about it, and they thought it would be a good idea. So they called a meeting with all the ethnic groups, and we started it.

EL: *Did you ever meet her?*

MK: She used to be with the school board. She's retired now.

EL: *Miyo, your most memorable moment in JACL is?*

MO: Is getting citizenship for our parents. That was during my tenure, and it was great. We did work really hard. We started a speaker's bureau back then. We had more members. I wonder where they all went.

EL: *So those classes and the speaker's bureau? And they all got their citizenship.*

MO: Tremendous, yeah.

Citizenship Class teachers: K. Miyaya, Horiuchis, and Miyoshis
[ChaptAct]

Toshiko Shimoura

interview by Scott Kurashige & Emily Lawsin at the Shimoura residence in Southfield, Michigan. February 3, 2003

My parents are from Kumamoto [prefecture], on Kyushu Island. My father came to this country early, and he went back to Japan to get married. He married my mother and they lived there for a few years, but he wanted to come and find a home for his family and get settled. Because my older brother had already been born, he left my mother and my brother in Japan. And as soon as he located a spot that he liked, my family moved out to California. My mother came on the last boat in 1924.[1] I don't know why, but she came in through Seattle and then took a train down to the Bay Area.

Originally, my parents were on a farm—not a big one but a small one [where they were growing different kinds of vegetables]. All of those [farms] around the Bay area were small. If you go to the [Central] Valley, you go into the big spreads. The neighbors were very friendly, very open. There were a lot of Swiss, Mexican, Portuguese. California had a lot of the southern Europeans there. These were the neighbors around there. And they were all very, very friendly.

I grew up in Fremont, that community right in the Bay Area. I was a sophomore in high school when the war broke out. Well, I'll tell you, when the evacuation order first came out, I was really ashamed of myself. I thought, "You know, I'm not like everybody else. I'm less than everybody else." I just felt like hiding someplace. You couldn't go to school like everybody else, you had a curfew and all this bit. But after we got to camp—and being a teenager, you're not concerned about livelihood, for one thing—you're not concerned about what's going to happen to you after the war is

---

1. *The Immigration Act of 1924 severely restricted migration from Japan to the United States.*

Toshi Shimoura as an infant [Shimoura]

over. Is there a possibility of being sent to Japan? Those were our parents' concerns, not children's concern. So maybe I was too naïve to appreciate all that.

I know there was a lot of pointed discussion with my parents all the time and among their friends. I used to listen in on some of that. I used to think, "There are problems, but thank goodness, they're not immediate problems for myself." Because you're fed and you're housed—as primitive as it is, you're housed. But in retrospect, I thought it was a horrible, horrible period. Because I think that, generally speaking, it had an effect on the security, the inner security of a lot of the Nisei; I think that there's a certain amount of apprehension. You know, I thought like everybody else, "How are they going to treat us?"

We were first put into Tanforan, the racetrack south of San Francisco. There were people who actually lived in horse stalls. They white washed it, but then, you know how it is with whitewash. You just rub it a little bit, and it all crumbles down. It was really a terrible place. Then in the inner circle of the racetrack, they put up barracks, and so we were fortunate enough to get one of those units in the inner circle. But the mess hall situation was horrible because here are all these people and only one dining room. So it seemed like we spent hours in line trying to get some food. By the time you got through eating, it's time, practically, for the next line-up. So that part was really, really bad. Then the latrine situation was terrible. They were inadequate; there weren't enough to accommodate all the people there, so that part was very bad. Then of course, you know we had to grab a canvas bag and stuff it with straw to make our mattresses. My sister was allergic. She was wheezing, and she was asthmatic and everything. And to sleep on all that straw! She was coughing and choking and sneezing all night long. That really demoralized my mother. She was a stoic person, but that really got her. I saw her crying for the first time when that happened.

We were there from April until August of 1942. Then groups had to be transferred out to Topaz, because we were all being shipped to Topaz, Utah. The train ride was something else again. They made us pull the shades down, and their rationale was that this way, you're protected from the public's anger. But I think, more than that, it was that they didn't want the public to know that we were being transported there. It took us a couple days to get into Utah, then to get into Topaz. There we were put onto these Army trucks. These trucks had benches and panels over the top. And we were hauled into Topaz. But the camp was not completely constructed, so there was no such thing as a road; there was just all dust and dirt. We were assigned our barracks and rooms. We were a family of five, plus my mother and father, but we also had a widower Japanese man and his daughter, who my mother was raising almost like her own child. So that's two more. So we were given two of the inner units, which were a little larger than the outside units. We also had a person who lived in the end unit, whose wife was blind; they were an older couple. My mother felt responsible for them, so we occupied the end unit and the middle two units.

My mother would insist we come back and have meals with the family. There were a lot of them who just ate with their friends, but she put her foot down. She said, "You have to get back to have meals with your own family." So we did that. My mother did not work; she felt like she ought to be home, to make sure the children aren't going to go too far afield, and so she stayed home. They did a lot of craftwork. Topaz used to be a lake, a dried-out

Toshi's Family
[Shimoura]

lake bottom. So if you dig about three to four feet, you come across a thick layer of shells. So they were digging up the shells and bleaching them, and making different things, crafts with that. In fact, a lot of my mother's things, I understand, are in the Oakland, California museum. They have a small section there on camp craftwork. My brother thought, "Well, it's a good place to leave them," so he contributed that. They did a lot of knitting, crocheting, handwork. A lot of the young people, including myself, did a lot of that too.

The men had jobs inside or outside the

camp. My father didn't know what to do. First, he was going to get a job as a watch man inside the camp. Then he decided it was so boring; he said he wanted to go outside the camp. You had to work on the farm then, so he went out of the camp and worked on the farm. One of my brothers decided that it would be interesting—they raised cattle too for use at the camp—so he got a job minding the cattle. He was riding a horse, minding the cattle. That's the kind of job he had.

I had a group of friends that, as I say, to this day I'm in touch with; they're scattered somewhat, but most of them are in the Bay Area. Every time I visit there, I make sure I touch base with them. I had a penpal in Ohio. So we used to write back and forth. I'm sorry I lost track of her. She moved, and I didn't get her forwarding address, so I lost track of her. It would be very interesting if I could locate her and talk about the old days.

They had school dances. They had different church groups that met in certain barracks. So from that standpoint, I think that lives were enriched to a degree. Topaz was a relatively peaceful camp. Some of the camps had some protesting groups there were some problems in Poston and some of other camps. Topaz was relatively mild that way. We did have a lot of problems when we had to sign the citizen's... no, the Loyalty thing, you know, the *yes-no* Loyalty thing. There were a number of residents, particularly the *Kibei* who felt very strongly that it was unfairly worded and you were stupid to say "yes." I remember we talked about it a lot at home. My mother, in particular, said, "You're Americans; your future's in this country. Why do you want to break that at this point?" So we all said yes even if the wording of the questionnaire was faulty. And it was faulty: how can you give up your allegiance to Japan when you didn't have an allegiance? We went through this

discussion at home; we all decided to vote yes. I'm glad my parents felt that way. There were some Nisei who were torn because the Nisei wanted to say yes, but the parents wanted to say no. And even between the mother and father, there was division, feelings. It created a lot of problems. I remember that really very clearly, how groups would huddle together and discuss it, come home and discuss it again.

Soon after we got there, the residents, those that were college graduates and in charge, developed a school—very primitive but a school. We started going to school there. They brought in a number of outside teachers, but most of them were conscientious objectors. They were Mormons, because we were in Utah. They spent their war years teaching in camp. They were very nice, nice people.

We had a science club. We had no animals to dissect or anything, so some of the guys went out and caught bullfrogs. Hard to forget that—we had to boil them out and then reconstruct the bone and study the bone structure and things like that. And I thought, "How primitive!" Science just fascinated me, and also math came fairly easily, that's why.

I was very fortunate to have a good Latin teacher. Her name is Toyo Kawakami. She had seven years of Latin, so you can imagine how thoroughly she knew her Latin. I had a couple years with her, and during the summer, a few of us were really interested. She said, "You know, if you will meet during the summer, we can study it beyond what you've studied so far." So we did that for a while. Do you remember—they had the hearings in different parts of the country? I drove a bunch in my station wagon, full of Nisei, from here to Chicago. So there was Toyo; she was a librarian at Ohio State. She came there to say her part, I've been in touch with her through the mail over the years.

I think it was three, four years ago, my brother was here, and I said, "Kiyoshi, do you mind driving with me to Columbus, where Ohio State is? I want to look up Toyo Kawakami." He said, "Yeah, sounds great." So we drove down there—what a wonderful experience that was—to see this teacher. She lives by herself in her old age. At that time she was pushing ninety. She's written a lot of poetry and things like that, and she was trying to get an anthology of her work together. It was a real good visit with her.

I graduated from Topaz High School in 1944, Summer of '44. My parents were anxious that I go on to college because they said, "There's no use just wasting your time here. We don't know how much longer we're going to be stuck in this place" and all sort of thing. And I was anxious to go on too. So fortunately the American Friends—and I have to thank them for many, many things—they were very instrumental in helping students, you know, locate themselves in the Midwest and the East somewhere. And I originally had planned to go to University of Connecticut, in Storres, Connecticut. They had accepted my application, and I was ready to go there. But the school, they had these notices put up on what schools were available tacked up there. You could pick one and hope you can get accepted at that school. You write directly to them and then send in your credentials.

But then I looked at the board where they listed the different schools that were accepting Nisei, and I saw Michigan State. I told my mother. I said, "You know, there's a school in Michigan that will accept." And she said, "Oh, that's closer." She said, "You'd better go there."

So at the last minute, I applied, and I was accepted. And therefore, I ended up in Michigan with the intention of transferring to [the University of] Michigan at some point. But by the time I'd finished a year and a half at State, the war had ended, and my parents had gone back [to California]. And so again, my mother said, "You're so far away. You rarely get to come home. Why don't you transfer?" So I transferred to Cal Berkeley, and that's where I graduated.

I know when I first went to East Lansing, got off the train, I wondered, "Now, how are they going to treat me?" You have that certain amount of fear in you because you feel the outside world is against you. I had a good experience there, and the first group that invited me to talk to them was the Friends. It was a home meeting; there were about twenty-five to thirty people there. They wanted me to talk about my experience in camp. They were very kind, very understanding; they made me feel good. Then I joined a People's Church there, an interdenominational church there. And there again, you're with really understanding people, and that was a great experience.

My parents' families were Buddhist. But when I left camp, my mother took me aside. "Wherever you're going," she said, "there will probably not be a Buddhist church. But in everybody's life, you have to have faith, and you have to have a base that will hold you steady. If you study another religion or another faith that you feel comfortable with and you feel the need for, don't feel that I'm going to get angry at you. You go ahead and make your move the way you think is best." So I was lucky that they were that understanding. So that's how I started going to the People's Church.

College was a fairly easy transition for me. First of all, I thought it would be difficult for me because I thought my schooling in camp was so lax, not up to standard. So I was little

Toshi's Father
[Shimoura]

bit timid about that. But after I got to college, I thought, "My gosh, I've had more math than these kids have had." Because I'd had some calculus, and none of these kids had calculus. They had advance algebra and that was about it—or advanced geometry, that was about it. So I didn't feel as intimidated as I thought I would be. Either I'm too naïve to feel any social pressure, but I didn't feel it. [To pay for college,] I had to work all the time. They gave us a stipend of $200 when we left camp. But, you know, $200 doesn't get you anywhere. So all the time that I was going to college, I worked. I worked in a home. I worked as a tutor. And then I also worked [as a grader]—they used to have, if you're doing fairly well in your field, you could correct papers. Yeah, then at Berkeley, I was a grader again, and then I was an assistant to one of the profs there. That paid me too. Then, during the summer, I was taking all these

classes, Japanese and different classes like that, and I got a job working in a home too. So I was doing whatever I could to stay ahead of the game.

I was in microbiology; that's my major. But I studied Japanese as much as I could. Every chance I got, I mean, during the summer, or wherever there's a spot that I could fit in. But to this day, I'm very happy that I did that, and that was on my mother's insistence. She said, "One of you [there were five of us in the family], one of you has got to learn the language. Otherwise we're going to lose our ties with the relatives in Japan." And so she said, "You do what you can with it." So I tried it. I'm not very good at it, but then I can speak enough to communicate. [When my parents got out of camp, they went back to Fremont.] Well, they had a house there, but, you know, when they went back, it was ransacked. I mean, there was not a thing in the house that was left; everything was gone. The doors were wide open. But then they decided they may as well go back and live in the house because it was theirs. A lot of the Issei found that their homes were no longer there, you know. Then they did not get the harsh treatment that some of the people had gotten. There [was] graffiti written on their homes and things like that. My parents told me that they didn't have that, so they were very, very lucky in that respect.

I moved back in '47. But I moved directly to Berkeley, so I never did live at home. When I got through Cal, I worked in Berkeley for about a year, and then I went up to Marysville to work. So I never really got home. When I first graduated Cal, I was at the Virus Research Center in Berkeley, California. But at one point, Dr. Brown—who was in charge of the Public Health Laboratories for the state of California—approached me and said, "You know," he says, "Toshi, you're young, you're single, you have no responsibilities around here. Why don't you go and run that lab up in Sutter Yuba County, up in Sacramento Valley? We have a fully equipped lab there, but no one to run it." So I went up there, and I ran that lab for awhile, which I thought was, you know, a great experience for me because, you're in charge of everything, and everything falls on your shoulders. It was a great experience for me.

From Marysville, I moved back to Berkeley; then I got married, so then moved out [to Detroit]. I met Jim, my husband, at Michigan State. He was on the GI Bill. He'd done his service in the South Pacific. Actually, he was drafted in Michigan; then he was sent to the 442 to train down in Mississippi. He trained with the Hawaiian Nisei. That was an experience for him because he had not grown up with Japanese. He said that for the first time, he was surrounded by all these Japanese. They were all billeted to go to Europe, to Italy; and one night, he said, someone called him, "Shimoura, come out."

So he went out, and he thought, "Now what did I do wrong?" It turned out that his godfather, Paul Rush, was in charge of the language school in Minneapolis. He had requested that Jim be transferred there. That's how he ended up at the language school. And he didn't know Japanese language at all. A lot of the teachers there were *Kibeis*, and they spoke Japanese really well. And some of the Nisei spoke Japanese, you know, enough so that they could pick it up. And Jim said, "Boy, there was class one to ten." He said, "I was in class at eleven." He struggled and struggled with it, and he tried to learn as much as he could; then he got sent to the South Pacific — to the Philippines, New Guinea, and Australia, places like that.

He came back, and they all had this free

education with the GI Bill, so he went to Michigan State. He transferred to Michigan afterwards, but he was there when I was there. I thought I'd never come back to Michigan, but here I am! We were married in Berkeley, then we drove out here. When I first came here, I didn't think I would ever get used to Michigan. And the weather! I wasn't used to all this cold. Well... I knew how cold Michigan could get, because I was in East Lansing. But on a permanent basis, I questioned it. But, you know, before you know it, you're in the thick of it, relating with your relatives. So you set aside your personal likes and dislikes and just kind of fall in line with everybody else. And that's exactly what I did. In 1952, there were quite a few Nisei who had come out of camp and lived around here.

After the war, the Nisei families that were in camps started moving out [this] way. And that was the big movement of people, of Japanese into the area. Until then, there was just a scattered, few here and there. When the Japanese, when the Nisei and their families started moving out this way, there was a kind of an enclave there at Cass and Canfield area, where there were apartments buildings that were renting to Japanese coming in. And so that was kind of like a cluster there. And then Central Methodist Church was a great gathering place. They opened their doors to all the Nisei and their activities. So a lot of the social activities, were held there. Right downtown [by the new stadium].

Then the JACL was formed back in 1946 to fill the social need more than anything else, of the Japanese, the newly arrived Japanese. Around the latter part of the Fifties, the Junior JACL was formed for the socialization of the Sansei in the area. Because they were growing up, apart from everybody else, and there was really no vehicle to get them together. And

Toshi's Mother
[Shimoura]

Junior JACL served that purpose. I know all my children went through that period, where they were members of the Junior JACL in those days. They have a different name for it now. They call them "Jays," I guess. But that was a good way for the Sansei kids to get to know each other, because in Detroit, we don't have a Japanese church, for instance, like in Chicago and wherever else, they have a church, and that becomes kind of a foundation for their community. But we don't have that here. We have a Buddhist church here, but it's very small. To this day, my boys will tell me, they said they were so glad

that they were affiliated with Junior JACL, because they said, "Whatever city we go to, there's someone, with some connection through the Jays."

Detroit in those days was still a very clean, beautiful city. The streetcars were running up and down Woodward Avenue, and you put on your hat and gloves and get on the streetcar and go shopping down to Hudson's, downtown. And then I was affiliated with St. John's [Hospital]. And the friends that I was able to find were all great people. Many of them are still my friends. But I had to get used to this inter-relationship between wife of the oldest son as she relates to her mother-in-law, and that was a new experience for me—believe you me. I worked at the microbiology lab for the city of Detroit, but only for a couple of years. My mother-in-law was very Americanized, but on certain things she was from the Old School. My husband was the oldest son, and therefore I was the one that was supposed to be taking over things. And so she required a lot of responsibility on my part. So it was a very busy time because of my children plus the responsibility I had with the family and everything. Well, we had our own place in Highland Park. We had a rented place. But his mother and father absolutely insisted I move in and help out. We lived there for ten years.

Many times I thought about going back into microbiology. That's one sacrifice I made, that I was not able to go back into the field. I just didn't have the time, not with all the children's activities and having to look after the needs of my mother-in-law constantly. When I first left camp, I was hoping that I could go into medicine, but it was a matter of money. In those days, you had to fill out the forms, and I looked at the form and it said, "sources of income." I thought, "No way I can do this." My parents were in camp, they weren't working. So that's why I went into bacteriology thinking I could do something with that. If I really had a choice, I think I would be interested in genetics.

My father-in-law owned a wholesale food business on Woodrow Wilson called the Oriental Provision Company. He would supply grocery stores and factory cafeterias. He had a combination of regular American and imported Asian foods. He came to Detroit as a single man in 1912, roughly, and he got a job right away with Ford. He worked at the original Ford Motor Company. He must have worked there twenty-some years. And as far as he knew, he said he was the first Issei that entered Ford Motor Company. He picked up English by going to night school while working at Ford.

My in-laws, the Shimouras, are from Tokushima, which is in the island of Shikoku. And my mother-in-law—I call her Grandma Shimoura—was from Kobe. And she has an interesting history too because it's rare for a young woman in the teens to go to college, but she's a graduate of Tsuda College, although in those days it wasn't called Tsuda. She was already fluent in English before she came here. In fact, I saw Tsuda University when I was in Tokyo, and I thought, "Wow, that's where Grandma went to school!" But it's very unusual for a Japanese woman at that generation to have graduated college. And she majored in English. But their English teachers were from England. They were missionary teachers. And, therefore, her ties with England were very strong through the teachers. And what's interesting is that her English had a British accent because of these teachers.

Right after the war, after the Nisei had settled in this area, my father-in-law helped them a lot. They used to congregate in their house all the time. He opened the door for a lot of people. In fact, at one point the Japanese government thought they'd like to recognize the Japanese in America who had contributed to the welfare of the other Japanese. And so there was a ceremony in Chicago. They picked out certain leaders from different communities; he was one of them, and he got this Order—Fifth Order from the Emperor—and a thank you gift. They call this the *Kun-Goto*. It's the Imperial Order of the Sacred Treasures. And it's a service medal, it's called the *Juri-Hosho*. It's for distinguished service to Japanese Americans, for Japanese-American relations and community service.

Even after the kids were born, we stayed with the Shimouras for ten years. It was a big house, but certainly not big enough to accommodate four children. That's why we moved out here [to Southfield]. We built this house 41 years ago. We were really interested in this lot because it's wooded back here, and we don't have a neighbor back here. *[laughs]* We looked in Livonia. In fact, we even bought a lot in Livonia at one time.

My husband said, "We're not going past Ten Mile." That was his limit. That is it. He said, "Don't look at anything beyond Ten Mile!"

I said, "Okay, okay." But I told him, I said, "You know, the school system is very good here, and the Lodge—you know, the freeway—is right there." And I said, "You can go in and out of downtown Detroit in no time." Mainly because the school was so good here, that I really was partial to moving out here. But he put the limit at Ten Mile!

He said that he didn't want to commute that much to work. So first, it was Eight Mile in Detroit. So we looked at houses around Northland, south of Northland. There were some decent houses there, but then I still wasn't satisfied with the school system, to tell you the truth. So I started spilling over into Southfield, and he said, "Well, you can go as far as Ten Mile, but that's it!" We built here in 1962. We started looking around '61, somewhere in there. And we sold that lot in Livonia, and we decided—I didn't want to go out there. It was near the racetrack and I said, "That is not the kind of neighborhood I want to live in." We didn't have a problem getting the lot. They were anxious to sell.

So, anyway, the children all grew up, you know, going to school here, and in those days, Southfield schools were in top quality. So I feel real grateful in that respect, the kids had a good education here. And the kids blended. They had a certain amount of problems in the beginning, but after a while, after they expressed themselves—especially someone like Jimmy, my oldest son, expressed himself very forcefully—the acceptance for the siblings became a lot easier.

When I first came here, I tried to register the kids in the local elementary school, and the principle looked at me and said, "You speak English so well! How long have you been here?"

Tula Kurashige and Toshi Shimoura, June 2006
Photo: Emily Lawsin

85

And I thought, "Oh boy, you need education!" That's why I became very active in the community, very active in the PTA, very active in the music group, in the different programs around the community because I thought, "Oh, these people just don't know what we're all about."

There were a few houses here and there when we arrived. That was kind of interesting because when we first approached the owner of this property, old Mr. Larges looked at us, and he said, "Are you a Nisei?" And I said, "How did you know that?" And he said, "Well, you know, I own the Checker Cab garage downtown." He said, "There a number of Nisei, who are mechanics down there." And he said, "That's why I know what Nisei are all about." And I said, "Well, that's amazing; that's marvelous."

But then he said, "But I have to tell you something." He said, "When you people decided to build here," he said, "the people in the neighborhood had a meeting. And they didn't know whether to accept you or not." And he said, "They decided, well, they look pretty good. They look like they're pretty nice people. It's okay." But we had to meet the approval of the neighbors.

One of the persons at this meeting told me this later, after we moved here. They said, "Did you know that we had to have a meeting to see if you people were acceptable here? "I said, "No, I didn't know that." I wasn't too happy about it. But then, you know, I felt like they were so good, I mean the neighbors were. We got to know them quite well, and especially when I got so involved in the school so much, I got to know people quite well in the neighborhood. And so, no, we never had a problem with that. But we did have to do some selling of ourselves first.

I became involved with the subdivision, for instance. I was their secretary for years, in the subdivision association. And sponsoring potlucks and things like that to get to know people better. And then I was a Girl Scout leader — my husband was a Boy Scout person — and so that way you get to know the community real well. And then, as the children got older, in high school and so forth, there was a junior symphony here, which was not just Southfield but throughout, regional. And Dick Brown was their director, and I got to know him quite well. And there was a parents' association connected with that, and I was president of that. It's been a comfortable community for the children to grow up in. But, there's been a big movement of people, especially when they had this thing about integrating schools. A lot of people moved out. There's been a big turnover of people. We have a very high African-American population now.

In the Sixties and Seventies, Southfield decided very early on that they were going to become an international community — that they're not going to be limiting themselves to just the white population. And so at the Parks and Recreation Building, they had a desk set up for any questions they might have for people who wanted to move into the community and are having problems. So they were encouraging, intermixture of the racial groups very early on. And so they were welcoming the blacks coming into the community.

[In the immediate neighborhood], a lot of the residents have moved out. In fact, at that point, some of the ones that felt strongly about the change in the color of the community went out to Brighton. When we came, the

Masao James Hirata and Tadae Shimoura
c.1915 [Shimoura]

neighborhood was highly Jewish and then very Catholic. There was a Catholic school across the street. And so St. Michael's was the attraction for a lot of people who lived right in this subdivision. Most of them were coming from Detroit. Let's see... the Jewish people were from Oak Park, moving out this way. And we were very grateful, because they really kept the standard of the school up. My children have a lot of Jewish friends because they grew up with a lot of Jewish friends. To this day, they're in touch with a lot of them.

So here we are today, with two of my children living here and two in the D.C. area. And they're all doing well. My battle cry was "Don't be a drag on society" when they were growing up: be contributing members of society.

Japanese Pioneers in Detroit

My father-in-law happened to be one of the earlier pioneers in the Detroit area. His name is Shimoura, James Tadae Shimoura, and he was from Tokushima in Japan, in the island of Shikoku. In 1910, he came in to Pennsylvania. He was interested in automotive from day one. And there was a small company in Reading, Pennsylvania, and he worked there for a while, but in talking to the owner there, he was told that if you're that interested in automotive, you should go to Michigan, to Detroit, where a man by the name of Henry Ford is doing great things. So he thought, "Well, that would probably be the best place for me to get settled."

The owner there happened to have a letter he wanted to mail to Henry Ford, and he said, "Oh, by the way, would you drop this in the mail for me." And so my father-in-law got the letter, and he noticed on the envelope, the address said "Edison Avenue." And he just remembered the number and the street. And so he came to Detroit and he was coming up Woodward Avenue on a streetcar, and he said that he passed Edison Avenue and he thought, "Oh, my goodness, Edison Avenue, that's where I want." He wasn't actually looking for the home, but he happened to come across this. He looked up the number, and he found the house and knocked on the door. Mrs. Ford answered the door, and she said, "Yes." She said, "We can probably use you, but you probably need a little training. My nephew Dahlinger is at the lab training right now. Why don't you join him?" And that's how he got started as a chemist at Ford Motor Company.

My father-in-law happened to be one of the earlier pioneers in the Detroit area. His name is Shimoura, James Tadae Shimoura, and he was from Tokushima in Japan, in the island of Shikoku.

And after working at Ford, he realized that there were great opportunities for young Japanese. Because, you know, Japan had been so far behind as far as technology's concerned. He wrote back to Tokushima and he encouraged some of his friends to come out. And several of them did come out. And they got jobs in the automotive factories. Several of them turned out to be very, very skilled tool-and-die people. They caught on in a hurry and they became very good at it.

The reason why my father-in-law went into wholesale food was that, you know, that Detroit was hit very, very hard by the Depression. And so at that time, knowing that the future in industry was kind of iffy, he decided to start the wholesale food business. The agricultural area wasn't quite so bad, but the industrial area was hit very, very hard. That when all the factory workers were in food lines. He decided that something more stable would be an every day item like food.

Before my husband passed away, and in talking to my sister-in-law—because they are the ones that grew up in this area—I itemized a lot of Japanese names and what these people have done in those olden days [before World War II]. There were between four and eight Japanese American men who worked in Shimoura's wholesale food business. Quite a few of [the others] were in automotive, but also there were a lot of them who were domestics. They were single men mostly, and they were domestics working in homes. In summary, I find there were five who worked at Ford Motor Company; three who worked at the Dodge Motor Company; two at Briggs Manufacturing; there were seven to ten food and gift store owners; two wholesalers; about twelve to fifteen domestic workers, single men working in homes; eight to ten draftsmen, engineer and tool-and-die type people; and then there were between ten to fifteen restaurant owners and waiters worked in restaurants. There were five who worked in country clubs, as cooks mainly. There was one gentleman by the name of Ono, who worked at Parke-Davis Research. They used to be in downtown Detroit. And then there were five who worked at amusement parks. They had concessions there, selling trinkets and so forth.

You have to remember that these guys were all single fellows. They came from Japan, and then in 1924, there was no more immigration in this country. And therefore, what do you do if you wanted to get married? In the case of my father-in-law, he went back to Japan in 1919 to find a bride. And he got married in Japan and brought over my mother-in-law, Tsugi. But there were many of them who decided maybe the future was back in Japan. One of them was Mr. Tamura, who worked for Dodge. There is a book that he wrote and I read; unfortunately it's in Japanese, but I could read enough that I could get the story. I think it was in the mid-Twenties, he decided that, rather than continue to live here, he'd like to go back to Japan. He was the oldest son, and he really felt the responsibility to go back. But he was a very innovative kind of a guy, and what really struck him in this country

was that in those days, Japanese parts were not interchangeable that well. They were not precisely, you know, made, and he was amazed how parts can be interchanged in an American radio, for instance. So he kept that in mind, [and] he says, "We've got to do something about this in Japan." So he went back and he started a radio factory, radio parts.

As a matter of fact, an interesting story is that the man who started Sony Corporation used to be a student in Tokyo that used to walk to school in front of his shop, and he would come in every so often to talk to Tamura-san. And so Tamura-san eventually said, "Why don't you come in and work here a little bit?" So he started working there, and that's how Mr. [Masaru] Ibuka got started in the electronics business—with Tamura's radio shop.

[Mr.] *Kitamura's* interesting. He was married to a Caucasian lady, and I think they lived a little north of here, maybe like Port Huron, Mount Clemens, [or] somewhere in that area. He also worked at Dodge Main—the main plant. But the interesting thing is that he was an acrobat that toured Europe before he settled down here. His wife was a local person here. He married her here.

I knew *Yutaka Toba*. He was from my father-in-law's generation also. Toba was a single fellow; he worked in the Gramm family as their chauffeur. And he used to stop by every so often. While I'm talking to him, he'd open the hood and he takes a towel and he's wiping the inside of the car. A true chauffeur—keeping everything shiny all the time. The Gramm family was very wealthy. I can't remember what business they were in, but they were in Bloomfield Hills. And I remember visiting him there, and the cook there—I can't remember her name, now—they had the little garden there, where they had fresh vegetables that they could use.

He was with the family for a long time. [He lived there on the estate.] There was an apartment over the garage, the help's quarters.

John Kazama married a African American lady, and they worked in a very rich home in Bloomfield Hills, also. Harry Arai was a single fellow, and he worked for a very wealthy family, but he also later started working for Shimoura's. Yoshito Tanaka and his wife, Sadako, had an adopted son; they lived in Grosse Pointe. They worked for the Semmes family, [who were] connected with the newspaper in Detroit.

Tsunaji Sato had a Caucasian wife. They had a daughter Sayoko; she and her family moved to Sacramento, I believe, so they're not around here anymore. He worked for the Dahlinger family. Dahlinger, I believe, was Henry Ford's sister. He was their person around the house. *Shoji Kawas aki* was from New York. He was a domestic in the Ford home. He worked also at the Ford Motor Company. My in-laws knew [him, but] he was gone by the time I entered the picture. George Endo worked for the Briggs family's dining room. You can imagine how huge the Briggs family home is, and he used to work in the dining room. *Frank Kojima* worked at the Briggs Manufacturing dining room as a cook.

Then there's Ben Akagi, their daughter Reiko—everybody calls her Elaine Akagi, very active in the Seattle JACL. She was very active here, but when she moved to Seattle, she picked up momentum, and she's very active there. But her father worked for the Shimouras. He's buried in the same area that my in-laws are buried in. He was one of these early ones that—you know, a lot of the Issei came eastward because they worked the railroads. But he was working in Ohio, in Lima, Ohio, in a restaurant as a cook before he came here to work for Shimoura.

James Hirata in kimono—haori+hakama [Shimoura]

I know that her mother's mother was a dance teacher in Seattle. She's one of those persons that taught dancing, and a lot of Japanese culture. And Kinuko was in camp, and Ben was here, working for Shimoura's, and he was looking for a wife until someone recommended Kinuko in camp. And that's how he got together with her.

There were a number [of men] that worked at the Aviation Country Club—way out where West Bloomfield is now. I guess one gets a job, then they tell their friends, "Come on, this is pretty good." Frank Ichida—he's another single fellow—he was a cook at the Aviation Country Club. He also worked at the Green Lake Country Club. Kenneth Shikata, another single fellow, worked at, he was a cook at the Green Lake Country Club. He also worked at some nightclub on the Boulevard in Detroit. Because they were single, I think that this was a comfortable place for them to work. Also, *Harry Yoshida* worked at the Aviation Country Club, and he had a Caucasian wife.

Frank Ebisuya ("Mr. Kado") is one of the early Japanese grocery store owners. He called his place *The Mikado*, but, you know, when war broke out, he decided he better change their name. So he changed the name of his store to *Ebisuya Food Company.* He also had a restaurant on Michigan Avenue, near Tiger Stadium. We used to go [to the store] and shop all the time because there weren't any other Japanese food stores there. Of course you didn't have any of the variety of now, but then it was the best you could do at the time. The restaurant was a

Tadae Shimoura at
Henry Ford's old house [Shimoura]

diner-like place right across from Briggs Stadium. And it was going quite well, because, you know, he got the captured crowd from the stadium. But the restaurant was before my time.

Eishiro Kaneko had a gift store. And he also had a Chinese carry-out place. Then there was a Takahashi, Gentaro Takahashi, who had a gift store. But he moved back to Seattle, too.

Tom Kadowaki was a draftsman; his wife, Yoshi, I got to know quite well. He was a draftsman by training, but they opened a Japanese restaurant on the Boulevard. So it was kind of a gathering place for a lot of the Japanese people on the Boulevard. They were east of Woodward, on Grand Boulevard. The restaurant was called Kadowaki's.

Raymond Hayashi, who was *Kato* in the Green Hornet program, was a partner with Yoshi Kadowaki at the restaurant. He also played Toyo at WXYZ Radio. He's an interesting fellow. I believe Kadowaki's was the first Japanese restaurant. It opened way before the war back in the Thirties. A lot of people would have events there. It was a hangout for all of the single men.

During the war, they closed up. That's when Yoshi started the Chinese carry-out, but they never reopened the restaurant. Yoshi was the primary person in the restaurant. Her husband was a daytrader; he was at the stock market all the time. And so the bulk of the responsibility fell on Yoshi's shoulders. The carry-out place was on Grand River, I think, where the Boulevard crosses Grand River. It was on the Westside.

Koyanagi was a cook, but he moved to Washington, D.C. and became a cook at the Japanese Embassy in D.C.. So when the war broke out, he was put into a special center where they put all the diplomats. I think it was in [West Virginia]—Greenbrier. From there, he was sent back to Japan with the diplomats. But it's interesting, because he didn't know what to do in the way of work in Japan. So my father-in-law, because of his connection with the Takenaka Komuten—it's the biggest construction company in Japan—so through that connection, Jack Koyanagi got a very good job there in Japan. I think Takenaka is still rated number one in Japan, or either one or two in Japan, as far as construction goes.

One that I'd like to talk about is *James Hirata*. James Hirata is a hometown boy that came up, but he turned out to be a very brilliant person. And as a matter of fact, if you go to the Detroit Institute of Arts, in the mural you'll find one Asian-looking face with a white shirt supervising. And in the brochure, it doesn't give his name, unfortunately. I tried to make the correction over at the DIA. I told them, "I know this, the history of this man, and I'd like to have you spell out his name in the next set of brochures." They told me they would, I don't know if they would or not. James Hirata was, especially during World War II, very necessary in the B-29 production over at Willow Run, the factory [where] they were putting out the bombers. It was a gauge machine that he was such an expert on. And so he was very necessary at the job. But because he was Japanese, the FBI used to escort him to work every day and sit beside him during the day as he worked and then, at the end of the day, would drive him home. They just didn't trust him in the factory there. But he was that important at that time. He said since he retired, and he went down to Florida, and he's passed on.

And there were others. There was a *Mr. Sasakura*, he was another one of those that did very, very well in engineering. In fact, if you're at all familiar with, you know, the wax carton that milk comes in, that's one of his designs. But, unfortunately, he couldn't get a patent on it himself because he was working for a company then. Also, do you remember the Tucker automobile? I think there was a movie made of Tucker. Well, Mr. Tucker went to Chicago to try to develop this car, and it was Sasakura that he took along as his engineer to work on this. So Mr. Sasakura was bouncing between Detroit and Chicago during that period. Unfortunately, the car did not take off, but it's an interesting history. And if you see the movie *Tucker*, there is an Asian man in there, and that would be Mr. Sasakura.

Taizo Kokubo, now there's a colorful one. He was an importer, and he's also a salesman of Japanese gift items. But he's actually an optometrist. And it was he who bequeathed money to the Japanese community. In fact, the JACL loan fund originated from the money that he gave JACL. He also left money for Japanese community use, and that money, because we couldn't get enough to set up a Japanese center, we helped furnish one of the rooms in Manoogian Hall at Wayne State University. They call it their International Center. The different ethnic groups were asked to decorate a room in the manner of their country. We asked *Hideo Fujii* (everybody called him Heidi), Heidi Fujii to design that for us, which he did. He did a very nice job. And there is a plaque there at the entrance of the room designating the committee that worked on that. And Heidi tried to use as authentic materials possible and we had about $40,000 to work with. So he put in very nice materials. Unfortunately, it was not kept up as well as we hoped it would be kept. You know, a lot of the wood, they grab it without realizing that you can stain unfinished wood.

Heidi [Hideo] Fujii was a very successful general architect. He was based downtown for a long time, and then towards the end, there, he moved over to Farmington Hills, I believe. I know he did the Michigan State University's medical school. He did quite a bit of work in the campus of Saginaw State. He said he was never able to do any work at University of Michigan. He graduated Michigan, but he said he never got any job there. Like myself, you know, out of camp, we went to universities or colleges in the Midwest. He's one of those that went to college in Ann Arbor.

The Takemoto Family, 143 E Vernor 1953
[Takemoto]

Eiko Kosai Takemoto

interviewed by Miyoko M. O'Neill
February 11, 2003

The first of the Kosai family to arrive in the U.S. was Shinya Kosai. He was born on July 4, 1862 in Shiga-Ken, Japan (which is about 60 miles from Kyoto). Shinya immigrated to Puget Sound, Washington in 1899. He moved to White River Valley around 1900. As one of the early settlers, he gradually acquired hundreds of acres of land in the Auburn area (located between Seattle and Tacoma). He started a dairy farm and gradually added berries to his farming. There were many apple trees on the farm also. Dairy farming was one of the most important early agricultural pursuits in the State of Washington.

Shinya's Japan-born son Kiichiro (born in 1888) immigrated to the U.S. in 1902 to join his father. Shinya's wife Suma immigrated to the U.S. in 1905 with son Gizo (8 years old). Son Suejiro (born in 1894) immigrated to U.S. in 1908 to join the family. They lived in a two-story residence with eight barns, sheds and garages. Shinya Kosai died of cerebral hemorrhage on July 7, 1919, and his body was returned for burial to Japan accompanied by his wife Suma and son Gizo. Kiichiro and Suejiro Kosai were two of an estimated 200 Japanese-American farmers in the White River Valley. The Kosai Family thus represents a historic socioeconomic pattern of development in the area.

Shinya Kosai's son Kiichiro and his wife Sumi had eight children. Frank Kosai, the eldest son, was named as owner of the farm. Suejiro and his wife Masa had two children. Masa Inouye Kosai came from Japan in 1918 to Seattle, then joined Suejiro at the dairy farm. Eiko was born in 1920 in Auburn, and her sister Mary was born in 1922. Mary was sent to Japan in 1938 to be with her grandmother Suma. She studied medicine at the Tokyo Woman's College in Tokyo. Mary worked as a physician at a hospital in Kyoto before returning to the U.S. in 1947. Mary Kosai Fujioka now resides in Oxford, Michigan. In the 1920s, the Kosai barns and other Japanese barns in the White River Valley were burned several times. People attributed these fires to arson, but they never found those who started the fires. Some believed it was anti-Japanese prejudice. The Kosai family was one of the 10 legal cases challenging the State's Anti-Alien Land Law Act of 1921. They were directly involved in a critical legal case over discrimination and land ownership. The Attorney for the State considered Kiichiro giving his interest to his American-born son Frank Kosai and becoming an employed foreman was a violation of the law and prosecuted him. However, the District Court and the State Supreme Court decided the case in favor of the defendants.

June, 1992. Jane Bertsch (right) recognizes Eiko and Ken Takemoto with an aware for 1,500 hours of volunteer service.

As a result of the barn burnings, Suejiro moved his family to Tacoma in 1927 where he purchased the Grand Hotel. After high school, Eiko left for Seattle and enrolled at the Charlotte School of Design. After a year, Eiko was asked to teach first graders in a Japanese American School in Tacoma. She taught every day during the week and worked at a gift shop on the weekends. The family stayed in Tacoma until the war.

After Japan bombed Pearl Harbor on December 7, 1941, President Franklin D. Roosevelt signed Executive Order No. 9066 on February 19, 1942 to evacuate all the people of Japanese ancestry (citizens and non-citizens) from the states of Washington, Oregon and California. They were considered military zones.

The Kosai families (three generations) were sent to Pinedale Assembly Center near Fresno, California. Then they were sent to Tule Lake War Relocation Camp in northern California. Kiichiro died in camp at the age of 57 on April 6, 1945. Frank Kosai was sent to Montana to work. His wife Aiko and their two daughters were sent to Minidoka Camp in Idaho.

Suejiro Kosai's daughter Eiko met and married Ken Takemoto at the Tule Lake Camp on May 5, 1943. Ken's father (Yoshitaro) operated a store in Sacramento California before the war. Mother, [his?] name was Yoshino. Ken's father had a stroke when the Sacramento Buddhist Church burned down. His father somehow felt responsible for the children who were burned at the Church. Ken was working for the State of California before evacuation. His sister Sadako Takemoto Nikaido and her husband relocated from Tule Lake Camp to Salt Lake City, Utah. Her husband worked for a produce house. Later, he was transferred to Cheyenne, Wyoming. Sadako died in 2002 at the age of 95 years.

Suejiro and Masa Kosai and the Ken Takemoto families were sent to Topaz Camp in Utah (September 1943). After three months in Topaz, Ken and Eiko Takemoto left camp. Originally, their destination was for Cleveland, Ohio. However, they got sidetracked in Chicago. Ken found that there were a couple of job opportunities in Detroit, Michigan.

This was in January 1944. When they came to Detroit, it was snowing very hard. They had never seen such a snow storm. It was an experience they never forgot. They don't remember any snow storm like that since. Ken landed a job at Charles K. Harris CPA accounting firm in the Penobscot Building in Detroit. While he was working there, a client offered Ken a job at the H.A. Powell Photo Studio.

Eiko & Ken Takemoto
[Takemoto]

Eiko Takemoto

interviewed by Miyo O'Neill
February 11, 2003

MO: *When did your grandparents come to the United States?*

ET: It was 1902. My grandpa came in 1902.

MO: *Then where did he go?*

ET: He went to Seattle. No! Auburn, Washington. That's where they started a dairy farm, rural dairy farm.

MO: *And your father?*

ET: And then my father come in 1908.

MO: *Did he come with your father?*

ET: No, I think he came later. My father came in 1908... He joined his father at the dairy farm, you know.

MO: *Uh huh.*

ET: Dairy farm...

MO: *Uh huh. What about your mother?*

ET: My mother came from Japan in 1918. Came to Seattle and that's when she joined my father. So both of them did the dairy farm. And then I believed they had berries, you know, strawberries and little farming.

MO: *And then, where were you born?*

ET: I was born in 1920 in Auburn.

MO: *Did you have any brothers or sisters?*

ET: I have no brothers, but I have a sister. You know, Mary.

MO: *Could you tell us something you might remember about your childhood?*

ET: Childhood?

MO: *Maybe about Mary going to Japan.*

ET: Childhood? I remember really green apples. *[laughs]*

MO: *Green apples?*

ET: Yeah, 'cause we had lots of apple trees. Mother and father had to go to the dairy. Certain hours you have to milk the cows. Mama says, "You eat lots of apples." *[laughs]* So maybe that's why I don't eat apples. I don't remember too much because you know I didn't stay in Auburn too long. I think I moved to Tacoma about 1927, I think. I don't even remember going to grade school. Maybe I did?

MO: *Going where?*

ET: Grade school.

MO: *Oh.*

ET: Maybe I did. And I don't remember the barns being burned either.

MO: *Oh.*

ET: That's when my father decided to sell it. I think it was lots of barns.

MO: *And then… where did you go after that?*

ET: After, Tacoma. My father operated a hotel. And we stayed until the war, 1940.

MO: *And when did Mary leave?*

ET: Mary left for Japan 1930… I can't remember. I think it was '38 or '39. Let's see, war started in December. She could've left in 1939. I can't remember… Getting old.

MO: *[laughs]*

ET: And she didn't come back till 1947. That's right, 1947.

MO: *Do you remember anything about your parents?*

ET: Parents?

MO: *Parent's family.*

ET: Parent's family. Not too much. Mother and father.

MO: *What was his father's name?*

ET: I think his father's name was Yoshi... tato... and... *[pauses]*... .I think his mother's name was Yoshino. And I think that he operated a grocery store.

MO: *Grocery store?*

ET: Called Kishugaki, I think.

MO: *Oohh.*

ET: Yeah.

MO: *Was it a grocery store?*

ET: A grocery or maybe a utility store. I don't know. One of those. And then, the father had a stroke because both of the streets got burned at that time. So, I don't know what year. But he says that when father worried so much that some of the kids must have got burnt, he had a stroke.

MO: *Oh.*

ET: And from then on, he was more than handicapped, I guess. You don't remember Sacramento? They must have had a dormitory or something, huh? That's many years ago. That's what he always says, papa got sick because he worried about the children that got burned. I was

always told that the children were not his, but he felt responsible for them.

MO: *Yeah. What camp were you in?*

ET: We went, you know, from Tacoma, we were sent to Pinedale.

MO: *Oh.*

ET: You know, by Fresno.

MO: *Then from Pinedale?*

ET: From Pinedale, we went to Tule Lake. Then we went to Topaz for 3 months and came to Detroit.

MO: *Why did you pick Michigan?*

ET: Why did we pick Michigan?

MO: *Yeah.*

ET: We had our tickets to Cleveland to tell you the truth.

MO: *Oh.*

ET: It was sidetracked to Chicago. There was a couple of places that had offered a job opportunities, so we stopped in Chicago and it came to Detroit.

ET: He applied at a CPA firm—don't remember the name in the Penobscot Building.

MO: *Did he stay with them long?*

ET: No, during his CPA job, you know, they go around checking the books. Mr. Powell said, "I want you to come work with me." Photography studio.

ET: That's how he went to H.A. Powell Studio. He asked. So that's where he worked until he retired. So he was what they called… secretary-treasurer for the H.A. Powell Studio.

MO: *And what did you do?*

ET: What did I do? When I came to Detroit, I went to work for the YW.

MO: *Oh, you did? [laughs]*

ET: I went to work for YW in the finance department.

MO: *Y-W?*

ET: Y-W-C-A.

MO: *In the finance department?*

ET: Uh huh. It was the finance department. There were couple of other Nisei working for YWCA. Doris Fujioka worked for Highland Park. I was working for downtown.

MO: *Who is she?*

ET: Do you remember Doris Fujioka?

MO: *Oh yeah!*

ET: She and [Setsu Fujioka] worked in Highland Park YWCA, and I worked for Detroit downtown.

MO: *Yeah.*

ET: Oh after, I had daughter. She was born in 1944. I didn't work until my youngest one, Bobby, was in high school, I think. That's when I started working again.

MO: *Oh.*

ET: Ken said, "I need somebody to help me," so that's what I did. *[laughs]* Only with agreement that I'd take the time off for meetings or anything else. I had to keep up the other activities, you know.

MO: *Yeah.*

ET: I'm too old really to get stuck in that.

MO: *[laughs]*

ET: So I was on my own time.

MO: *Did you use to work in the same place?*

ET: Powell, H. A. Powell? Yeah, that's when Ken was a bookkeeper. He wanted somebody to come and help.

ET: Oh, so I said only with agreement. *[laughs]*

MO: *[laughs] You had Judy in 1944?*

ET: And John was born in '46. And then Julia was born in '52. And Bob was '57. So at that time, when the kids went to school, I got involved in PTA, that's why.

MO: *And did you have… was there any discrimination?*

ET: Me, in schools?

MO: *Like after you came to Michigan.*

ET: I don't think so. I didn't think we had any. I think the only time was when Ken went into, you know, to see the ad for rent. At that time, housing was bad, you know?

MO: *Oh yeah.*

ET: But we did find places as we went along.

MO: *Uh huh.*

ET: Yeah. Did you know one of the buildings that some *nihon-jins* lived in were in the paper, brownstone buildings.

ET: Downtown, John R.

MO: *That's where you stayed?*

ET: No, I didn't stay, but I knew a couple of *nihon-jins* stayed in there. I think we stayed in the northern part of that, I think. We were—I forgot the address—forty-one-twenty or something. We stayed at John R too. You know, when we first came, we knew there was no housing. I don't know about all of you. How did you get your housing?

MO: *I… I stayed over at Sakow's.*

ET: Oh! You, that's right! I remember now.

MO: *They had a hostel.*

ET: Yeah, something like that. Uh huh. On Trumbull.

MO: *Yeah.*

ET: Oh. See when we came in, we stayed at the Grand Hotel on John R. The WRA told us that we could stay, so we stayed there until we found a place. Then we kept moving. You probably heard of 280 East Kirby. That's where all the Niseis were staying.

MO: *Oh.*

ET: Most of them were married couples, you know?

MO: *Uh huh.*

MO: *So when did you come to Michigan?*

ET: We came in January 1944 in the snow.

MO: *[laughs]*

ET: That was a snowstorm! I haven't seen snow like that since we came here. January we came, and then my father and mother came out, it was about August from Topaz.

MO: *It was in 1944?*

ET: In 1944. In August. Yeah, in August, my father and my mother came.

MO: *They had a hotel?*

ET: Hotel on East Warren, right on the corner of John R and Warren. It no longer stands there.

MO: *Uh huh.*

ET: But then we had some Japanese staying there too. I believe one of them was Kubota. Mr. Kubota was staying there.

ET: There was quite a few staying there. Then when my father died, we sold the hotel.

MO: *When was that?*

ET: So they gave up the hotel in 1954.

MO: *Okay, when did you start volunteering?*

ET: Well, I did lots. I started with PTA. You know, the local PTA. Then I went into what they called Detroit Council. At that time we had about two hundred PTAs, you know.

MO: *Wow.*

ET: Yeah. Did you have council PTA?

MO: *Yeah. I did. What did I do? I was treasurer for some time.*

ET: Yeah, and I did other little things too. Some of the groups are still living. Then as soon as I retired, I had a phone call from Detroit Receiving Hospital.

MO: *Oh.*

ET: Yeah. Because I knew the lady that was Detroit Council's PTA President. She knew I retired and I kept up my membership to the Detroit Council, now, what they call Detroit Receiving Hospital Service League. And she called me and she says, "You've been member, why don't you come and help us?" That's when I decided okay, I was thinking something simple. I went to volunteer and then Ken says, "Well, I might as well go too." *[laughs]*

MO: What did you do?

ET: Once a week we volunteered.

MO: *Doing what?*

ET: Well, first we went in to take a survey of all the patients that came in—wanted to know how they were served. "How was your doctors?" You know, "did you like your doctor?" Or, you know, questions like you asking me.

MO: *Huh. [laughs]*

ET: *[laughs]* And then Ken says, "Everybody has the same answers!" he says.

MO: *[laughs]*

ET: Which was true.

MO: *Uh huh.*

ET: Because they don't want to spend time with you, you know.

MO: *Uh huh.*

ET: Oh! I'm too busy. I have to go. "Oh yes! Everything was just fine, fine, yes, yes." So Ken finally says, "That survey is no good." He says, "Everybody gives you the same answers." *[laughs]* And so we knew about them. We did that for a while and went to help the service league. And what did we do? We did a candy... candy cart.

MO: *Oh..*

ET: With the patients.

MO: *Uh huh.*

ET: Yeah. And they still remember us. "Why don't you come around with a cart?" I said, "I don't have a partner... you can't do alone."
A boy stole money. If I walked out, there's nobody to watch.

MO: *Oh.*

MO: *So do you still do your volunteer work?*

ET: I still volunteer.

MO: *What do you do?*

ET: I take a lady from Grosse Pointe Unitarian Church with me. She and I both work together in the clothing department. The patient that comes in Emergency, you know, they have no clothes to go home in.

MO: *Oh.*

ET: You know, stockings and shoes. Shoes we give them. Anything that they need to be discharged.

MO: *Oh.*

ET: Especially in Emergency.

MO: *Uh huh.*

ET: I became one of the officers, you know, in the service league. We now call them now Auxiliary. So I've been on it for some time. I was a treasurer for some time.

MO: *[laughs]*

ET: But we both worked the ER. And then we got honors too.

MO: *Uh huh.*

ET: You know volunteering. It's surprising, yes. First, I think we got a … you've heard of a "Thanks for Giving Organization." That's in Wayne County, Oakland and Macomb. They honor people that were volunteers. So Ken and I were honored in that. And then another week we were honored for what they called "Governor's List."

ET: Just before Ken died, he was honored at the Detroit Athletic Club for being

80-plus. I said to a friend of mine, "How come?" "He's over 80 isn't he?" I said, "Yeah. What did he do?"

MO: *Oh.*

ET: Yeah. I was surprised. So what did we do? Aside from that, I go to Auxiliary meetings. And, we decorated for Christmas. We don't decorate anymore. We're too old. *[laughs]* We have hired a display company that does all the decorating.

MO: *For Receiving?*

ET: Yeah. Well, this company, it's a big job for them. And I hired her about ten years ago. She was just out of college. *[laughs]* And I said we had connection with her with Powell Studio. That's what it is. So I went to talk to her. "First year we bought a tree." And then everybody said, "You don't want to do it. We're getting to old." *[laughs]* Young people said, "Oh, it won't take too long. We will come and help." Nobody came to help.

MO: *Uh huh.*

ET: So, the lady said, "We decorate the trees all over the city, private homes and companies." I said, "Oh, well that's good." We had two trees decorated—one in emergency and the hallway at a cost of nearly $3,000—but it was worth it.

MO: *I see.*

ET: Then we had sales to make money.

MO: *Uh huh.*

ET: But that's what I do.

MO: *So what do you do besides from JACL and…*

ET: Hospital and Church.

MO: *Church. So what do you do at the church?*

ET: What do you mean? I joined the church in 1962 or something. Well, Ken, you know how he found Unitarian church. He was reading a magazine, and it says something about, "Are you Unitarian without knowing?" *[pauses slightly]* I don't know. That's how we joined it.

MO: *I'll tell you afterwards.*

ET: And then a Father from Detroit came over. He lived in my neighborhood and that's how we decided. And then we talked to Reverend Tsuji, I think it was. Ken says, "We're thinking about joining Unitarian because there's no [Buddhist] church." And he says, "I have to have something for our children." We did, Ken did stay at the Methodist church because the Reverend Wada—no, Tanabe—was out there. Remember?

MO: *Uh huh.*

ET: Cause he's from Tacoma. Ken took the kids. He took Julie—no, Julie didn't go, she was a baby yet—Judy and John. Then he went to doubt the education class, you know. He says, "I don't like it." So he stopped going, but he took the kids. The kids said, "If Daddy's not going, we don't want to go." *[laughs]*

MO: *Isn't that true?*

ET: Yeah. So meanwhile we looked into Unitarian church, and they [Buddhist advisors] said, "If you don't have it [nearby Buddhist church], I think you are making a good choice." So that's what we did. There's a pamphlet now about Unitarian Buddhism. Did you read it? So that's why we've been going since 1950…'60, I think…'62. 'Cause Bobby was about four or five when we started. So ever since then, we've been to church. Long time, huh? Almost 40 years. My goodness. Well, we've been here for 60 years. 'Cause Judy, she was born in '44. Well, it'll be 60 years this year. We came in '43. This is 2003.

ET: Sixty years. I don't know how many years you've been here, but…

MO: *[laughs]*

ET: Almost the same. Fifty-three, that's right.

MO: *What has Julie been doing?*

ET: Julie is a MD and in physiology. I think she works for the Los Angeles, UCLA Harbor City Hospital. She's affiliated with the school. And I think she teaches or lectures or something too. 'Cause my son-in-law says, "She don't say much, but she's up there some place. She don't even tell me," he says.

MO: *What does her husband do?*

ET: Her husband is a dentist. They got married in Detroit. Then after they got married, Jimmy said, "Mommy, mom and dad." He says, "Is it alright if we move to California?" 'Cause his mother and father just came from Japan. Mother was born in Japan.

MO: *What was their ethnic background?*

ET: Chinese.

MO: *Chinese?*

ET: But mother was born in Kobe, Japan. And then father was some kind of engineer who made all the tunnels during the war, but then they've been around the world. She told me, "All my children are born in different cities 'cause daddy had to move and we moved." *[laughs]*

MO: *What's their names?*

ET: John works for the city, Oak Park.

MO: *Oak Park?*

ET: Uh huh. I don't know what he does. He never tells me exactly what he does. I think it has something to do with a computer. He's married to a Caucasian girl, you know.

MO: *What's her name?*

ET: We call her Beth, but I think she goes by Maria, I think. She's an automobile engineer, some kind of exhaust or something. And then Judy. Judy is in Kalamazoo. She's a physical therapist and works for Kalamazoo School Board. And her husband is a schoolteacher. He's quite active with the city, and Kalamazoo is a small town, you know.

MO: *Do they have any children?*

ET: Oh Judy, has two of her own. So actually three girls, one's adopted. John has two adopted Korean Girls. And then Bob is divorced. But he's raised his children. They wanted to go with mom, so...

MO: *Oh.*

ET: Yeah. With that interracial... *[laughs]*

MO: *Two. Two boys?*

ET: No, he has boy and a girl.

MO: *Oh, he raised... He's raising them?*

ET: Miko graduated high school last year. She was young and she didn't know she was graduating. She didn't go senior, year, just junior. She's home studying. Her parents have to teach them. So when it came to graduating, they told her counselor that she's graduating. But she said, "You still got senior year." So Bob says, "She's got more than enough credits."

MO: *And the boy is younger?*

ET: The boy is older.

MO: *Older? Wow. What does the boy do?*

ET: He works with family business. I guess you call it, huh? 'Cause if grandpa is a contractor for the pavement, big jobs in the highways. So all the family is in the business.

MO: *Did Bob work for them too?*

ET: No, Bob works for General Motors.

MO: *What do you think of the Nikkei community here?*

ET: Do we have a Nikkei community? *[laughs]*

MO: *I guess we're all pretty scared.*

ET: We're scared, aren't we? We don't get together too often, either. I don't know about you. Maybe we should. I don't know.

MO: *I don't know.*

ET: Clearly, we don't seem to be getting together all the time.

President Bill Clinton presenting at the WWII
Medal of Honor Recipients Ceremony, June 2000
[Okubo]

James K. Okubo

Nobuyo Okubo (1920–1967)
Medal of Honor Recipient – June 21, 2000 (Posthumous)

James (Jim) Kazuo Okubo was born in Anacortes, Washington in May 1920. His father was Kenzo Okubo from Hiroshima, Japan. His mother was Fuyu Kanzaki from Fukuoka, Japan. Mr. Okubo worked as a cabin boy, then as a cook on ships coming from Japan to the United States. Mr. Okubo decided to stay in the U.S., met and married Fuyu, and they settled in Seattle, Washington.

Mr. and Mrs. Kenzo Okubo's first born was a daughter named Toshiko. She was born in Japan and came to the United States to join the family when she was in her teens. The remaining six children were born in Anacortes, Washington. They were: Hiram, Sumihe, Tomi, Hime, James, and John (died at 13 of leukemia). Later on, the family moved back to Seattle, then to Bellingham.

When Mr. and Mrs. Okubo had five children, they added the youngest four children of Mrs. Okubo's sister (Mrs. Kunimatsu) when she suddenly died from a stroke. They were Saburo, Shiro, Isamu, and Takeko (who was only two years old).

Mr. and Mrs. Okubo opened a restaurant (Sunrise Cafe) in Bellingham, Washington. James went to school in Seattle and Bellingham, Washington. Jim graduated from Bellingham High School in 1938. He was active in football and was a member of the ski club. James was attending Western Washington College of Education (and in the summers, he worked in the Alaskan canneries) when Japan bombed Pearl Harbor on December 7, 1941.

When the war broke out in 1941, James and his brothers as well as his cousins tried to volunteer for the U.S. Army, but they were rejected. Only Hiram was accepted because he was drafted earlier and completed his time in the Army before.

After Pearl Harbor, President Franklin D. Roosevelt signed Executive Order 9066 on February 19, 1942 to evacuate all people of Japanese ancestry from the West Coast.

The Okubo family was sent to the Tule Lake concentration camp in 1942. At the Tule Lake concentration camp in 1943, the Okubo boys and the cousins (Kunimatsu boys) volunteered for the military. James (age 23) was sent to the quickly organized Japanese American 442nd Regimental Combat Team (RCT), as well as Hiram, Sumihe, and Isamu. Saburo was sent to join the Military Intelligence Service.

Father Kenzo Okubo died at the Tule Lake concentration camp in 1943. The rest of the Okubo family were sent to Heart Mountain concentration camp in Wyoming. After two years of incarceration, the family was allowed to leave and settle in Detroit, Michigan. Mrs. Fuyu Okubo passed away in Michigan. James was assigned as Tech 5th Grade Medic with the K Company of the 442nd RCT. James distinguished himself by extraordinary heroism in action in France and was recommended by his Commanding Officer to receive the Medal of Honor. He was downgraded and received the Silver Star instead because he "was a Medic and not a combatant."

S SGT Hiram Okubo with the 442nd RCT came home disabled. PFC Sumihe Okubo with the 442nd RCT came home disabled. Isamu Kunimatsu with the 442nd RCT was killed in action.

After the war, James joined his family in Detroit, Michigan. He enrolled at Wayne University in Detroit. There he met Nobuyo (Nobi) Miyaya who was also attending Wayne University and later became his wife. Jim was obtaining his pre-dental requirements at Wayne University. After James received his bachelor's degree, he went on to University of Detroit School of Dentistry. He received his D.D.S. degree in 1954. After graduation, Dr. Okubo opened a private practice with another dentist. He also started teaching at the University of Detroit School of Dentistry. James later became Chair of the Anatomy Department.

In the winter of 1967, the James Okubo family (wife Nobi and three children) was en route to a Michigan skiing area when they were involved in an automobile accident. Unfortunately, James died from that accident.

Nobi Okubo received a phone call in 1999 from U.S. Senator Daniel Akaka (of Hawaii). He informed her they were reviewing the files and attempting to upgrade her husband's Silver Star to Medal of Honor. It would require a time limitation waiver from Congress. Congress authorized the upgrade to Medal of Honor on June 15, 2000.

On *November 11, 1999* (Veterans Day), the *Detroit Free Press* front page reported "the late Japanese-American instructor at University of Detroit is in line for highest military honor."

February 3, 2000—JACL Detroit Chapter Newsletter, Volume 54, No. 1. Article honoring James K. Okubo. "Congressional Medal of Honor pending for Detroit 442nd War Hero." On May 7, 2000, Mrs. James (Nobi) Okubo spoke about her communications with some of the people who have been instrumental in trying to have her late husband's award upgraded to the Medal of Honor.

February 9, 2000—*The Observer & Eccentric* newspaper, Birmingham, Michigan. Article entitled, "Honored at Last"—World War II hero with Oakland county ties receives nation's highest honor.

June 21, 2000—Ceremony honoring Asian American medal of Honor recipients at the White House. (22 recipients—12 from the famed 442nd RCT). Mrs. James (Nobi) Okubo, her children, her grandchildren, and relatives were at the ceremony.

July 17, 2000—*Bellingham Herald,* Bellingham, Washington. "Medal of Honor comes late for ex-Bellingham resident." Medic James Okubo, whose family was interned during war, saved dozens of lives.

September 2000—members of Dr. Okubo, University of Detroit Dental class of 1954 honored him by inviting Mrs. Nobi Okubo to their class reunion to speak to them about the Medal of Honor ceremony in Washington, D.C. They also wrote about it in the *Journal of the Michigan Dental Associates* of November/December 2000.

March 25, 2001—Dedication ceremony of t/5 James K. Okubo Medical and Dental Complex at Fort Lewis, Washington. It was a historic event that honored an American, a Nisei veteran, a World War II hero, with the dedication of a $5 million Medical Clinic and a $5.5 million Dental Clinic in his name.

Honorable Gary Locke, Governor of the State of Washington stated, "James Okubo is our home town hero." Ceremony was highlighted by strict military protocol hosted by Camp and Ft. Lewis Commanding Officer Lieutenant General James T. Hill and his fine staff of soldiers. Over three hundred people attended. U.S. Army Chief-of-Staff Eric Shinseki gave the main address.

November 7, 2001 — B*ellingham Herald,* Bellingham, Washington — "Bellingham High School alumnus James Okubo saved dozens of lives." First recipient of Bellingham High School's Distinguished Alumni Award at school assembly. His wife Nobi accepted her husband's award.

May 2003 — *Detroit Free Press,* Woodland Cemetery in Detroit. Dozens of U.S. Military representatives presented Nobi with Combat Medics badge and the Bronze Star on her husband's behalf. The ceremony was marked by a gun salute and the playing of taps. This would have been James Okubo's 82nd birthday.

May 6, 2003 — Dedication of Okubo Barracks at Ft. Sam Houston. "The facility at San Antonio, Texas is 'The Home of Army Medicine' and the dedication in the name of Medal of Honor recipient and Army Medic, James Okubo, is a very fitting tribute to the American hero."

July, 2003 — Re-dedication of Medal of Honor Memorial in Riverside, California. James Okubo's name was added to the granite walls inside the courtyard. Medal of Honor Society, March Air Base.

Mrs. James (Nobi) Okubo and her children resided in Walled Lake, Michigan. Three children have all been successful and are independent. Nobi believes that her husband James exerted

James Okubo receiving Silver Star, Biffontain [Okubo]

a strong influence on them as well as pushing them into outdoor activities. Two of the children reside in California, and one now lives in Colorado. Nobi now resides in Colorado near one of her sons.

Nobi still attends the 442nd RCT reunions where the veterans still remember technician fifth grade medic James K. Okubo.

118

Okubo Family
[Okubo]

JACL Picnic
[Miyao]

Max Koga

Max Koga was born in Seattle, son of Shizuko Tarnai (from Osaka, Japan, 1921) and Jingo Koga (South Japan, 1905). His mother, Shizuko was born in Japan and raised by her grandparents and came to Seattle. Shizuko's father was bilingual and was a court translator. Max's father Jingo worked in and later owned his own restaurant, serving non-Japanese food. Max is one of three children born to Shizuko and Jingo; others are Stanley of Peoria, IL working for Caterpillar Company and Joyce of Portland, Oregon.

In 1925, the Koga family moved to Yakima Valley, WA to start a restaurant. It was from Yakima that they were evacuated during World War II and spent the war years in the Heart Mountain Relocation Camp.

While in Heart Mountain, Max worked on a farm that produced beets, potatoes, peas, and asparagus. He was drafted into the army in 1944 and trained in Camp Blanding, FL. After training, he was sent to France to join the 442nd Regimental Combat Team.

His service in Europe included southwest France near Italy. After the Battle at Bruyeres, he was sent to Italy to fight in the Po Valley and battles north of Po Valley. Max was in the Infantry and was wounded and hospitalized in Italy. Because of this, he was not among the 442nd soldiers who received a warm welcome upon their return. Instead, he returned quietly by way of New York.

Because his brother Stanley was by then working for Caterpillar in Peoria, IL, Max went to Chicago to be near Stanley and entered Bradley College under the G. I. Bill. He majored in

Engineering in 1948, but there were no jobs open to him. He settled for menial jobs around Chicago. There was a job offering by the government in a munitions depot which he took. This led to a job in Detroit at the Detroit Arsenal where he worked for five years. He was then hired by Ford Motor Company as a safety engineer and worked there for thirty-two years before retiring.

An emphatic statement made by Max: While working at Ford Motor Company, he was made very uncomfortable by disparaging remarks made behind his back. His coworkers did not back him up for fear of retaliation. No one took up his cause. The clergy was most understanding.

He married Yuri Shimokochi in 1952. Their son, John, went to the University of Michigan and played clarinet in the University of Michigan marching band. Currently, John, married to Angie, is in computer work in Knoxville, TN. Max and Yuri's first home was in an apartment in Royal Oak. They bought a home in Troy in the 1970s and continue to reside there in their retirement.

124

Frank Kuwahara

Toshiko Shimoura & Mary Kamidoi

Frank Kuwahara was born in Sacramento in 1921 and at the age of two returned to Hiroshima, Japan with his family. In 1938, he returned to the U.S. alone and lived in Sacramento, CA until the evacuation of all Japanese Americans in California was effected. He was first placed in an Assembly Center in Marysville, CA and later sent to Tule Lake Relocation Center and confined there until the end of World War II.

Frank returned to Sacramento and after six months was drafted into the U.S. Army Infantry. Later he was transferred to the Military Intelligence School in Monterey, CA because of his bilingual ability. He graduated from the MIS in 1947. Because he was alone and had no family to visit, he came to Detroit, where his future wife, Agnes Fujii, had relocated from camp. He married Agnes in 1948. The U.S. Army then sent Frank to Japan (1948-1950) to study at the Intelligence College in Japan. He served as a translator/interpreter during the War Crimes Trials in Tokyo.

After his military service ended, he returned to his wife in Detroit. He discovered the true taste of prejudice while looking for a place to live and finding work. Even menial job offerings were closed to Japanese. His first job was at a Jewish Fish Market.

While looking for an apartment, he wore his army uniform, but was repeatedly told that the apartment was rented already while the "For Rent" sign hung in the window. This was in the neighborhood of Cass and Canfield. On the city bus, the bus driver did not open the door on his signal but went on for a couple of blocks to let him off. One bitter experience was when he didn't have the right change and asked the driver for change. The bus driver took his dollar bill and threw it on the floor. Frank retrieved it and put the whole dollar into the change box, paying much more than the regular fare.

Frank did finally get a job at Chrysler Corporation on the night shift. While boarding the bus, he was called "Chink" and pushed aside. His temper flared and he was about to punch the person, but a Native American Indian who stood behind him restrained him and told him that this was a "no-win" situation, a situation he had been in many times and that Frank would have no chance. Frank admitted that this was the first time he cried in public.

After fifteen years at Chrysler, he was laid off in 1962. Luckily, he was able to get a job at an automotive supplies company that made clutches. Chrysler did call him back, but only for a few years. Realizing the uncertainty of employment in the factories, he then decided, with the persuasion of James T. Shimoura, to start his own business and called his Japanese food and supply store Kuwahara's Trading Post. The year was 1967. It was located near Detroit's Chinatown. On many occasions, he had bullet holes in his front windows, shot by disgruntled Chinese.

The Kuwahara Trading Post was moved to a location in Birmingham and again to the present Noble Fish Store in Clawson. Upon retirement, Kuwahara sold his Noble Fish store and moved to Mt. Clemens, Michigan. They spent the rest of their remaining years in California.

Linda Fukuda for Far Eastern Festival, 1970
[ChaptAct]

"Mr. Kado" *(Frank Ebisuya)*

Dorothy Kuroda

My father and mother, Nowo and Momoyo Fukuda, entered San Francisco, California on May 13, 1919. They travelled to Sedalia, Missouri where my father had been living at 133 Ohio Street. From Missouri they moved to Lincoln, Nebraska where my oldest brother, Harry Yuji, was born in March of 1921. From Nebraska, they moved to Slick Creek, Oklahoma where Tom Minom was born in February of 1923. After a short stay in Toledo, Ohio they moved to Lincoln Park, Michigan where my father and his partner, Frank Ebisuya, opened their own restaurant on Fort Street. My sister Mary was born in Lincoln Park in April 1926. My parent's final move was to Detroit, Michigan to the area that is called "Corktown." I was born at 2016 Eighth Street on February 28, 1929. After the house on Eighth Street was torn down, we lived for a short while above a bar on Michigan Avenue which is now known as "Nemo's." My father and his partner opened up their restaurant on 1438 Michigan Avenue which was located a ½ block east of what was known as "Navin Field" now known as [the former] Tiger Stadium. They named the eatery "Nicko Lunch" and moved the family upstairs to reside.

The restaurant was located across the street from the Trumbull Police Station, which was torn down when Michigan Avenue was widened and was next door to a night club called "The Corktown Tavern," which closed and was divided up into several smaller stores.

My father passed away the same year I was born. In 1935, while my mother and my sister, Mary, visited my grandmother in Japan, my brothers and I stayed with our father's ex-partner, Frank Ebisuya.

At the restaurant, my mother worked as a cashier while my brothers helped out by peeling potatoes during their summer vacation. There were two Japanese waiters, a Tom Urabe and a Kenneth Shigata; however, I do not know what became of them.

Shortly after my mother returned home from Japan, she remarried my father's ex-partner, Frank Ebisuya. Although he was my step-father, Frank Ebisuya was the only father I knew and had always referred to him as "my father." He passed away in March of 1964.

Franklin Elementary School—where I had attended until the fourth grade—is still standing and can be viewed from the expressway and is currently being used for adult education.

Beside the two men who had worked for my father, I can only recall three other families—the Shimouras, Kanekos, and the Kokubos. I also remember two couples—the Kadowakis who owned a sukiyaki restaurant and the Kawasakis who worked for Mr. and Mrs. Ford as domestic servants. When Mrs. Ford passed away, they were remembered generously in her will and retired to Japan shortly after.

In 1938, we moved to 3316 Fenkell where my father opened up a wholesale/retail chop suey business called "Mikado's." When the war with Japan broke out, he had to go downtown to the FBI office for questioning, and as he was exiting the building, some newspaper photographers took his picture and printed it in the newspapers. As a result, my father's wholesale business suffered because many of the restaurant owners refused to buy from him forcing him to depend on the sales from the retail business. He also decided to change the name of the business from "Mikado's" to "Kado's." All of the family members worked in the restaurant—my mother helped with the cooking, my two brothers delivered and cared for the bean sprouts (which included growing and cleaning), while my sister and I answered the phone, waited on customers, and assisted wherever we were needed (i.e. cleaning the celery, filling shoyu vials, etc.).

During the war, some friends of my father's came to live with us because they had lost their jobs and had no place to live. I can recall some of them, such as Harry Midzutani, who had been a cook for a railroad company in Sandusky, Ohio and a gentleman, who I only remember as Frank, and his friend, a Mr. Sato, who was blind. Mr. Sato passed away. While my two brothers were in the service, Harry and Frank took over their jobs and worked for my father until the end of the war, when Frank found another job and moved away.

Harry stayed on with my father and rented a nearby room when my brother Tom discharged from the service and had returned home. Harry passed away in 1959. My father gradually phased out the chop suey carry-out and started a Japanese food and gift shop.

With the influx of Japanese from the relocation camps, he expanded his Japanese food line and had instituted a delivery service. Both of my parents were active members of the JACL. My mother passed away in August of 1983.

While living on Fenkell, I attended the Custer School through the eighth grade, the Post Intermediate for the ninth grade, and then graduated from Cooley High School in 1947. I then attended Wayne University (now called Wayne State University), and received a bachelor of science degree in pharmacy in 1951.

On Thanksgiving Day of 1946 I met Frank Kuroda at a mutual friend's house — a Mr. and Mrs. Shimizu who were living on Hamilton in Highland Park. Frank and I were married on June 28, 1952 at Augsburg Lutheran Church, which was located at the corner of Dexter and Keeler. The church was later torn down to make room for the expressway. We lived in Detroit in an upper flat on Clements for 1½ years before moving to our current residence in Allen Park in December of 1953.

We have one son, four daughters, three grandchildren, and one great-grandson. Frank's parents lived with us for a short time in the 1960s before retiring to Japan. They both passed away while living in Japan.

Frank Ebisuya

Mrs. Ebisuya playing samisen
[Shimoura]

"Concentration Camp" marker,
Crystal City, Texas.
[Hirozawa]

Yuji Morita

interviewed by Cathy Zheng, 2005

CZ: *Can you tell me a little bit about how your life was when you were growing up?*

YM: Well, I lived in the far side of San Francisco, which is not associated with Japantown. In fact, I lived basically in two different neighborhoods: one in the western half of San Francisco and one downtown San Francisco. I attended grammar school and junior high and Lowell High School, which is at that time and still is the all-academic high school—the oldest high school in the western U.S.

CZ: *So were you born in America?*

YM: I was born in San Francisco, right in the middle of Chinatown. *[laughs]*

CZ: *How did your family decide to live there or raise a family there?*

YM: Well my father came to the U.S. in 1907. I guess initially to go to school, but when he got here he decided to work instead. He went back to Japan in 1918. [He] did not marry the woman he was supposed to and chose my mother instead. And he came back to the U.S. through Seattle and settled in San Francisco. They operated a general merchandise store right in the middle of Chinatown and that was where I was born.

CZ: *Oh wow! So growing up did you relate yourself more with the Japanese Americans or the...*

YM: Most of my classmates at school were Caucasian people, but San Francisco is pretty cosmopolitan. There were students who were descendents of White Russians, some Jewish people. I don't recall any blacks in my classes, very few Orientals.

CZ: *Did you experience any discrimination at all when you were growing up?*

YM: I'd say... I really didn't encounter blatant discrimination. After high school, we didn't participate in some things, such as dances. Again, because there were so few Orientals.

CZ: *Did you live in California all your life?*

YM: I lived in California until 1942, when the evacuation occurred.

CZ: *What happened at the evacuation? What were your feelings and your reaction to the evacuation?*

YM: Well I didn't see any necessity for the evacuation. Wondering what was going to happen because I had just graduated high school and I was eligible for the draft. Until the war started, I guess I would have gone in the army, if the war hadn't happened.

CZ: *How long were you in the internment camp?*

YM: Well, I was in the assembly center for three months in Pomona, and I was at Heart Mountain Relocation Center for one month in mid-August or mid-September in 1942.

CZ: *What was it like living there? What were the living conditions?*

YM: Well, we were in the Pomona assembly camp during the summer from about May through mid-August. The Pomona assembly center was a part of the Los Angeles County, so some of the people were in the re-painted, whitewashed horse stalls. My family was in the barracks. Six of us, my parents and my two sisters, my brother, and myself were in a room twenty feet by twenty feet. We slept on cots and a ticking filled with straw. I guess a couple friends I knew were cleaning out a recreation building. We were paid thirteen dollars a month. With all the free time, we played bridge practically every day *[laughs]*.

CZ: *What was your family's initial reaction to the relocation camps and how did it change afterwards?*

YM: Well, my father, while I was growing up in grade school and junior high, worked as a houseboy basically, cleaning houses for a living. And about mid-1930s, my parents decided to open a cleaning shop. We sent out for the clothes to be cleaned, but my mother did the alterations. My father ran the ironing machine. That's where we were when we got sent to camp. When we got out of the camp, my father didn't want to set up his business again. He was into his fifties by then. So he went back to work as a houseboy.

I guess they were doing pretty well because I can remember before the war that the man who we rented our home from said he liked the Japanese people because they always paid their rent on time. I guess my father got along with the people whom he worked for. One of the people whom he worked for was a stockbroker, and after he died, I learned he had a fair amount of stock he had saved up. And he had been taking trips to Japan, and I think once around the world, so he couldn't have been too poor. *[laughs]*

CZ: *So did the whole relocation camp have any affect on them in any way?*

YM: Well, many of the Japanese American families, the kids scattered all over the U.S. My older brother had been going to the University of California. He was in his senior year when the evacuation occurred and he was also in his first year of med school over there. The president of Heidelberg College in Tiffin, Ohio was able to get him a job at the Deaconess Hospital in Detroit—that hospital being related to the church that the college belonged to. He was able to go to medical school and

graduated at the top of his class in 1946. He stayed in Detroit and worked at a number of hospitals. At the time of this death in 1976, he was associate chief of staff at Beaumont Hospital in Royal Oak.

CZ: *So did you have to take the loyalty test at the camp?*

YM: No, I was out of camp well before the loyalty test took place. I was glad I didn't have to take it. *[laughs]*

CZ: *If you had to take it…*

YM: I don't know how I would answer the two controversial questions *[laughs]*.

CZ: *So you didn't stay in the camp very long, right?*

YM: No, I was not in camp for very long. In fact I knew I was getting out, and I missed the bad winters of Wyoming. I was just there during the summer time and the camp was not very organized. I passed the barbed wire perimeter for a whole month while I was there.

CZ: *How long did your whole family had to stay there though?*

YM: Well my brother got out probably in mid-forty three. The older of my two younger sisters, she got out probably in '44. She went for about nine months to Baldwin-Wallace College in Cleveland, Ohio. After graduating high school in camp, my youngest sister, the youngest one, went back to San Francisco, went to Lowell High School. So all four of us, attended Lowell at one time or another and graduated from there.

cz: *What happened after that?*

YM: Even before we went to camp, I knew I was going to get a scholarship to attend Heidelberg College in Tiffin, Ohio, which is a church-related school. There were five of us from San Francisco who received scholarships to go there from a mission church which they ran in San Francisco.

cz: *Did you end up joining the army after awhile?*

YM: I attended Heidelberg College for two years. One summer I stayed on campus and another summer I worked in Buffalo, New York. At the end of the second school year, they had reclassified all Japanese Americans as 1-A, so we were eligible for the draft. I decided to not return to school since I could be called up at any time. I ended up working in Buffalo for six months. Subsequent to that, I got drafted in December of '44. I was put in the enlisted reserves, so I didn't report to duty until April of '45. I spent eighteen and a half months in the army, primarily attending one kind of a school or another.

cz: *What was their treatment of you in the army? Were you treated differently than other people?*

YM: No... I was not in a segregated unit. They took infantry, basic training in the replacement center, and I thought I would be sent to the 442nd. Instead they sent me to the army specialized training program, and I attended the North Carolina State College (now University) for three months. Since the war had ended, they closed that program and transferred the whole unit to the signal corps in Missouri. From there I was in a radio repair

school. That camp closed, and they sent us to Fort Monmouth, New Jersey where I completed the course in radio repair. At that point, they put me in another radio repair course just to fix large transmitters for long distance locations. And I was just one of three students in that class. The other two fellas were graduate engineers, and I had finished a couple years of college. When I finished that course, the war had been over for over a year, and they asked me if I wanted to re-enlist or get discharged. Of course I said discharge.

cz: *What did you do after you got discharged?*

YM: After I got out of the army, I went back to California to visit my parents, but decided not to stay there. After the war, many Orientals had become professionals, but none of them could get jobs out in the West Coast, so they ended up working for their family on the farms or other kinds of businesses, which had nothing to do with their professional training.

cz: *Why do you think that is? Do you have any personal knowledge of why they couldn't get any jobs that they were qualified for?*

YM: Well that was just discrimination. Orientals had been excluded from immigrating into the country back in the '20s. There weren't as many Orientals then as there are today.

cz: *When did your parents get out of the camp?*

YM: Well, my father went back sometime to San Francisco in either late '44 or early '45, to look for a place to live. My mother and youngest sister went back after he found a place.

CZ: *Was it hard for your parents to start up again, because I understand that when you have to go to the camp, you lose practically everything.*

YM: Yeah, I'm not really sure how hard it really was for them. I know they didn't want to start up a business again, and so he went back to working as a houseboy. They seemed to get along all right. The older of my two sisters who have gone to Cleveland, became a dietician. She interned in Portland, Oregon. She came back to San Francisco, and she was a head dietician at the student health center at the University of California in Berkeley. She subsequently quit that job because it got to be almost all paperwork and dealing with a number of new employees all the time. She went to work for Pacific Gas and Electric utility in San Ramon, California at their research and development center.

CZ: *Now you said, it was kind of hard for Japanese Americans to find a job that they were qualified for. How easy was it for your sisters and brothers to find a job?*

YM: Well apparently, it got a lot easier for us to find professional jobs after the war ended. People recognized that Orientals have been highly discriminated against. It still occurs, but it is not as blatant as it was before. The other thing is, with all the industries that moved into California because of the war, they were looking for qualified people.

CZ: *So when did you move to Michigan?*

YM: Well after visiting my parents, I decided to look for a job in the east. And I arbitrarily decided the city of Philadelphia, and I flew there. After six weeks, I found a job at a chemical plant in their standards laboratory, where they tested the products that they made at that plant. During the course of looking for a job, one of the chemical plants I went to turned me down, but before I left the plant, the president of the plant called me in. I talked to him for about an hour about my experiences. So that was kind of interesting.

CZ: *What would you say are some of the major differences that you experienced in Michigan and in California?*

YM: The differences?

CZ: *Like in Americans' attitudes towards Asians.*

YM: Well, I traveled extensively since I've been here in Michigan. Even at that time, I've been in something like a half a dozen different states, where very few other Orientals were around. I didn't really come across any blatant discrimination of any sort.

CZ: *So would you [say you] didn't notice any difference in Michigan versus California?*

YM: It was much easier to get in to associate with different kinds of people here in Michigan than in California. Particularly at the university. I arbitrarily wrote to about dozen schools where I was in Philadelphia. At that time, it was very difficult to get into state boarded schools because they were catering to most of the veterans from their own states, and I was a little surprised to get into Michigan. I attribute that to having transferred rather than starting as a freshman and also to the fact I had gone to a prestigious high school. *[laughs]*

CZ: *So when did you attend the University of Michigan?*

YM: I attended the University of Michigan from January of '49 through September of 1950. I stayed in school all that time, including the summer sessions, and I got my degrees, one in a bachelor's of science and engineering in '49 and master's in 1950.

CZ: *Seeing how the University of Michigan is today, how would you describe the changes that went on since you were here?*

YM: The university student body probably at the time I was here was about twenty-five thousand. Now it is thirty-five thousand. So it has grown tremendously. The curriculum has changed substantially, and I thought I rather got a pretty good education here.

CZ: *Specifically, did they have a lot of courses related to Asian studies back then, Asian history studies, Asian cultures, things like that?*

YM: I am not really certain because I was in engineering school, and our curriculum was completely differently. I suspect the Asian studies had more to do with histories about the countries themselves and not about any of the Asian population in the U.S.

CZ: *What was the size of the Asian population back then compared to now?*

YM: Well there was a fair number of Japanese Americans, but I didn't know any of them. I don't know about the other Asian cultures. Certainly there was no Vietnamese here at that time. I'm sure there was a sizeable Chinese population, but I'm not sure how large it was. The first year I was here, I stayed in a rooming house with a number of students from the Philippines. I thought I might have trouble, but I got along really well with them.

CZ: *So what did you do after college?*

YM: I went to work in the Engineering Department, doing calculations for a man who was getting his PhD, when he went out to Willow Run Laboratories, which was then part of the university. At that time it was called the Michigan Aeronautical Research Center. I went with him. I stayed there working full-time in the 1950s. I thought I'd stay there for a couple years and then look for another job. I did interview, in fact for one aircraft factory out in California, but then after seeing a huge room full of desks, I decided that was not my style. I stayed with the Willow Run Laboratories. I worked in a large number of fields, including the iconic warfare sensors, mine detection, navigation, and I got to travel all over the United States. They separated with the university during the Vietnam War around 1971. Subsequently they have been bought first by a company called Veridian and now by General Dynamics. They are not located in Ypsilanti. But I retired from the company, let's see... about fifteen years ago.

CZ: *Did you end up getting married by any chance?*

YM: I married a girl I met at work and been married since 1960. We have four children, two girls and two boys.

CZ: *I understand she's Caucasian? Did you have difficulty with that? Did your parents think different?*

YM: No, there were no objections from either side of the family so we got along pretty well. Of the four children, one of my sons went to Japan after he finished the American University. After working here in Ann Arbor for about a year, he went to Japan to teach English at a junior high school for about three years.

CZ: *Did your children, do they know anything about your Japanese heritage?*

YM: My kids are very well acquainted with their background. Especially the one son who's been over in Japan. He earns a living now as a translator, not only in Japanese but all the Romance languages. *[laughs]*

CZ: *Do they speak the Japanese language?*

YM: Well, he can speak Japanese, but the other kids can't. *[laughs]*

CZ: *Do you speak Japanese?*

YM: Not really.

CZ: *So when you were growing up, your parents didn't speak Japanese to you?*

YM: Well, a lot of the Japanese kids went to a Japanese language school after regular school, but we lived too far from Japantown for that. My parents tried to teach me, but I don't think I ever got beyond say third or fourth-grade level. It's been a long sixty years since then.

CZ: *Did your kids go to Japanese language schools?*

YM: My kids? No.

CZ: *In general, did you get any reaction for being in an interracial marriage?*

YM: I've never had any problems being in an interracial marriage.

CZ: *Do your kids think of anything of it?*

YM: My kids seem to get along with everybody.

CZ: *So do they identify with the American culture more? Do you think?*

YM: My kids are interested in all kinds of things. We've gone through a Smithsonian exhibit on art from the Edo period in Japan. That was several years ago, and they've got all kinds of books on Japan.

144

Nob Shimokochi
[JACL]

Nob Shimokochi

interviewed by Soh Suzuki at the Shimokochi residence. February 5, 2004

Both of my parents are from *Hiroshima-ken,* and they were in the country, in Kamiseno. Somebody in the town of their neighborhood went to America, worked for a few years, came back and had made a lot of money. Of course, probably it wasn't a lot of money, but the exchange rate, perhaps, made it seem like a lot. I wonder if there was a drought at the time that made it economically very difficult because it seems to me like a large percentage of Japanese immigrants were from southern Japan. My father came over to America first somewhere around 1905, and his father told him to go to a mission, although whether it was a Methodist mission or a Presbyterian I don't know. His port of entry was Seattle, and he went to a mission where they gave him a shelter and food until he got situated. Exposed to the Christian religion there, he was converted.

I don't know what kind of work he first started on, but he did mention that he had a job at a lumber mill, where he graded the oaks to be cut. Then he drifted down toward Los Angeles. He didn't care for agricultural work, although I'm sure he did a lot of it. The only kind of work a Japanese could do was agricultural work, gardening, working as a house servant—menial type of work. Not only did they do the kind of work most Americans wouldn't do, but they also couldn't just go to a store or company and ask for a job because they wouldn't be hired. So they either worked at or for a Japanese company or even started a company that dealt within the Japanese community.

I think there was a cutoff date for Japanese immigrants in 1923 or something like that, so my father went back to Japan, got married, and came back. My sister was born in 1924, and I was born in 1928. The first job that I remember my father having was selling supplies for the Los Angeles Farmers Supply Company. His clientele was Japanese farmers and it was a partnership with a man named Harada. It was pretty good until the Depression hit. Then people were unable to pay for their personals that were bought on credit, the company went out, and the partnership dissolved. My father bought a mom and pop grocery store, and he had the back of the store modified into living quarters and we lived back there.

In the thirties, you had to live very frugally. It was really tough living when you didn't get paid because you still had to make sure to pay the rent, the water bill, and gas bill, and live on what was left. My mother became very adept, a real expert, at stretching the dollars. We saved money for a long time, and we bought a washing machine and then a refrigerator. Our family car was a pickup. The pickup in those days weren't big ones like today. My father was the driver, my mother was on the passenger side, my sister sat in between them, and I sat on my mother's lap. That was our family car. On Sundays, my father would pick up kids like a school bus and then take them to Sunday School. In the back of the pickup, my father had put in seats, the back seats from a car, probably from an old car that didn't need the seats anymore. That's

where the kids sat. Today you cannot do that, but back in those days it was a common practice.

We gradually bought a few luxuries like a refrigerator and we had a piano that my sister played. I still remember the name on it: it was a Baldwin. When the war came, we had to get rid of everything. This guy wanted the piano and he offered twenty-five dollars. He went to his relatives to see if he could borrow some money from them, but he couldn't. He only could come up with ten dollars, so we gave him it for ten dollars. Like our refrigerator, we just gave it away because all we could take was all we could carry. They gave you like six days notice to evacuate. There were posting notices on utility polls on the corners telling everyone what the limits of that zone was, and everybody in that zone would have to come with only their belongings and gather at a certain point.

So we sold our stuff early, packed up, and moved into our church, the Japanese Union Church, I think it was called. And in other zones, some people gathered at the Union Church, and some people gathered at the Buddhist temple. On May 9, 1942, soldiers with old-fashioned "soup bowl" helmets and yellow Springfield rifles put us on Greyhound buses. I think there were some *hakujins* who came to say goodbye and brought coffee and donuts. The soldiers put us on these

Greyhound buses and told us to put down the shades so we couldn't tell where we were going. We ended up at Santa Anita racetrack, which was on the outskirt of Los Angeles in our area, so it wasn't a long trip.

The people who came first got stuck in horse stalls. They were really unsanitary and stinky, so we were lucky that we didn't get stuck in one of those. They ended up with something like 18,000 people there. They had built these shacks in parking lots. They put us in these shacks. Rooms were really tiny, and they put beds, these army cots, on the floor. I guess there were some smaller rooms and some medium-size rooms, depending on the size of the family. We got a room for four people, but it didn't leave us much space for walking around. They gave us what they called "picks." They were cloth bags, and you filled the picks with straw for your mattress.

So, there were 18,000 people and three mess halls to feed all the people. And all the mess halls didn't have the same capacity. They averaged three thousand a piece, so maybe some of them fit four thousand, some of them maybe two thousand. Anyway, people who were used to sitting around at a dining table for a meal found out that in a concentration camp you needed to make huge changes and get used to it quick. We had to stand in the line for a long time outside of the mess hall in order to get in. That was really hard on the old people and mothers with little babies because in Southern California, the sun gets really hot. And we were fed food that we weren't used to. For example, I was used to having milk every day and they wouldn't give me any milk. Because, I guess, they wouldn't give it to you after a certain age, and I was tall for my age, at least for a *Nihonjin* kid. Babies got their milk from what they called milk stations and at

certain time of the day. They had a schedule for passing out milk, and as you know, babies don't eat on schedule. For salad, they would cut a head of lettuce into six sections and pour vinegar on it. It was tough getting used to the food. One of the common dishes was called cabbage sauerkraut. It smelled like *tsukemono*, but it was really sour.

Spotlights would sweep all night as soon as it got dark and the lights went on. It was kind of hard to get used to it.

Then they had barbed wire all around the camp with guard towers all over and guns pointing at us. Spotlights would sweep all night as soon as it got dark and the lights went on. It was kind of hard to get used to it. At night, we would be trying to sleep and the lights would come and flash in the eyes, going through the cracks and through windows. The walls had these big cracks in it. You could hear anything the next door neighbor was saying, so we didn't have any privacy.

I remember my friend, Tom Robinson; he came to visit us. He stood in a caged area for a quite a while in a hot sun. He was a seventeen-year-old black man who worked at my father's grocery store. He was the only one that came to visit us while we were in camp. I lost contact with all of my other childhood friends. There was a big shack with a screen going down the middle, and there was a chair on one side and a chair on the other side. That's how we would meet our visitors. We would speak for a few minutes, and then everybody got up and went out, while a bunch of people came in.

Everybody was put to work, except for kids. I guess I qualified as a minor, so my mom didn't have to work. But my sister was seventeen, and she had to work in the mess hall. My father worked as a census taker. Every night he would go down to a certain assigned number of homes and count the number of people. Everybody had to be home at nine o'clock. I recall there were some commotions about working. There were men who worked over in the grandstand, and they were paid like seven cents an hour. I think the camp officials wanted them to work a lot of extra hours. And they refused to work the hours or something like that because the men felt that they were forced to do the work.

I remember that every Monday, police used to come and do shakedowns, inspections. They would open up all of the belongings to see if there was anything that they considered contraband. They would take things like kitchen knives, screen blazers, carpenter tools; anything that they would consider as weapons. They would repeat this every Monday. It was very humiliating. Some things, like blankets and things you got stuffed and tied in a bag, it's really hard to get in and get back out. We had to keep doing it over and over. Young mothers had brought electric hot plates to warm the baby's milk. And the police took those away. One of the rumors was that some people got so angry that they chased the police out of the camp and started a riot. I don't know how true the rumor was.

Back then, in those days, there were a lot of rumors. They say *uwas a. Uwas a.* The government started investigations and found a lot of irregularities. People who were Caucasian worked in mess halls, and they were stealing sugar and meat and stuff like that. We were supposed to be getting some kind of allowance, like three dollars a month, to buy our essentials like a soap and toothpaste, but somebody was keeping it. Of course, the people who were doing these things felt patriotic by doing bad things to us.

Anyway, looking back, there was no due process at all. Absolutely not. There was no hearing. We weren't charged with anything, and they incarcerated us. They couldn't tell the difference between us and the pilots that bombed Pearl Harbor. To the government, we were all the same. We were considered enemy aliens, even though we were born here. And the government tried to increase the hatred of the Japanese. They got the media to hype up stories, even got Hollywood to participate in making movies that would increase the hatred. In the papers, there were a lot of false stories about how we were all spies, that we were all committed to the emperor of Japan. They got people very nervous and there was war hysteria.

The thing was, Hawaii was bombed, so the defense was completely demolished, and it was two thousand miles from the West Coast. So they were very vulnerable to the Japanese attack. But, there was no subversive activity by the Japanese. There were thoughts of incarcerating the Japanese in Hawaii, but because they were one-third of the population, if they put them away, the economy would collapse, since there would be nobody to do any of the services. So they left them there, but in the U.S., it was completely defensible. They said that we were a threat to the national security. It doesn't make any sense. But that was the rationale at that time. And, back in those times, all the governments, local, state, federal, all way up to the top—the judicial, legislative, executive—they all were anti-Japanese and used terrible words to describe us.

In recent years, I read about how rotten the Japanese were treated in this country. There were lynchings, and there were a number of cases where people would go at night to a bar and bring guns and take all these people on a truck and drive hundred, two hundreds miles away and drop them out and tell them don't come back. I never realized how bad things were, and I never was able to ask my father why he didn't go back to Japan. A lot of Japanese settlers sent their kids to Japanese language school. Even though

Left to Right: Scott Kurashige, Toshi Shimoura, Mary Kamidoi, Nob Shimokochi

it was very expensive thing to do since at the time everybody was so poor, they did it, I think, because there was always a chance to go back to Japan. I really wonder why my parents didn't go back. I think if you look at the statistics, a lot of people came over, but there weren't that many people who left during the war.

We stayed in Santa Anita until September [1942], or the end of August. Probably, it was the first part of September when they put us on a train and they shipped us out. I guess Santa Anita was just a temporary place to put us while they were getting permanent camps built. We went up onto those mountains. We crossed the Great Salt Lake and there is a track that goes right over it. All during the time, we were sitting in these bench seats in a passenger car. You could lie down on those bench seats and sleep. I forgot what kind of food we had—sandwiches or something. We couldn't go to the dining car because it cost too much money. And, of course, people who worked in the dining car were complaining because normally passengers tip,

but nobody was giving them tips. They were paid very poorly, and their income depended on tips. But we couldn't give them any money.

Anyway, we got to Heart Mountain, Wyoming and we were there in about the first week in September. A week later, it snowed. That winter, the temperature went down twenty degrees below zero. We were from Southern California, so we didn't have the kind of clothes you needed. We had to order clothes from Sears, Montgomery Ward's, and Spiegel's. Heart Mountain had about the population of ten thousand and that made us instantly the third largest community in Wyoming population-wise. Our post office became a branch of Cody. Cody was a town of twenty-five hundred. They had a very low volume of mail. The postmaster gets paid by the amount of mail he has to handle. When we started ordering our stuff through the mail, he didn't have enough space. So he got a huge pay raise.

When you were in the camp, you had no

feeling about the outside. I remember, on the radio, they used to talk about Big-horn Basin. And then, when I was going up the mountain and looking down, I finally realized what Bighorn Basin was. The mountains make a kind of big bowl-like shape. And, that's what they call Bighorn Basin. But when I went back to Heart Mountain, I went over that summit. I could see fifty miles away, a little bit on the horizon. As we went down the road, there would be a lot of small towns, where the elevation was more than the populations. Anyways, when we got to Heart Mountain, it wasn't such a nice place, but it was a lot nicer than Santa Anita. There was more privacy, and the rooms were bigger. Instead of a 3,000 person-capacity mess

When you were in the camp, you had no feeling about the outside.

hall, it was three hundred.

At Heart Mountain, barracks held twenty-five people. The two end apartments were for families of two or three, the next two was a room for five or six, and the two middle rooms were for family of four. Sometimes, we took bachelors and put them in one room. There was a communal facility, which had a laundry room, ironing room, and there was a men's bathroom, a women's bathroom, and in the middle, there was a boiler room. It was kind of a little H-shaped building. Every block had the same configuration, as far as the layout. Sometimes we didn't have hot water. The cold water was hard to get used to for showers. Also, in the camp, there was no between-meal food, unless in the morning you could get a couple of pieces of toast and put jelly on it and then take it home. Or you could maybe in the evening, make a *nigiri* or something like that and eat it. But, other than that, no between meals. Food was always hard to buy through the mail.

The thing that we had for some fun was the Boy Scout movement. The Boy Scout movement was sponsored, I think, because it expressed character, and character-building was important to Japanese culture. We used to go to camping in the summertime. Heart Mountain is in the middle of a big desert with sagebrush, tumbleweeds, cactus. In the fall, when the winds started making dust storms, the dust used to come into our rooms. You could see the tumbleweeds go like fifty miles an hour. That's how you can tell how fast the wind is going by, seeing how fast those tumbleweeds go. Winds always came from the north, and we had to walk south to the school. So when we went home, we walked against the wind. You had to walk with your back to the wind. That's how we used to get home. But you had to lean way back into the wind, or else every time you took a step your foot came out at the same place. When we got home, there was no hot chocolate or hot soup or anything. We were frozen stiff by the time we got home, although it wasn't really a long distance. The school was almost centrally located. When everything is concentrated like that, you never have to walk very far. At the most, I think, the farthest distance I walked was three-quarters of a mile.

Our high school athletic teams used to play some of the surrounding towns. Softball, baseball, football—we used to beat them all. There was no turf to play on, just dirt. We didn't do so well in basketball because height makes a difference. There weren't many towns around, so they came from maybe a hundred miles away or two hundred. One team we played was Deer Lodge from Montana. Poor guys, we beat them sixty-three to nothing. And then, there was a town called Sheridan. They used to come and play baseball, football, and things like that. I didn't realize it back then, but years later, when I went to Sheridan, we found out that they had

152

to go way up the big Heart Mountains, and come down on the other side. They were about one hundred miles away. That's a real high mountain that you had to go over.

I guessed the people who lived in the area felt resentful, bad. Our school did better than theirs, even though I remember we used to have school inside the grandstand. The city donated some books. On Sundays, we had religious services in the grandstand. That thing was so huge that one group used half and the other group used the other half. The people in the area put up a sign on the road saying that at one time there were ten thousand people living here. But they were claiming that we weren't concentrated and that we had a modern high school and that we had modern plumbing. They didn't say that the modern plumbing was only in the outhouse. Maybe they felt guilty that there was a concentration camp. I don't know.

We went to Ohio when we left camp in 1943 or 1944. The government said, "We want you out of here." At first, we didn't know where to go. The people on the West Coast said, "We don't want you back." And there were people who did go back, and there were a lot of hate crimes. We didn't hear about any hate crimes if we went to the east, only if we went west. So we went east. But, the thing is, in the camp you

have a degree of security; you know you got a roof over your head, and you got food on your table. If you left, they gave you twenty-five dollars and a free ticket on the railroad. They would tell you that you cannot come back. To leave the camp without having a job or place to live is a kind of terrifying feeling. Leaving camp was more painful than going in. My father had a friend who went out earlier than we did, and when we were leaving camp, he decided to go back to California because his business was in orchards. He wanted to start a business. He offered his job in Ohio to my father.

So we went to Chagrin Falls, outside of Cleveland. Things didn't work out there. It was a job where my mom and dad were like servants. I would help cut the grass and things like that. Then my father heard about a job in Royal Oak, Michigan as a church custodian, so he took that job. We have been here ever since. A lot of people came east to New York, Philadelphia, Chicago, Detroit, places like that. After five, ten years after the war, they slowly went back to California. Some of them stayed.

There was a church in Detroit that tried to organize the community. There was the JACL group. And Peter Fujioka, he did a lot to make the Japanese American community. Leaving the camp was a tough experience for many of the people, but we got away pretty easily compared to others. A lot of people went back to California, and it was a terrible mess. There were housing and job shortages because millions of people had gone to California before the war. People, like families in the South who were starving to death, went over there and got high-paying jobs. California had a lot of shipbuilding and aircraft work, plus other kinds of work for the war effort. A lot of people made a lot of money, but suddenly we didn't need any more airplanes, and we didn't need any more warships. So all the people were laid off. In the meantime, ten million soldiers and sailors were coming back from the war. All during the war, they had built no homes. There were no living quarters available and no jobs available. The people from the camps were going there. A lot of trauma, a lot of trauma. People were really hurting. Many families had to break up into pieces.

Look at the Japanese people, and how after the war, they had nothing. They started from zero, and pretty soon, they got jobs, found a place to live, and got an education. They got good jobs, as engineers, and lawyers, you name it. They achieved. Here is the despised hated minority that didn't become a burden on society. We didn't become criminals to the same degree other people did. We paid our taxes, and took on responsible jobs. We have a number of representatives, federal representatives, and senators, disproportionately large numbers. But you see very few Japanese names in the news. I think we could be very proud of our return, or I shouldn't say return, but our achievement for where we are now.

I think Japanese family culture made a very good impact. Character training, perseverance, *oyakoko*, *ganbare* were all very important. We were proud to be mentally tough, and I think that the suicide rate was very low. I see in today's generation that the kids are not mentally tough. They are soft; anything can make them cry. *Nintai*—we don't have that either now. Unfortunately, I think we are losing the Japanese culture. Even in Japan, they are losing it too. Too much *zeitaku* (luxury). For the Japanese, at least from what I learned from my parents, there was delayed gratification. You have to work hard for a long time to get something. My parents worked a long time. You know, they earned small wages, but they were able to buy a refrigerator.

That's the message I have for the younger generation. They got to look into the Japanese family culture of that time. There was a lot of character building. *Nanakorobi yaoki*—that's what held us all together. That's what brought us up from being way down there. Most other minorities don't have that that kind of culture trait, so they stay a burden on society. And education was very important, because that was the source of power. So even back in the days before the war, when companies would not hire Japanese people, they still went to college and learned special skills. A lot of them went into agriculture. And at Heart Mountain, we had people with agriculture degrees, so they were able to grow a lot of our own food. We grew enough cash crops. Even today, people cannot match the dollar values of those crops. Back in those days, even if you got a degree in teaching, you couldn't get a job teaching. But the Japanese still got their education, and they became self-reliant. And self-reliance is another character trait of the Japanese.

I think they did a really a fabulous job of getting their respect, especially the soldiers who fought in the war. Despite what Americans thought of us, as being subversive and disloyal, they were very loyal and very brave. A lot of times, when they looked into service, their fathers told the boys, "Don't do anything shameful." Honor was very important to Japanese families. So, when these soldiers got these words from their fathers, they went out and performed with unusual courage. The 442nd had the highest number of awards of any regiment. They received only one Medal of Honor, until President Clinton awarded them some more. I guess they didn't believe one regiment could or should be getting that many. Definitely the big thing that Japanese Americans got to be proud of is their character.

View of Camp
[Miyao]

From the Diary of an Issei Interned in Heart Mountain

From the Personal Archive of Nob Shimokochi

Note from translator: It is a beautifully written diary. Through each entry one can sense the life of the Camp in Wyoming quite vividly. Here and there I could not quite make out the kanji, but generally his writing was very clear.

—Asae Shichi

1 *(p.167) Original spelling says Partemai... from Mark 10:46-52*

February 15 Tuesday

Today I read a book by Forsythe on the nature of the Cross (translated by Takayoshi Aso). Although it was a very difficult book, I was told that the book contained the essence of Christianity and so I read it with much concentration. It was not an easy book to understand. I knew that the book required relatively extensive knowledge in order to grasp (its meaning). I tried hard so that I could understand it. Maybe because of that or because my head was clear this morning, I did understand it deep in my heart. That's what they call "*shin-doku*" (reading with heart), I think. I was very pleased, and my heart was filled with joy.

2 degrees below zero in the morning
20 degrees in the daytime

February 16 Wednesday

I want to be a true Christian and I read hoping to obtain the deep mysteries of Christianity. Mr. Aso explains that one can understand all of life once one gets to understand the Cross of Christ. The Spirit which is the Truth exists only in one point (?) between the Heaven and Earth, but that one point is the Christ's Cross of Redemption, the pivotal point in the moral world. In this Spirit resides... the Life of all life, eternal Action... The Cross therefore is at the very center of Christ who is the central moral person in the whole mankind.

20 degrees in the morning
25 degrees in the daytime

April 15 Saturday

The Youth Patriotic Corps that Nobuyuki belongs to had its celebration today since today happens to be the full one year for the Platoon 333, and I attended since I was invited as a family. They told us that there are 26 young members. Recently the Platoon got a leader by the name of Fuji-se. They showed quite an accomplishment, and won the first place in action at the General Center Association meeting. They demonstrated tonight their very brave and lively spirit. As parents we are concerned about how our children behave, but I was pleased because as I watched, (my son) was doing okay although he may not have been the most distinguished. The meeting was adjourned at 11:30.

April 16 Sunday

Since there were only 4 people cooking for about 250 people the cooks seemed very busy. Those of us who were helping were also extremely busy, with no time for ourselves. Since we have gotten so busy of late, a few people quitted work. There are some who seem to be dissatisfied. When I examine myself, I have no complaint. People might think bad things about me or say bad things but it does not hurt me. When one realizes that people almost never say good things (about others)... I have such insight into life... then it is useless to have complaints. When one looks heavenward and keeps going, one can get magnanimous.

30 degrees in the morning
45 degrees in the daytime

June 14 Wednesday

Around 5pm suddenly it grew cold, and the sky was pitch black as if being painted with *sumi*. Then we heard thunder, and thought it started to rain. It was in fact not rain but pea-sized hail. It lasted only for about 10 minutes, but as we watched, the roofs and the ground started to look white as if covered by snow. So this is truly Wyoming to have hail in the latter part of June. The newly planted crops must have suffered some damage. The weather in Wyoming is really unpredictable. If one thinks of making a living, farming is truly difficult. Now suddenly the temperature has dropped.

June 15 Thursday

It was decided that The Jerome Center, one of the ten Centers, was to be closed down. Therefore 500 people were to come to our Center, and they arrived at 4pm today. The weather was getting cold just now, and we might have some rain today, so people will realize that Wyoming is a cold place. Since the beginning of June, we've had rain almost every day. As if by schedule, thunder starts in the afternoon followed by rain. People don't mind a little bit of rain though. Both the young and the old get together, organize baseball groups as if they don't feel anything and keep playing. It sort of looks like each and every one does not think of improving oneself.

August 15 Tuesday

A farewell party was planned today at our Mess Hall as Mr. Nago(?) is going to be relocated again. We two attended it. We felt we should because he is Nobuyuki's Scout leader, and also a member of our Union (United?) Church. The war situation is getting increasingly worse for Germany. According to Mr. Fujii, within two months from now either surrender or peace movement will take place. As I think of a lot of things, I need to consider re-relocation. Of course in my mind I am preparing myself (unclear) for it. Some day soon we will have to relocate.

August 16 Wednesday

I wrote to Masunaka and Shimpei Nagao whom I haven't written for some time. It took me about four hours writing two letters. I wrote about myself and how I've been feeling recently. I went over four pages! I wrote about re-relocation problem, the War situation in Europe, conditions in Japan, and how Japan will have to face an increasingly difficult situation as the War in Europe comes to an end. What Japanese people don't like is the defeat of Japan. I wrote about unconditional surrender (of Japan). Maybe I wrote too much, I'm afraid, but I wrote what I believed.

38 degrees in the morning

October 14 Saturday

Tonight we went to see the movie that Mrs. Watanabe told us about, *The House of Seven Gables* written by the famous author Nathanel (original spelling) Horthome. The hero, Pynchon, was rich with two brothers. They fought over their property. A life obsessed with material things cannot find happiness in the end [unclear]. I interpreted that (the movie) was teaching the meaninglessness of such life. I took Nobuyuki along with the intention of educating him. I explained and advised Nobuyuki to become a warm-hearted person *Ningenteki Na Ningen*, not a materialistic (person).

October 15 Sunday

Although I want to communicate to Nobuyuki what I think about his education, it is difficult (to do this) in detail. That side does not understand Japanese, and I don't understand English. Wishing to communicate somehow, however, I explained to him using some simple Japanese. The goal of a person is not in gaining material things, especially like gaining monetary wealth. It is, rather, in building Nobuyuki's own character *Hinsei*. Even if he graduated from college, if he becomes a machine-like person, it is a failure as a person. That's what I told him.

December 25 Monday

We were able to celebrate Christmas whole heartedly. The whole family surrounded the stove quietly, talking about spiritual things, encouraging Nobuyuki *[It looks like he first wrote 'faith', but went over and wrote Nobuyuki.]*. The talk was about putting good things inside the heart… the right thought! The thought turns into flesh and blood. It is the Truth. Such thought will go down to influence children and grandchildren. Our daily effort is not futile. The thought [grounded] in the faith in God has everlasting life. One who seeks truth has everlasting life… we talked about these things, and were filled with joy of the ones who believe in God and were deeply moved.

17 degrees below zero.

Mary Kamidoi at an Office Party, 1952
[Kamidoi]

Mary Kamidoi

One Step Ahead and Who You Know, Not What You Know

interviewed by Melanie Carbine
November 10, 2003

MC: I am here to interview you on your travels from the time your parents came to the United States till the present time.

MK: My father was born in Hiroshima, Japan on October 15, 1880 and came here on October 24, 1899 at the age of nineteen years old with a younger brother that had just turned eighteen years old and six other friends from Japan. They first went to British Columbia and they decided they would work on the railroads because that was work for them. When the railroads were done, they all felt there should be a better life and jobs in San Francisco, CA. At that time, the Japanese immigrants faced quite a bit of prejudice, i.e. not able to live where they wanted to, send their children to any schools, job limitations, etc. So by word of mouth, my father, his brother and friends decided to go to the northern part of California (Stockton—known as the agricultural area). By now, all the men are realizing the hardships without a wife. So my father and a few of the men decide to send for wives. I understand that my father's family knew my mother's family and at the age of twenty-three became his wife. She (Chiyeno Kinoshita) was born on September 5, 1890, in Hiroshima, Japan and came to San Francisco, August 10, 1914.

In the northern part of California there are a lot islands in Stockton [there farmers] raised celery and asparagus. My uncle decided he would import friends from Japan and head a celery farm. In the meantime, my father decided he would like to own a pool hall with his uncle. Shortly after, my uncle had gone to San Francisco to pick up his help and was hit by a car and killed instantly. That meant my father had to take over his farm and live on the islands.

There were many islands and we lived on Sherman Island. After a short time, my father decided he would move on to another island called

Bouldin Island #27 (where I was born) to run a camp raising onions with an acquaintance, Mr. Sakata. My father was a very restless and independent man and after a few years decided to leave the island and started a tomato, pear, and almond farm. The farm was very close to the San Joaquin River and after a few springs of flooding, he decided to move to the northeast part of Stockton to raise strawberries and vegetables. I can remember my mother with every move, questioning my father why we moved so often. In those days, we had to do whatever your father chose to do without any questions, and I give my mother so much credit for all the work that went with uprooting the family so many times. Of course, while our parents were working the fields, all the younger ones had numerous chores to do. My job was to have the *furos* (hot tubs, today) ready when they came in from the fields. These tubs were not heated by electricity, so we had to keep the wood burning continuously. So often, I would go astray with my friends on the way home from school and forget about my chore, and when I got home, it wasn't a happy situation at all. I guess I might have taken after my father with his independency and faced the

consequences many, many times (too many to count). When walking home from my friend's home, it would be so dark. And I had to walk over a long bridge that had tramps (homeless) that lived under the bridges cooking their meals in tin cans, and I never had any fear. Of course, you wouldn't think of doing things like that today. I guess I was like a problem teenager, and my older siblings often asked my mom where I fit in. How I survived is a mystery. We lived on this farm until World War II broke out.

MC: *What happened after World War II?*

MK: When the war broke out we became *Family #6928* (not the Kamidoi family) and were evacuated into the Stockton Assembly Center which was walking distance from our home. Shortly before the evacuation, my youngest brother was kidnapped by the Filipinos and kept for three days. That was such a traumatic experience for our family, and I can remember shaking so much from being scared. He would never discuss the ordeal and took it to his grave. We assumed that he might have been warned not to talk about it. You can imagine what a parent's feeling would be. Helpless. This was the fairgrounds, as well as the race track for horses. Since the barracks were not ready, most of us had to live in the horse stables. We would scrub and scrub our stables to try to get the smell out; it was impossible. So often, when I went to the Detroit Race Course, Northville Downs, or Hazel Park Raceway, I would often look over at the stalls and sort of grin and say to myself, "You horses don't have it so bad." It really brought back so many memories and there is no way that you can forget. I was only eleven years old at the time, and I still remember most everything that happened. And when I speak to my friends (Americans), they cannot believe that I can talk about the horrible situation and not break down. I say to them that my life has to go on and I can't dwell on the past. Most Nisei that I know will not speak about this period of their life, even to their children. There are only three of us in the JACL that will speak to high schools, middle schools, churches, universities, clubs, etc., about our experience when asked. We believe this is an eye opener to the public and have to let the students know first-hand, since they will not learn any of this from their history books. (Hopefully, in the near future the books will have more information on what took place during World War II.) After about six months in the stables, we were sent by slow-moving trains on a long journey to Rohwer, Arkansas. It took four nights and five days to reach our camp. In certain areas, we were not allowed to open the windows and had to pull down the shades, supposedly, for our protection. The camp was built on swampland with rows of barracks and zillions of "chiggers" that would burrow under our skins, causing us to constantly pick them out.

Rohwer had forty-one blocks (I was in Block forty-one closest to the front entranceway and the administrative buildings). Each block had twelve barracks with a total of seventy-two rooms. Our family was given two large rooms because of the size of our family—twelve in total.

After about a year or so of helping to clean more land and building what furniture he could with wood that was thrown away, my father decided to work at a tomato nursery in Kalamazoo, MI with a number of other camp internees that were restless. They had to sign a contract to complete the job and when the government sent us letters telling us of the closing of the camp, I contacted my father and he

*The rally
"It's Not Fair!"
close-up [ACJ]*

along with the others were not able to leave until their contract was fulfilled. Therefore, we were the last families to leave the camp. Since my brothers in service had checked out our home conditions in Stockton, they found there was no home for us to go home to. So word of mouth among the families left, We were told that a man (Mr. White, a large landowner) would like to have the internees work his land in Painton, Missouri, a community that had never seen an Oriental. This little town was about forty miles from Cape Girardeau, Missouri, and one hundred miles from St. Louis, Missouri. What a time we had trying to be accepted in the school system. The children on the buses were so nasty and cruel, putting it mildly. There were about ten of us kids on the bus, and most of them were a little older than I was. I guess being brought up to

be the quiet, polite people that we should be, the older kids would just try to ignore all the harassing out of fear, since we were outnumbered. One day, I must have said to myself, "that's enough" and stood up in the bus and started yelling at the kids that were being nasty and surprised them all with my English. The two Bird boys—neighbors next door—were the instigators, so I paid their parents a visit when I got home from school. The parents were very apologetic, and as of the next morning, the boys could not have been nicer and fought for us when others picked on us. (I found out that the boys got a "lickin" after I spoke to their parents).

My parents and the other Japanese parents thought I was crazy to have done what I did. I said, "Oh well, it took care of the problem." My biggest complaint was that the bus driver did not stop all the harassing and kept driving until we got to school. Now that I am older, I am assuming he was afraid himself or he was a bigot and enjoyed seeing the kids harass us. Shucks, I should have gotten on him too. They always threw the line "Go back where you came from" at us. Through all of this, the Bird family ended out being the nicest neighbors.

What a time we had trying to be accepted in the school system. The children on the buses were so nasty and cruel. One day, I must have said to myself, "that's enough" and stood up in the bus and started yelling at the kids that were being nasty and surprised them all with my English.

After my brothers were discharged from the Army, my brother Tad decided to come to Davision, Michigan (borderline of Flint, Michigan) because he had a friend in the Army that had relatives that would help us get on our feet. Again, we faced a certain amount of discrimination since they were not used to seeing Orientals. They raised onions, peppermint, and spearmint leaves for oil. After a very rainy spring when the farm was flooded and lost most of the peppermint and spearmint roots, my father decided he would like to move on to Capac, Michigan (outskirts of Imlay City where the land was rich muck dirt) and started raising carrots, parsnips, and soy beans. Again, this was another community that was not used to having so many Orientals invade their territory (four families) and starting farms that they were not used to. If you shopped at Wrigley's store for groceries, you would have been buying carrots that were bagged from my dad's farm. The farm was in operation until my father passed away in 1972 at the age of ninety-three years old. (He had become a citizen at the age of seventy-two.) After that, most of the land was leased out to various companies to raise soy beans.

I did not live in Capac. I went to schools Davison (borderline from Flint) and Flint. I was recruited from the Flint Business College in 1951. My sister and I were hired into the Accounting Department at the Rouge area. We were the first Japanese women working at Ford Motor Company at the time. At that time, it was not such a long time from the end of World War II, and we worked with many young women and men that had lost a loved one in the war.

Again, we had to face a terrible few years of discrimination and distrust from our coworkers. I guess that was understandable, but they did not know that we were just as American as they were. It was so degrading to be followed around everywhere (right to the ladies' room door), and it made me so mad. Along with my sister, I wanted to quit so many times. To be stopped and asked by hourly men on the line every morning if I could speak English — by someone that could not speak English as well as I did — wanting to know how long I have been here from the "old country"! They were both of Polish descent and from Poland. How dare they! I told them I was here for three years, and I had already been going up and down the stairs for ten years. That was a puzzle for them to figure out.

Being I was able to speak English, they started to bring me pies, cakes and fruits every day. Of course, I didn't eat any of their stuff and gave it to my coworker, Gordie. He really appreciated it since he was not able to afford to buy lunch each day (he was living at Boys Town on Fenkell) and thought I was sharing my lunch with him. After weeks of him thanking me, I told him the truth, and we had a big laugh and became best friends. He asked me what I told them if they asked me how the food was. Of course, I said, "It was really good." I think they missed me on my days off according to my lunch mate, Joyce.

After so much of this harassment and discrimination, I decided I had to do something — whether it was for my good or get fired — and decided to speak up. I felt that I was recruited by the company, and the recruiter knew who and what we were and still hired us. I asked myself, "Why am I tolerating all this?" Because of my stubbornness and determination, I was going to be accepted or fired. I finally went to my boss and the plant controller with my complaint, and they were shocked with the treatment we were having and issued a communication as to the treatment of his employees. He would not tolerate it and told me to see him if I had any other problems. All the coworkers tried to figure out how this communication came about (whispering among themselves). Of course, I wasn't going to be the rat-fink — a phrase used for "tattlers" at that time.

I became friends with my boss's secretary and very friendly with the controller's secretary, and my coworkers realized I was in with the right persons, so be nice to Mary. My sister Jean was quiet and not outspoken as I was and very unhappy with her job conditions. With all the complaining we did when we went home to visit my folks, my dad decided to inform us that if we quit, we could only live at home until we found an apartment because he "did not raise quitters." I thought, *shucks*, that was my intention and go back to my old job as a bookkeeper at an Olds and Buick dealership — live at home and I would be rich not having to pay rent. I thank my father for his wise words for making me stay for thirty-seven years at Ford and be able to enjoy my retirement checks. My sister quit after a few years and got married.

At the time we were hired, we lived with family friends, Mr. and Mrs. Kumazo Ambo on McGraw off of Linwood and Wyoming. They thought it would be great, since they had a young son that was home waiting for them to return from work each night. This couple worked at the famous Devon Gables Restaurant in Birmingham along with quite a few other Japanese men and women. That only lasted only a few months, since our schedules did not coincide with theirs since it was a long ride home for them—no freeways in those days.

We tried to buy a home in Dearborn to be close to work, but Dearborn would not sell to Orientals and be responsible for any problems we might have encountered. I later met Mr. Al Miller, who had baby sat Orville Hubbard and knew the family well and would talk to Orville about my situation—I told him to forget it.

We moved into various apartment houses and finally decided to rent a home on West Grand Boulevard next door to *Hitsville, U.S.A.* with three other girls we met along the way. We often sat in our large front window and watched all the little black kids going into Hitsville and never questioned what was going on. They became the famous singers of Detroit—Diana Ross, Stevie Wonder, etc. How naive, unconcerned or uncaring could a bunch of young girls be? After a few years of living together, we decided to go our own way. I was living in northwest Detroit

Mary Kamidoi, 1961 [Kamidoi]

and the riots were 2½ blocks away (Steel and Meyers). And after the riots the neighborhood started to change for the worse, and all my neighborhood friends [were] starting to sell and move out of Detroit. I was transferred to the Livonia Transmission Plant on Plymouth Road so decided to move to Livonia in 1970. I purchased one of the first condos built in Livonia—5 Mile and Farmington Road. What did I know about buying a house or condo—ZILCH—but I lucked out.

I was accepted quite well because they found out that I was an appointee of Mayor McNamara as the Secretary of the Human Relations Commission. At that time, the Appalachian regions were having lots of economic and poverty problems, so I was able to travel for the City to check out conditions and how the City would be able to help. I lived in Livonia and ran the complex until 1980, when I decided to move to a larger condo in Westland, which was closer to my job.

Again, life was not easy being at the Livonia Plant since there were so few Orientals living in Livonia and Westland and none working at the plant. Whenever the car slump hit the auto companies, it was a bad situation for me. It was then that I realized I probably would be facing more problems from the hourly workers. Yes, they did come to my office to tell me that my people are taking their jobs from them. I asked, "My people?" and "Who are you speaking of?" I was born and raised here in the United States. I said, "Maybe, if the plant manufactured quality products and not have to scrap most of them made in this plant, we wouldn't have so many problems trying to keep the plant open." Japan was manufacturing better quality transmissions and shipping them to the Livonia Transmission Plant that were installed in most Ford cars — the start of 'Japan Bashing'."

Sadly, Vincent Chin, a young Chinese engineer was mistaken for Japanese and killed by two Chrysler laid off workers. American Citizens For Justice was formed and drew the attention of everyone throughout the United States through the newspapers and TV stations. After a long drawn out period of marches, hearings, and trials, the two men were found *NOT GUILTY. JUSTICE* — what about Mrs. Chin? When you deal with hourly workers in any

manufacturing company or auto industries, you will find a different breed of people to deal with — especially, when there are layoffs and overtime is cut off. Greed, I would say, is the word ,and nasty.)

Lucky for me, I had a job where I was in contact with most of the managers, especially the plant manager and general manager, and they told me if I had any problems to see them because I was just as good as the next person and don't let them take that away from me. The plant manager was a huge man, who intimidated everyone with his size and mouth (not good). And one day I challenged him doing the right thing, and he and I became good friends. My boss was not happy with him giving me gifts on holidays, which was against Ford policies. I told my boss, "The next time he brings me a gift, I will tell him I cannot accept it because of you complaining." His answer, "Don't you dare! He will fire me." The general manager would come to my office and was very nice to me. I think the plant manager had something to do with it.

So often, coworkers, managers, and secretaries would ask me how I can work for my boss — much younger than I was and a jerk. My answer was very simple, he needs me and I don't need him because he doesn't even know what my job is. My worst dealings were with the hourly workers from the plant since our plant was in bad shape and rumored that it may close down if the quality of the transmissions did not improve.

At that time, Japan was also making transmissions and sending them over to the states, better quality, which was a sore spot for the hourly workers. (Yet another

"Who you know and not what I know."

reason for the "Japan Bashing.") I have to admit; I did drop names once in a while when things got nasty. I was very nice to the security officers and the maintenance crew, who were looked down on and really appreciated me treating them as equals. They would have done anything for me. During the hourly strikes, I had my office cleaned and vacuumed and security looked after my office. No one else got service. My coworkers wondered why I was special. My answer was, "It doesn't cost anything to be nice." Again, the ol' line is "who you know and not what you know."

I retired after thirty-seven years of service from the Livonia Plant and have so many tales to tell about the life at a large manufacturing company and the people you deal with. These are people worried about their jobs, layoffs, and greed. I witnessed many of my friends laid off, and I was very fortunate not to have been picked for a layoff. In fact, I use to ask for a layoff during the summer months of July and August during the changeover. My friends sat by the pool and even collected unemployment. Isn't that hard to believe? I have to say I enjoyed, hated, and regret some of the tales I could tell. I still meet with a group of friends every month for lunch that sometimes extends to dinner because we have so much to talk and laugh about. Of course, they never let me forget the fact that "I had it made" and "got away with murder," since I knew all the managers. I always tell them I learned to "be one step ahead of everyone" and lived by the rule—*"who you know and not what I know."*

MC: *What are you doing since you retired?*

MK: Living here in Westland and even before I retired, I have been on the board of directors and making most of the decisions on what to do with the problems occurring at the complex. Of course, you always run into co-owners that may be anti-Oriental until you educate them.

I always seem to run into uneducated co-owners that think I am from the "old country" and think I don't know what I am doing and in a very nasty way would say, "Why don't you go home where you came from?" They have found out that this "foreigner" is not the nicey, senile lady that is going to overlook their nastiness and not backing off. So hard to make them understand we have rules at a condo to follow. After a while, your skin gets awfully thick and everything rolls off. They're the losers.

Just before I retired while I was in St. Louis, Missouri, visiting friends, I decided to drive down to the Rohwer Camp in Arkansas, not knowing what I would face. I drove into McGhee, Arkansas (just outside of the camp site) and met some wonderful ladies that had been planting flowers and weeding at the cemetery. They were shocked to meet me and the boutique shop owner wanted me to have lunch with her—of course, I did and had the best fried chicken her daughter brought to us.

After leaving for the camp site, there was a lot of construction on the road, and I couldn't find the entrance into the cemetery. I stopped by an old shack (I remembered the shacks along the railroad tracks when we were in camp), and an elderly crippled black man came to the door and was so shocked because

Vincent Chin, a young Chinese engineer was mistaken for Japanese and killed by two Chrysler laid off workers... the two men were found NOT GUILTY. JUSTICE—what about Mrs. Chin?

his grandpappy that lived there told him about all of us "disappearing off the face of the earth" when the camp closed. The man and the kids were so polite and nice to me. It was a hot, sweltering day (I don't think the rental cars had air conditioning), and he insisted that I have some lemonade his granddaughter was mixing with chunks of ice. It was the best lemonade. Usually, I do not accept anything from strangers but I guess I was desperate for something cold.

Also, I stopped on the trip to the camp to visit a friend that lived in Cape Girardeau, Missouri that I knew when I lived in Painton. After not seeing her since I left Painton, it was such a great reunion. Thinking back, I guess I was so young to even think of the problems I could have faced traveling alone or I wasn't too smart. Oh well, everything turned out fine, except my friends in St. Louis were furious when I got [back] because I had to spend a night in Cape Girardeau.

I was very happy to see the graves were in good shape and able to read the headstone markings. The tank and statue of the eagle had few cracks and was beginning to show their wear. Names of the deceased internees and soldiers that were killed in action were still very legible. Since then, a group of internees from all over U.S. had gathered for a reunion in the late 1980s, and the state of Arkansas has declared Rohwer camp a Historical National site and will be taken care of by the State of Arkansas.

Two things from camp that I will never forget is the baby-sitting job for a three-year-old boy that had a beautiful, gorgeous blond mother and a teacher of Indian descent from Wagoner, Oklahoma. The mother of the child always asked me to play outside with the boy and if it rained to bring him into the recreation room. I noticed she had so many different men coming and going and just thought, "She sure has a lot of MP friends." Of course, at that age, and in those days, you never heard about prostitutes or gays, etc. I realized as I got older that she was a prostitute—no wonder she paid me so well with silver dollars, which I still have. Also, she always had goodies baked for her son and I.

Live and Learn.

Mrs. Essie Jane Avery was the wife of the Mayor of Wagoner, Oklahoma. She was always on my back for talking in class, and I did a lot of eraser cleaning. She was a very robust woman with a bun and kids made fun of her. When the camp closed, she returned to Oklahoma and began writing to me and we kept in touch with each other until she passed away at ninety-three years old. When her daughter informed me of her passing, I asked her why her mother would leave her home and be our teacher. She said her mother thought what happened to us was so wrong and wanted to help in any way that she could to make things better for us.

MC: *How do you feel about all the hardships you and your family went through?*

MK: Since I left California and lived in camp, through all the hate, discrimination, harassment, and hardships, I have to say that it has made me a much stronger, very independent and caring person towards the less fortunate. And I've learned that life is not a bed of roses and you have to go on with life and not keep dwelling on the past injustices. Of course, there are a lot of Nisei that would rather not talk about that period of their life, even with their children—*wrong*.

We, the Nisei, Sansei, Yonsei, and a few fifth generations should be very proud and hold our heads up high to our parents, grandparents, and great-grandparents for teaching us to endure regardless of the obstacles and hardships we might have to face. We would not dare to say *we can't* because *they survived* and taught us how to survive through all of our good times and bad times.

Toshi Shimoura and Mary Kamidoi, 2012
Photo: Emily Lawsin

Above:
Wayne State Japanese Room
[JACL]

Center Left:
Bell Creek Park JACL Picnic
[Miyao]

Center Far Left:
Eiko Takemoto, JACL Picnic
[Miyao]

Bottom Left:
Peter and Doris Fujioka
[Fujioka]

Bottom Far Left:
Mr. Hopping, 1952
[JACL]

Above:
Maryann and Kids at the Barrack,
c. 1943
[Mahaffey]

Left Top & Center
Far Eastern Festival, October 1972
[Miyao]

Left Bottom:
Reagan signing the Civil Liberties Act,
August 10, 1988
[Yamazaki]

Top Left:
Toshi Shimoura's Parents' Wedding
[Shimoura]

Top Right:
Tadae & Tsugi Shimoura
[Shimoura]

Bottom Left:
Patsy Mink [JACL Act]

Bottom Right:
Family [Hirozawa]

Above:
442nd veterans
[JACL]

Right:
Mrs. on the phone
[Okubo]

Bottom:
Running children
[Takemoto]

Miyo O'Neill, 1956
[President]

Ernie Otani, 1992
[President]

Jan Ishi, 1977
[President]

Roy Kaneko, 1955
[President]

Scott Yamazaki, 1972
[President]

Min Togasaki, 1963
[President]

George Ishimaru, 1969
[President]

Valerie Yoshimura, 1995
[President]

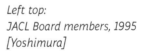

Left top:
JACL Board members, 1995
[Yoshimura]

Right top:
JACL daikon harvest, 1960s
[BoardMem]

Left center:
Peter Fujioka, Toshi Shimoura and
Doris Fujioka, c.1942
[Miyao]

Left:
Mayor Mariani and Walter Miyao, 1952
[JACL]

Top Left:
JACL Board
[JACLAct]

Top Right:
Yo Kasai, President
[JACLAct]

Right Center:
National Convention:
Okuda, Montanti, Satou, Bohn, &
Masaoka, 1964 [JACLAct]

Right Bottom:
Iwao and Mary Ishino
[Ishino]

Above:
Installation: Terry Yamasaki
[JACL Act]

Top Left:
Shig Wakamatsu
[JACLAct]

Top Center;
Installation: Ken Miyoshi, 1955
[JACLAct]

Left Center:
New Year's Eve.
[Kokubo]

Left Bottom:
Picnic
[JACLAct]

Top:
JACL Picnics
[Miyao]

Top Right:
JACL Dance Club
[JACL]

Center right:
New citizens, JACL Eastern-Midwest
district council convention, 1955
[JACL]

Right Bottom:
JACL Dinner Dance at
the Hotel Fort Shelby, 1951

Top Left: Governor Romney,
M. Nagano, S Shirane, 1964.
[JACL]

Top Right:
Mr. & Mrs. Taizo Kokubo
[Kokubo]

Bottom Left:
Man with Army Uniform
[Ishino]

Bottom Right:
James Okubu, Italy
[Okubo]

Blossoms and Bridge in Japan
[Miyao]

Natsuko Sugawa

interviewed by Asae Shichi, 2003

AS: *This interview is with Natsuko Sugawa in Bloomfield Hills, and we would like to find out how she has grown up in the diaspora of Japan. So where were you born?*

NS: I was born in Taichu in Taiwan. Taiwan was a colony of Japan at that time. I was born in 1943, January 16th. January is supposed to be in winter, but Taiwan is a very hot country, so my father, probably teasingly, he named me, Natsuko. That means summer. It's opposite in idea of January. Actually I like my name very much.

AS: *So you are brought up in that surroundings. So what is your father doing there. My father is a medical doctor who is a surgeon. The reason he was working in Taiwan was, he was assigned as a chief of surgery department of state hospital of Japanese, under the Japanese—how do you say governed? So that was the reason he brought his family to Taiwan. I happened to be born there, while he was working there. So your sisters and brothers were born there too?*

NS: My brother who is the oldest. He was born in Tokyo. My elder sister—this is a kind of story—my mother was almost at the end of pregnancy while my father was assigned to move to Taiwan. There was no airplane at the time, so going by boat is the ordinary way. Well since my mother was almost at the end of the pregnancy—that was a big liner of the company, they said no because if baby is born during the trip then ship company is responsible to throw the party, which is very costly so they said no. But the CEO of liners, happens be my father's uncle. So my uncle involved, and my father was given the permission to take his wife with him. Luckily for the liners, my mother gave birth after she reached to the port here in Taiwan. That was the story. I thought it was very funny.

AS: *That is amazing.*

NS: So my elder sister's mother is here in Taiwan because of that special condition. So then my father's job was in Taichu. I think they call it Taichung now, where a couple years ago, several years ago, a big earthquake hit. Taichu is known as like a neighborhood. I think it is very like a cultural city. It's almost middle of the island. As an island member, few scenes I remember. It was already wartime, but my few memories wasn't really very scary one, first one. And nothing as I remember, I was scared because I was too small. But that is already later, my parents often talked about as a matter of fact kind of a way. It was wartime, and one day my father was given a paper and a surgeon is needed to treat all these soldiers sent back from all the southern islands of the battlefield. So my father, at the age of forty-some, who has to become, how do you say, *guni*, military doctor. And so then my mother had my brother, my sister, and me—"I", I should say. One maid from Taiwan, some how do

you say, like an Indian kind of person—really not the Chinese, more like the original...

AS: *Mountain people?*

NS: Yes. And my mother was in charge to look after all of us and we lived in a big *kansha*. It is provided by Japanese government, big house. And we have a big yard and the stream was going across the background, but all this airplane from this U.S. raid started after my father was taken away. The air raid comes so what we had was so-called in Japanese *bokugo*, but that is nothing, anything like President Clinton has. We just dug a hole in our backyard. It is just kind of a hiding place. So what I had was, as I remembered, this new water comes up every day, so my mom...

AS: *Inside this?*

NS: Yes, inside of the hole. She has to prepare at any change when the siren goes on. She has to bring the kids down to the hole, so water should be always kept along. So twenty-four hours and you don't know when. So my mom says, always checking the level of the water, and with help she bucketed all the water always. When the siren goes on, she said, since you know that *Katsui-san* is someone's daughter. So my mom always said, "Send her with me." I was a baby so first, then two kids, then my mom. Atame [head] is thick of enough, they said, that the blood doesn't go through. So she said she laughed, you know. When such a case, you get special mystery power.

AS: *It was a long time it lasted.*

NS: Finally it was my father's order: "Okay now, evacuate the city, it's too dangerous." Okay, so my mom and three children are sent to the mountainside by the train. So I think it lasted for maybe one year or so. In meantime, my father was working in hospital. She heard all this rumor, it's a big air raid, and the middle hospital was burned—destroyed. My mom had no way to contact my father. She thought that maybe he's gone. So but, much, much later, my father kind of wondering and came visit my mother and us. I think, how you think, I think embracing you know, he's survived and we survived.

AS: *So about this life in the mountains. What do you remember about that?*

NS: Well the life on mountain, I really don't remember much, but one scene I can clearly remember is occasionally my mother asked someone to look after my brother and my sister, and she and I went back to town, the city to check the house. Maybe because she casually told me later, maybe that's why I can remember that scene. She took off the mountain and on the train, but somewhere in between to Taichu, air raid sirens goes off. So everyone has to leave the train and hide out. Well, I think, the whole night, I think my mom had all the feelings that kids behind the mountains, and you never know what will happen. So when she told me of this one, I can remember some scenes that was only things remember I can recall of this particular mountain life. Actually, so 1943, August 15th came, and my father and my mother both knew clearly, from the beginning through, my mother's brother, who is a navy officer, he visited my parents right before the war started. As a navy man, they have their own idea, and casually he was permitted to speak of his own feelings and opinions without worrying. My father told us when uncle, actually my father's brother-in-law, right—because wife's big brother. When he came and chatted, just he said this war is a no way; it's a no way, it's really, truly no way. But still whole nation is facing and there is no way to stop also. So my father always said so from the beginning we were doing something impossible. Actually I am very happy that my parents who was drowned of this idealistic miracle, where it happened to a nation in Japan. Well it really gives me a clear chance when it was over and whole nation, including the people who lived in Taiwan, faced now to a whole different world from the yesterday.

AS: *It was '45?*

NS: 1945 in August 5th is the surrender of the day. I don't know when we came back from mountain, but we have still home, which wasn't destroyed. So we came back to that *kansha*, the wonderful building was still okay. So we came back. So we kind of sit-and-wait kind of condition, I think, it was. But I am not bragging, but I am so glad I was born under the parents who know what's fairness. My father treated any patient no differently. He was most fair person that people say. So he really treated any difficult patient even Taiwanese farmer's wife—whomever came to him. He had big name *onna-noko* association which he created. So once the war was over, he often laughed and said, you know when things are going well, people forget and take it as it for their own grant—take it for granted you say? My father said, but watch out something happens, and it is all opposite.

Luckily for us, my mother and father, are such honorable character. They were always fair to everybody. No matter what happened. He was. My father and mother was very respected by neighbors. So when I heard of this one, I was educated so nicely. Not because of the special condition you act differently; you act always the same no matter what. That, I was given as a child. I am a very lucky. So life in Taichung now, Chinese regained power, and all the people, the Japanese who used to use all that privilege wonderfully had miserable life now, but for us, it was okay. We don't know how the life will be, but in the meantime since my father's fairness, it was given a chance to open a small clinic because there are nowhere regulation at that time and so then you still have to live or eat. So no government anymore, so you have to use your head to survive. My father is a medical doctor so he decided, "Okay next step become clear someday, let's just make what I can do." My mother later, and laughingly said, "So we wrote a letter of advertisement and the arrow to the direction and we pasted to areas: Haichon clinic is this way." *[laughs]* I thought, you know, "What the hell? Is he mad?"

AS: *So they did what they could do.*

NS: Yes! Instead of whine or depressed or anything. I was happy to hear this.

AS: *So you did hear about your neighbors or whoever, who were not treated nicely after the end of the war? The Chinese would come and...*

NS: That's right. The one incident my father jokingly said, Transportation was a *jinrikisha*. The chief of the police who used to use run for his power but denied—no more. Hey... ."

AS: *You can't ride...*

NS: I don't want to take you. No thank you. The rickshaw man is refusing. But of course my father said, "Oh always I was treated fair." That's another clearer episode to teach me well. Another episode was already my mind was functioning because what is happening in mainland China, that Kuomingtang and Mao group. But Kuomingtang was so big at the time, so my father took this Japanese emperor's picture no more, right?

AS: *And he got the picture with Chiang Kai-Shek?*

NS: And he is very clever to put his family. He put Chiang Kai-Shek's picture instead of Emperor Mai. It was a brutal time. All the gangs. I don't say Chinese, but it was Chinese, right? It's always looting as the things happens. My father expected this would happen. So now that's why he had idea to prepare. The one night, four gangs walk in and closer. It could be worse. It's almost like everybody smiles when everybody talks of this memory. My mom said—whispered to my brother who's about six or seven now—"Yujin, go jump over the fence and tell the next door neighbors we are looted. Gangsters here. So hurry up!" So my brothers, I think took off. Then four gangsters really came into the room. One guy acknowledged my father, "Dr. Hayashi! He's very fair guy, right?" Then he said, "Stop!" Then he saw the hanging, picked up the Chiang Kai-Shek: "This house is not the one who we have to disturb. Let's go." [laughs] So they left without harming anyone, taking anything. This episode, I really love to think about it.

AS: *But I'm sure you have been scared.*

NS: I am so sure. This case, I thought about my father's wisdom. And really, how smart of an attitude. He was thinking ahead to protect us.

AS: *Right. And also your neighbors!*

NS: Yes. I think so!

AS: *It's quick thinking.*

NS: I think so! I'm glad. So not too many things, but a few stories. Later I learned it's always a story of survival. What implanted in my mind was fairness, you know, to live. Fairness, I can never forget and that's soaked into me. So 1945, the war was over, winter came, and we didn't know what was going to happen. And 1946 spring, without any pre-information one day such-such part, that this area will go back to Japan. So you only have eight hours to prepare, so you didn't prepare to what you hear. And whole big house, all this wonderful things parents accumulated for a lifetime, all these things my mother brought from Tokyo, well, of course, you cannot take it. You are not permit to take any precious things. Since my mother is only daughter whose father was a navy officer high rank, who traveled all over the world a long time ago, my mother had all the wonderful precious stones. But that is not permitted to take it. So my mom said, I had a whole sack all kinds of stones, but then...

AS: *Precious stones.*

NS: Yes, you know, it could change to money—big money—but cannot take it because the rule was whole group was responsible for each other. If anyone who breaks the rule, whole boat, people on the boat, will be stay back again. So my mom decided abandon this whole thing. That one friend: "Someday when the time becomes peaceful, I'll give it back, in meantime I will keep it for your safe keep." Well that's the end of the story *[laughs]* because life is not that easy.

AS: *So your mother gave those things to people she knew.*

NS: Yes. I mean whole one person, just the whole thing because she offered to keep it, but that's okay. And furniture was no question. What was permitted to bring my mom said, "Three kimonos for one person." That is only the things you can carry. Three kimonos for one person and no pictures, no other things, no money—only certain cash and kimono. So funny thing is one lady who knew my mother had so many kimonos came and "If you go back to Japan, if you give me this and this, then I will be part of your carrier to take your kimono back." She was a kimono maker too so she sewed—underneath of one kimono, she sold another kimono, hide it, and counted it as one kimono. Isn't that clever? I knew this lady later. I met many times, but that's the way other people hate someone who has more. She gets something also in reply. Within a few hours prepared, my mom said, "Strange thing is when you in such condition, you don't think what is more valuable as money, you think about valuable for the memory." So when I was cleaning up the house much, much later as a grown up, one day I found a very funny case, it is all dried out human gallbladders.

AS: *Gallbladders?*

NS: Yeah!

AS: *Human?*

NS: Yes! And I asked my mom, "Mom! What are they? Why it's here?" My father in Taiwan, there are so many patients whose—in Japan you don't see that kind of patient—but my father was so curious and always has the mind to study, so after the operation, he saved. I don't know.

AS: *Specimen?*

NS: Okay. He is a very neat guy and he studied and you know. He has a way to do it. He made it, and it was his stuff!

AS: *And he took that back?!*

NS: Not he! My mother! My mom saved for him.

AS: *Instead of dress?*

NS: My mom said it was his important things because he treated patients and he always thinks about case. And this was his stuff that was so precious. *[laughs]* He brought them back! I mean not he, my mother's idea! I think you know, "What a sweet mother!" *[laughs]*

AS: *Did you remember anything about getting on the boats and things like that?*

NS: Yes. I think my father was suffering from malaria. My big brother was suffering from malaria. I was suffering the malaria. My sister and my mother wasn't. Those three patients automatically suffered a high fever. Anyhow, my sister had a little tiny knapsack, you call, backpack. You know my mom had a new bottle of Chanel, which she got through her big brother who is a navy officer. When he went to Paris before the wartime for his sister, he brought the perfume. A long time ago, my mother kept it and never used it. And she had it and suddenly now, she had to go back. Instantly she thought, for his memory, she took the bottle of perfume and put in my sister's backpack and a few teacups. She said her mind wasn't working so she just wrapped it in a newspaper and stuck it into the backpack and the perfume bottle. When the boat arrived to the Kagoshima port, she was exhausted and forgot what was in the compact, and she threw because...

AS: *She threw it away?*

NS: Yeah because Miyako was so tiny and she carried all the way, this backpack. "Ah hurry up! Take it off! Hurry up! Relax!" my mom said, you know. I felt so sorry she was carrying all the weight and took it off. My mother was pregnant with my younger sister and she kind of threw it down and crashed! Everything crashed in the backpack! *[laughs]* This backpack, I remember that it lasted for years and years and whenever we picked, this Chanel perfume smell years and years! That is the one thing than coming back on the boat, my father is a doctor so he was assigned a ship for I don't know how many hundred people, but the boat is not made for a passenger boat so it's almost no convenience. Most of the people stayed under the boat and deck. Few people who strong enough stayed on the deck. It took for how many days they said? It's, how do you call it?

AS: *Torpedo?*

NS: I think it was still floating here and there, but I think they tried to clean up and some unlucky boat, it was peace time, but you know struck with torpedo and steerage. But our boat was okay.

AS: *Perished.*

NS: Perished! Our boat okay and I think Kagoshima, maybe four or five days kept it very slowly, but another things, maybe I'm bragging in a way, but I am so proud because I am, you know, the way my parents were. We had a big jar. How do you call it inside? It's glass.

AS: *Like a thermos?*

NS: Thermos. Yes, it's a big thermos, and my mom couldn't throw away much, much later. "Mom it's such dirty!" You know, "Some thermos, why don't you?" She said, "I can't." And she told me the story. She had this big thermos carried the water and took with them with, you know, family—then on the boat and lots of people like me or my father and high fever. So no convenience, nothing. And lots of said, "Water, water." Can you see the picture? My parents are not selfish at all. So my mom said you know that she mend cotton that she just soaked and gave to those with the high fever and suffering with their mouth. You didn't think about, you know, hygiene. They only think about give some comfort. So after a few days of the trip, then my mom said, "Everything was so sticky." Can you imagine? Now it was... You don't think about it.

AS: *You don't think about it.*

NS: They were always the one who shared.

AS: *Ready to share.*

NS: And this boat trip was not easy, but we survived.

AS: *Yes, that's a great story. So then you came back. Do you remember anything about coming over to the land after days on the ocean?*

NS: Alright, we arrived to the ports of Kagoshima. One picture clearly I remember in my mind is my mother was pregnant for my younger sister. She was probably about eight months pregnant. Well, anyway one thing is my elder sister who had a backpack, which my mother, just not thinking, she said, packed with few English-born China tea cups and one perfume bottle which her big brother is a navy officer brought back from Paris years and years ago. But when they landed to their port, fastest thing my mom did was taking off the backpack from my sister's back and just thinking, "My little sweet daughter, you carried all the way this heavy stuff, you must be tired. Okay let's take it off." Then she threw it to the ground and with a crash sound. That sweet talk we carried many years of that scene and that smell of the perfume from all that backpack lasted for many years. It was memory.

AS: *And what did some other sister or brother carry in the backpack?*

NS: My brother was quite ill. He carried back a few probably... I think it, you know, this is very another smile it gives me. My father was very scholastic surgeon, and all the patients he treated and many Taiwanese patients had very different diseases from Japanese. So my father collected... Oh I did? Oh, okay sorry. Think I repeated.

AS: *I think that's fine.*

NS: Anyway, my brother, probably those stuff. My father probably was in charge so I think he had a thermos with water. The thermos lasted for years and which saved many people. That was a memory. And the thought brought back some memories years, years later, many years. And the Kagoshima, first night, first day, I was on the top of the truck already, and this some young man reaching down and helping my mom climbing up the top of the trunk—I mean the truck. That is a scene I remember. My mom was quite you know...

AS: *Heavy...*

NS: ...Very. That some guy was reaching down—my mom wasn't afraid, she kind of really hopped. The sugar, everybody said in Taiwan that Japan has no sugar, no rice, anything, no food, nothing, so my mom would kept thinking, she said, how lucky we are in Taiwan because we really don't suffer any kind of food, even after the war. My mom had some idea, "Okay let's bring some precious, so-called precious sugar to give to family." Well I guess such a time, all the confusion people suffered and some too clever people get some wrong idea. Very first night she said, "All the sugar was taken." I think that was every day things because most people from Taiwan probably brought back the sugar. So people who looked after those things, we call it, the evacuator. I think they took the advantage. That's one thing. Another thing such a time, people can have the wrong idea. That's the teaching my mother gave me. Such a time people could have the wrong idea. Not necessary you will have, but some people might have. That's good education.

195

AS: *Instead of blaming these people, your mother said that this was just the times and that's how people become. Then you get settled and...*

NS: Yes, and the first true settle, my father's family who was doing well in Fukuoka. First you know, we went to my father's oldest brother, my uncle, my oldest uncle, who's a lawyer, big-shot, we don't care. We said, "Hello, we're home." The second brother was a doctor and whose wife is paralyzed. So it's a big house, little countryside of Fukuoka, and he invited us. "Okay, until you find permanent settlement, stay with us." I think I see the two different character even in the same family. My second uncle, since his wife is paralyzed, my uncle was just like a Buddha—very peaceful person. So we were taken in, under his wing. First week we stayed with him and we were provided white rice every day. So my mom thought, all the rumor that Japan is suffering that any food, just people starving, that was a rumor she heard in Taiwan. Mom said, "I thought it was a big lie." We ate rice every day for first week.

Anyhow, we were provided housing by uncle. We moved out from his house and my mom visited my uncle, I mean whole family visited. After we moved out, they were eating very—how do I say, "not so great food" I said another teaching. When you do treat without saying anything, just to do.

AS: *She had the best...*

NS: No explanation, nothing. Only action. That's another great teaching I got.

AS: *What a great teaching you got!*

NS: And Mom's explanation is wonderful, very detoured, but it gave me all this clear scene and image. Then my mom gave a birth. Another big thing is, such a time, war time, terrible time, a war of confusion, something we cannot image, have any image right now under such a time. My mother was from Tokyo and my grandfather was a navy officer who was a very high ranked, but in a way, my grandma said, fortunately died on the *tatami* because he was struck with stomach cancer and died just before the war. So my grandma was a widow living in Tokyo and her two sons both are taken away—officers, both are officers, so gone. And Tokyo was air raid. Grandma had made from Gifu prefecture, and my grandmother didn't have any place to escape. She was a very proud woman and so she was in Tokyo. This helpful man offered. "Madam, if you like or need place to live and escape from every day danger, please come stay with us." But while she was preparing to move some of her stuff—air raid. That big air raid in March. She lost completely everything. Only a few packages she sent before hand.

So my mom came back. Rumor Tokyo is banned. No way to know about old mother, and so she said, "You know such a time, no telephone, nothing, no light, nothing. And you don't want to worry. It doesn't help you," she said. She said, "It doesn't help you." She had a great skill—decision making. And really in her mind, she put it in action—very crisp. And she is most gracious, beautiful person. She doesn't whine. So anyway, my mom, actually, I remember too—maybe I was with my mom—sitting by the window of this little apartment, and one kimono with umbrella and one lady's walking very *cha-ch-ch-ch-ch-ch*—very quickly. But the lady is not a worker or anyone like that because she stands out so differently. Stands out. My mom, looking down and just tilting her head, "Someone, hmm, who could be?" That was her mother! My grandma. So later what went on was Tokyo was bombed. My grandma was not injured… luckily. So she put the sign—mail, temporary address is such-such prefecture, such-such-such. She put the sign and left Tokyo, went to this Gifu place, borrowed some little, you know, place. I think she lived there.

Now the war was over, it was March, then August. War was over, now her mind was started clicking. Not seeking two sons who went to war, more like seeking if they are—Taiwan most likely safely—they are alive at that time. When and how are they coming back from Gifu to Nagoya. Nagoya is a place—big station which has all this information who evacuate from all over: from Manchuria or Korea or Taiwan or some maybe from Philippines. So from, how do I explain such a… I love my grandma. It's very inconvenient transportation right? It's just crowded. It's just terrible. Inconvenient time. But she took train every day, every day from Gifu to Nagoya by commute, every day. (Right now it's only for maybe thirty or forty minutes.) Maybe hours and hours of ride. She said, "Commute every day to check the board from which area which boat carried who—every day. So August, December came and January came, then springtime came, and we came back in the spring. One day my grandma saw the sign such-such boat from such-such Taiwan from such area brought back these people. So my grandma had no way to call or anything. She just took off. [laughs] It was already hot time and I think maybe around time my younger sister was born in July.

Maybe after she even she was born, just about. It's already hot time. No wonder she was wearing white kimono.

AS:	*Summer.*

NS:	Yes, summer. But isn't that so nice. The people who has action! No whine, nothing. Do it. So she just hopped on a train to unknown place. I think it is very hard to believe today.

AS:	*Yes, yes, yes.*

NS:	I think when more and more confusing time, this kind of courageous action is a very effective. People depend and rely on each other too much these days.

AS:	*Yeah, right.*

NS:	And they say it should be good. It should be that. No! I thought it was great.

AS:	*First do it.*

NS:	Yeah and my grandmother did, and so they found each other. And another embracing, you know? So anyway, then my father, when my mom was giving birth and everything, he needed a job. So he once belonged to Tokyo University Medical School, 3rd Surgery Department, so-called. So my father took my brother to Tokyo in meantime. My mom's handmade jacket my brother was wearing. The train was so crowded, while he was sleeping somebody reached over and stole his jacket. Such a time. So my father took my brother, and they went to Tokyo. So my father is a character again. He respected Dr. Olski so much. So he went, visited, and said "I have sweaty palm." Then Dr. Olski, who was a guest of honor of my wedding, said to my father, "I can give you two offer." One is Nishiki hospital The other one is—how do you say in English?

AS: *Mental house.*

NS: Mental hospital. So my father grew up by the ocean. He always had a wonderful, warm weather location to grow up so he decided Nishiki was offering a better salary, but he chose better climate for less money. So he took this job. And when my brother already—maybe he still carrying, the two pencils, he never use it. I asked to my brother, "Brother, why don't use this pencil." "This is my journal pencils," he said. "This is given by Dr. Olski, when I first time visited with my father." Isn't that sweet memory?

AS: *How old was your brother?*

NS: I think he was about seven or eight. I think so. So anyway my father again, back to Gifu. You know this is important, my mother just gave a birth, so she cannot move right away. My father took a job, took brother, and my elder sister. I think he was a really responsible man. He didn't pick up by himself. He took two kids and moved into new area. Again, this was government job so we were given nice housing. Anyway, my father started a new life with two kids—alone. It's very unusual in Japan.

AS: *Yes!*

NS: Amazingly, this was my family.

AS: *So this is where you grown up.*

NS: So my mom, after she delivered the baby. I remember this scene because I was four

years old, four-and-a-half. I was quite capable to remember. And I went to the area my two grandmothers were living. Very first time, I ate corn. We were suffering, we always hungry, right? And countrysides, still farmers providing good, fresh foods. That's the memory.

AS: *I think that in all of your stories, the great big scenes of transitions. You have faced many big changes. So I would say, I would say that the next big change is when you got married and got out of this, house from the Hayashis into the Sugawas.*

NS: Yes.

AS: *According to the good Japanese tradition. You are married and you have to live with the whole family of the husband. So probably you can pick a few stories.*

NS: Well, we had quite a free idea and modern idea and tradition. Beautiful tradition, yes. Ugly tradition, no! That beautiful or ugly—I kind of have an idea according to how we can keep up your individual pride. Woman and house combined? Actually, I never agreed. I never called myself, I am a wife of a Sugawa. I denied over such a self-recognition. I happened to be married to Sugawa. So I am his wife, not Sugawa family. So this was a great tool. All my life, it was very greatest tool.

AS: *Very unusual in Japan.*

NS: Maybe. But not in my family. So no matter what happened, I always had clear idea. Sometimes so many things undesirable but oh, that's okay. I am not saddening to anyone. Maybe I am helping need to fill that I am actually giving my hand, not serving. That's just a matter of how you think. That is so helpful. *[laughs]* That's the way I naturally started my new life. It is completely different people, completely different philosophy, completely different value. I could have victimized myself if I want, but I didn't want to. So I guess maybe, in some old-fashioned eye, I was a very tough person. But my philosophy was if you disagree and exchange a nasty word, it is time to say completely goodbye. If you don't have that much clear idea, then you won't throw the darts. That was clear picture. So it saved me, it really, it building up my pride—now in better shape really.

My husband and my elder son was born there. Then he finished Post-doc studies and earned another PhD title besides the M.D. Finally I felt okay, my patience time in many ways was over. I thought well then a job was given by the university and went to Kofu for one year. Which is big countryside at the time. I felt it was so great. I felt it was so great. It's so country! And really completely, I felt great. I still think of Kofu time as the best year of my life after I married.

AS: *Get away from your in-laws.*

NS: Yes. That's intuitive. It's more like a healthy distance. Then Tokyo University was under the fire of that particular year. And his department decided to change so many things and recall my husband back to university. It was quite a disappointed things happen, but, anyhow, my husband kept thinking he wanted to come to the United States. He was maybe in his studies—in maybe for he was focusing English too, but he never explained to me. So one day, he said, "Let's go to United States for one year." Then my mind said, "Only one year? Okay, one year." I had a

wonderful life in Kofu. Another one year in life in America. I'm young. I never studied English, I mean real-life kind of English, but English studied a lot as a student, English grammar, and read a few short stories. Basically I am a Japanese literature; Japanese language was my major. I said, "Well I don't know if life takes this way." If I knew it is so, I probably took English major. It was such a popular things my time already. I am quite sometimes against with very light so-called...

AS: *Fad.*

NS: Fad. I kind of take it light of that because of my father. You know, "Everybody does it so I do it." I had that feeling, so most of my classmates all took the English major course. I rather took Japanese with *[laughs]*, now what? Is it against me? I have to go to America, but it's too late to worry. So I'm like my mom, I drop to worry—already let's go forward. One year, it's not too long. With one boy, it's okay. Then my mom always thought I am a great reader. That was my hobby. I never was one who goes out and spend time foolishly. My personality maybe wasn't given that way, my mother taught. "Is she going to be alright? She's not the one who just go out and making noise." Later she said that. "Are you sure mom? Do you really think so?" She said, "Yes! Because you are not the one who goes out and play around."

Anyhow, I happen to be a quite, you know, thinker, so mind was clear. I think it helped me. I came with my husband, two luggage—big luggage—no help. We landed in San Francisco. My husband was so upset, worry the porter and he is not a good helper anyhow. "Ah! I can't depend on—why I should depend on them?" Got

199

angry. I don't depend on him, then it's okay. Two days we spent in San Francisco. First television program was Captain Kangaroo.

AS: *What year was this?*

NS: That was 1969, July and we entered San Francisco, seventeenth. So seventeenth and eighteenth we stayed at San Francisco. Right in the middle of *nihon-machi*, Japanese *Nisei-san* was running the hotel.

AS: *Oh! What was it Victory Hotel?*

NS: Maybe they named it—not any longer. Many times come back, no longer. But I always go back to same place to look around, to walk around. Second day, we took bus tour, and bus driver was speaking English. That park, Golden Gate Park, and so we were in and he was speaking English. Very simple phrase. I heard what he said *[laughs]*, and I said, "My English is not so bad. I can hear what he said."

AS: *How delightful!*

NS: *[laughs]* I thought I'd be okay. So we arrived to Detroit, nineteenth. My husband never asked anyone anything, so we arrived and it was two years after the riot, right? Many of my friend in Japan said, "Why Detroit?" Well, I read the newspaper over there have riot all over in America. But since, you know, physically we didn't know anything. We just came, right? And still my hobby isn't worry. Nothing is dangerous, right? *[laughs]* You know how to be protecting yourself. Airport picked up the taxi. At least the JBSB made—how do you say, another

appointment?—reserved hotel in downtown. It was called Diplomat Motel. Still I see that building—no more than motel.

AS: *JTB right?*

NS: JTB! Yes, JTB.

AS: *Japan Travel Bureau made that reservation for you, right? Yeah.*

NS: They reserved actually. So my husband, anyhow managed to tell the driver, "Take us to Diplomat Motel." It is still a building in there. It is I-94 and Woodward corner. It's just by the campus of Wayne State.

AS: *That's where your husband is going to be studying.*

NS: Yes. I think the JTB people studied to take, you know, reserve us somewhere close by. The very first day, the small television was airing the scene from the moon. Moon landing day. That is a nice memory—very first day in Detroit.

AS: *So you stayed in that motel for sometime or did you get settled soon?*

NS: We didn't know what to do. My husband just found a way to go to university, but once he focused he forgot. My husband took the Kondo from Keio University. I don't know he got and he just a kind of send away in Japan and someone told my husband Dr. Kondo and many other Japanese doctors studying, researching under Dr. some-some and in Wayne State. So my husband had one information Dr. Kondo and telephone number, so my husband called. He was a good Christian. He came right away, maybe four days after we arrived. It was time that we cannot have money, and we don't have money from the beginning, but also it's the limited dollar was permitted to take, right?

AS: *Bring from the government position in Japan.*

NS: Yes, yes, so you cannot survive too long. *[laughs]* So he was very kind. He and other doctors all lived near Highland Park in one building. He said, "We are all together, so therefore we can leave. But since the riots, air raids, dangerous, so you would never walk around. But you come with us." They are just on their way to move down to Baylor, Texas. But, you know, they had another month, one month, so they said, "One month is long enough to decide the permanent place. In meantime, I arranged my landlord, so you are permitted to live one month." With his English and the kindness, I was saved. And moved into Highland Park, the big apartment—most of us, Wayne State students. And it was, how do you call it, studio? One room. But I thought it was great. And Dr. Kondo took me to like a Kmart place. It wasn't Kmart—another name or something. It's called, you know, a chain store, not the department. Like a Kmart, you can buy things cheap. So I bought blanket and pillow, and he was so kind. Without him, actually I think life was much more sad. It was going to be, but our time was great! Always I appreciated him. This gracious one person. He saved me.

AS: *Then after you get settled, meaning that in that apartment, and then you were doing your shopping every day?*

NS: Well, you know, one day I walked a little to [mail letter to] my mother. Telephone was too expensive, so I cannot call and this difference of the time, ours, just unthinkable. So I walked a little, and I was going to step out of the building and now Mrs. Kondo said, "Where are you going?" "Oh! The corner of Woodward and this street." It is Glendale, it is called. I still see the sign when I take Woodward. Mailbox over there. I am going to drop this mail. She said, "Don't you ever do it!" I asked, "Why?" "No, if you need to do it, wait a minute. I will get my baby. I will walk with you." I said, "What do you mean?" "That is rule number one leaving here too dangerous. If you need to step out building, make sure invite me." "Okay?" So then she had a whistle with her. Still it really didn't hit me how dangerous, or so people say, because my husband didn't have car and he was with somebody to downtown. In meantime, before we buy a car, other doctors from Osaka University or Kobe University or many different universities, doing one research under the one grant. Most of they poor, so they have very old car, but everybody has all the cars. Then they said, "I walk up, my car is gone." *[laughs]* And "Oh yeah! Okay, why don't you come and ride with me?" That's the way they share each day. Then usually those old stolen cars was found somewhere. All the gas was spent. They didn't break or anything. They used it and leave it. That's the time, but people are so funny. They say, "Oh yeah?" And they share and no fuss. So anyway my husband was introduced another one, and we kind of look for the car. We bought a car. We just drove around and nothing, no idea. *[laughs]* Nothing. We just saw the sign "Children welcome." Sign for one apartment. I said, "Okay." That was in Roseville. It is very far east. We didn't check anything. My husband didn't ask any help.

AS: *What kind of an apartment was it?*

NS: Of course we looked for the cheap apartments. When we moved in, three Indian families from India, most old white Americans I say, but many are underprivileged sort of. A few has a good education maybe. Most are not. So background why the Indian people were educated, but no money even for rent—sort of same thing. But I never felt I come to this country to take as my country, so temporary feelings. So just a little things, Mr. Kondo and others moved out of Michigan, we moved into new place. Then the telephone conversation. I lost all the contacts, right, because—I don't know—I had no guts yet to practice English. One of them, Mrs. Gana—it's a student, the wife of student at Wayne—once called me, Roseville apartment. Oh, how panicky I was *[laughs]* because when she said, "Did you go grocery shopping?" I'm sure she asked that, but in my mind, I became so panicky. Then first time, very first time, I was sad. First time I was sad and no teacher, no condition, and how am I going to make myself be free from worry? I had one book of conversation textbook from Japan—one page written in English, another page is Japanese. Since I have no helper, my mind was working at how to help myself. Yes and so whole textbook I already read. It's kind of stupid conversation, but it's every day things. I can read it. So with my way of pro-nunciation, I read whole book. I try to put emotion. I try to carry the conversation as it is written. It helped.

AS: *So how long did you live in that Roseville apartment?*

NS: Hmm. It was supposed to be one-year promise. Terminate lease. What's going on? We don't have money to go back to Japan. Well I knew *[laughs]* how—oops. So second year, we wanted to move to V.A. Hospital Los Angeles because there were famous doctor there. My husband still sort of a student, so he wanted. Then he asked me. I said, "Choichi, I spent so much energy to fit into this life so far—this far. If you say are moving, only way to get going back to Japan. Another move I am not permitting you." Besides he was offered a little better salary and he decided to… he had a great respect from the doctors here. Instead of to be student, he was respected. He liked it! He lost the chance to go back to Japan. And the second year passed. Okay, I just didn't want to have only child because my husband is only child, and his father was only child. I didn't want to have only child, so I wasn't afraid. I think it was better to have another child. *[laughs]*

AS: *So now you have two sons.*

NS: Yes, and the second one just because since I didn't know when I would have another baby. Better off to have chance to have the baby here. So I just go ahead and have a baby. And third year came, so '69, our moving to Roseville. Baby came '71, February, but we decided because we lived in the second floor. I have to keep telling kids [whispering], "Don't jump, don't jump, don't jump!" Thinking about people below. I said, "Choichi, I cannot look after two kids—healthy way by telling kids not to do it. We need place that kids can run." So then, a friend of mine,"Natsuko, in America it's very easy to buy a house." I said, "It's unthinkable in Japan. Building house or buying house is lifetime things." "No America is easy."

So I hold my heart, trusted Helen and her husband, I said, "If so, will you help me?" I showed all my savings account notebook and checking book. I just opened up everything. This is all! *[laughs]*

AS: *So you built a house?*

NS: Yes!

AS: *So this is the house!*

NS: The first house in Sterling Heights. Of course no cat and no animals. I had no idea, but, anyhow, wonderful kids to run! *[laughs]* And I explained to his parents, in American culture, buying a house is not a permanent idea. It is very temporary. People buy and sell all the time. Therefore, don't be so afraid that you worry that we are not coming back. It is only to raise kids. When we go back, don't worry, we sell the house and come back to you. When his mother died, I cleaned up whole big box, hundreds of letters I sent. She kept them.

AS: *So you are still here.*

NS: I'm still here. I just didn't want to make them disappointed by telling we are not coming back. I acted out, it's temporary. That was toughness to think, and it's unhealthy, I tell you. It's difficult. You cannot have both. I cannot declare myself that, okay, eventually it's going to be temporary. Right now this is apartment. If I declared that decision earlier to myself, I think redo my life in America. I think much healthier feeling I created, but that was the past. My mom's, "Every doctor went to America and stayed. Out of ten, nine would not come back. What are you thinking?" "Mom, I don't know. He won't say, no matter how much I knock the door."

AS: *So it was all up to the husband. So it wasn't your decision?*

NS: Yes, but those are very tough things. But in the meantime, I was learning English, and there is a "Sesame Street" program on the TV every day. By flipping the channel I found it. It was the greatest textbook! If you are not to really given the circumstances, very kind environment instead of whine. It is my family tradition: You create it.

AS: *You do it!*

NS: Yes! So that I did. This Indian family close by, particularly Maya. She came one day, "Are you the one whose Japanese moving to apartment recently?" I said, "Yes." And we chatted. And I studied English as a student but never this practice. One day she took me to her apartment and showed me channel—was it 2? Channel 4? "General Hospital." So popular. And she was pointing Dr. Such-such used to be married to this head nurse, this and that, she explain-ed. So since then I switch on, I listened to the conversation and this station and what kind of vocabulary exchange. It was a thrill.

AS: *Great study! Hmm.*

NS: It was a thrilling thing not just a stupid story. How to use it, you know? I think I gained this language power quite early. When I had a baby, I had a small coin-sized—so-called half is English/Japanese, another half is Japanese/English—one small pocket dictionary. I had that dictionary with me. I went to hospital. My husband you know left me. *[laughs]* And I said, "Sure! I am not in the wild of Africa. I am in the middle of America, in a top-notch hospital. Why should I worry?" Only a few vocabulary.

203

[laughs] I need to pre-study. So I pre-study. I remembered, and when I was by that from the tiredness and the painkiller was given, I think I was knocked out, quite deeply. Next day, after the baby was born, I had very small memory of the birth, you know, and I asked the nurse, "How did I manage? I don't remember much. How did I manage?" She said, "You know when I asked you do this, do that, you replied in English." I said, "Hooray!" I was so into the reality. *[laughs]* It gave me, you know, "You can do it if you want!"

Miyoko at Swarthmore College, c.1943
[Bassett]

Miyoko Inouye Bassett

This chapter is drawn from three sources:

[1] Miyoko Inouye Bassett's presentation at the University of Michigan, February 21, 2005

[2] Her presentation to a Friends gathering, July 3, 1995

[3] Her presentation given at the Swarthmore College War Years Reunion in June 1992.

In life there may be certain profound events that you may want to suppress in order to get on with your life. Our internment experience was one of these, which we rarely talked about, even to our children. Few people asked about it, even among our friends. But there was the lingering feeling of discomfort and feeling that it had not all been put away. What can we learn from it? What can we do about it? We thought about it from time to time.

We slowly started questioning about what really did happen. The injustices seen around us made us more aware that ours too was a major injustice worth talking about, worth informing people, and being vigilant, and seeing that what happened to us must not happen to anyone again.

After 9/11 it did start to happen again. We identified with the Muslim and Arab people who were targeted with anger and hatred. They were falsely linked to the "terrorist" just as we were linked to Japan, the country of our cultural heritage. We were as shocked as anyone with the attack on Pearl Harbor, and deeply saddened also with what happened on 9/11. The anger and hostility directed to Muslims and Arabs were similar to those which we experienced. The sudden taking of Rabih Haddad from his family here in Ann Arbor, without hearing or trial, and not initially informing the family where he was taken—also happened to many leaders of the Japanese community. National security and patriotism were touted loudly. My speaking out today is to describe the difficult experience of the Japanese internment and examine the injustices imposed not only to the citizens of this country but to our non-citizen parents and others as well.

My parents were Japanese immigrants, settling in Sacramento, California where my two older brothers and I grew up. My father came to America in the early 1900's, returned to Japan to get married, and my parents settled in Sacramento where my father with three other men ran a furniture store in the Japanese part of the city. My mother, who was the principal activist in the religious realm, was introduced to Christianity upon arrival in America. In her new home, she found comfort and spiritual support in her church, and this was reflected in her family and our family outreach to the community. However, she became dissatisfied that the church did not carry out its mission very well, and in her spiritual searches we visited and learned about other religious communities. For a while she conducted Sunday school for us at home, inviting some neighbor children. She also taught us Japanese language at home, and, with other children joining us, our home became a Japanese school.

My childhood memories are those of growing up in a Japanese community (but wanting also to be integrated), being taught and absorbing Japanese culture, going to a racially mixed grade school, and of being a part of a religious family and community. As with many immigrant families imparting the culture of the country of our origin was important as we were growing up. Respect for the elders, for authority and for citizenship were important values. My parents considered themselves as fortunate guests of America, and they appreciated the citizenship of their children. Duty, perseverance and patience were other values which were stressed.

After Pearl Harbor, on December 7, 1941, of course there was a crisis in our communities. Leaders were rounded up and their families were not told where they were taken; they had to cope for themselves without their fathers. My parents had their suitcases packed just in case, my mother because she was involved in teaching Japanese, and my father because he was involved with martial arts training of young boys. Every time the doorbell rang we feared that they had come to get my parents. Home searches were conducted by the FBI looking for "evidence" of our ties with the enemy country. With this fear in mind, our family burned many letters from Japan, papers, photographs, and books Contraband—guns, swords (family heirlooms for some), radios, and cameras—all had to be turned in to police stations. Curfews were later declared, from 8:00 PM to 6:00 AM. At this time, my oldest brother, Bill, was studying at the University of California in Berkeley, my next oldest brother, George, was in junior college near home, and I was in my junior year of high school. Travel was restricted to five miles, and my brother had to return home from Berkeley. Because of the intense anti-Japanese climate, we feared that some change was going to happen to us, but we did not know what to expect.

On February 9, 1942[1], President Roosevelt declared Executive Order 9066, which gave the army permission to move us out of the western defense zone on the grounds of "military necessity." Reports of espionage and sabotage by the Japanese were falsely reported to the President. When would this move happen? Where and for how long will we be sent? What should we take with us? We began in earnest to dispose of our belongings—house and its contents, cars and our businesses. Moving sales at which our things were sold at ridiculously low prices were difficult. My father's store had buyers who backed out at the last minute making it necessary to dispose of it for almost nothing. We were told that we could take only what we could carry, in two bags or suitcases.

We were given two weeks notice to appear at a certain area to be taken initially to an assembly center, usually a state fair ground or a race track near our homes, waiting there for a couple of weeks to a couple of months until more permanent internment camps were hastily built. Ten camps were built, and we were sent to Tule Lake in northeastern California. We dutifully complied with these governmental orders, not wanting to make waves nor have the government question our loyalty. There were only three people who contested the constitutionality of the curfew and internment. These cases went to the Supreme Court which turned them down; however, years later the federal courts reversed their decisions. The Supreme Court has not revisited the issue yet.

There were fifteen thousand of us at Tule Lake from the states of California, Oregon, and Washington. We lived in blocks of tar paper covered barracks, four families to a barrack, twelve barracks to a block with a central dining hall, a central bathroom and a laundry with scrubboards, no washing machines. Our room was twenty-by-twenty feet, with a central pot-bellied stove, a single light bulb hanging from the ceiling, and five metal cots. Partitions of cloth were quickly put up in our rooms and in the bathrooms. We were not allowed to have any public gatherings, and we required to speak English only. Camp newspapers were censored. We were not allowed to take photographs and not allowed to have absentee ballots.

We tried to live normal lives under these circumstances. Education was very important to the Japanese, and before schools were formally established, older college age siblings were teaching their younger siblings and their friends. Later certified teachers were recruited from the outside and a formal school was begun with a set of curriculum which I'm sure underwent a great deal of discussion. I had my senior year in the camp school, and graduated from the Tri-State High school in the first graduating class of four hundred students. An ecumenical church was established and activities for youth were programmed. Sports such as baseball and volleyball became major events, not only for children but for the whole community.

There was concern about the many college students whose education was interrupted by the internment. Clarence Pickett of the American Friends Service Committee was asked by Milton Eisenhower, the director of the camps, to do something to help the students continue their education. AFSC and a group of college and university presidents organized the National Japanese American Student Relocation Council. This group helped approximately 3,500 students to go to colleges located outside the restricted areas, mostly in the East

Coast and in the Midwest. It was no easy task to match the interested students to these schools located in communities which would accept Japanese students, to get the necessary government clearances to leave the camps, to get school transcripts, find scholarships or grant aids and references. They said they wrote about twenty-five letters for each student they helped. Early in our internment my brother, George, was invited to go to Swarthmore College. The President of Swarthmore happened to be the chair of this council. It was a major event for one of our family members to embark alone on a train trip across the country to an unfamiliar location. He was given $25 and a ticket to the college by the government and arrived there safely and settled into his studies. He soon informed the college that he had a brother back in camp, and inquired whether he could possibly join him. The next semester my oldest brother, Bill, was indeed able to enroll, however needing to repeat his junior year. They were both warmly received by the students and found their studies to be a challenge.

When my brothers were together at Swarthmore, they decided to write on alternate days so that we would hear from them each day - penny postcard crowded with information. Yes, there were skip days. My father kept each of the postcards and letters, numbering each one as they were received, and I have had these to reread again. My brother wrote, "The students here are selected for their scholastic ability so they really travel in their studies." "I spend a lot of time at night thinking what's going to happen to us after the war is over. I also wonder why I was selected to come where I never expected to and when I never expected to. You can be sure that I'll do my best to prepare for whatever task I am faced with." "We Nisei have an obligation to give American democracy another chance to overcome racial prejudice and to work for international understanding in spite of the discrimination we have experienced."

In another vein, George wrote about his first Thanksgiving dinner away from home. He was invited to President and Mrs. Nason's home for a wonderful turkey dinner. "I had quite a stomachful except the part usually filled by rice was still empty." That was the Japanese part of his stomach.

There was a great concern by the government about the loyalty of the internees since there were no hearings or trials to determine this prior to our internment. The year after we were interned, the government decided to require each of us over seventeen years of age to respond to a questionnaire with thirty questions. Pivotal to and controversial were two questions which they felt addressed our loyalty. *Question #28*[2] *asked:* "Are you willing to serve in the armed forces of the United States?" *#29:*[2] "Will you swear unqualified allegiance to the United States and faithfully defend the United States... and forswear any form of allegiance or obedience to the Japanese emperor or any other foreign governmental power or organization?" People who answered affirmatively were considered to be loyal and those who answered negatively were disloyal and dangerous. There was great turmoil and division between family members and between friends who responded differently. Qualified responses were not acceptable. The government decided to segregate the disloyals into one location, in Tule Lake, and transport the affirmative responders to other camps to make room for the transfer of the *No-No*'s (as the negative responders came to be called) to Tule Lake. Divided families and qualified

211

1. The correct date is February 19, 1942.
2. The correct questions are Question #27 and #28, respectively.

responders of the questionnaire remaining in Tule Lake had a very difficult time. Our family was sent to a camp in Arkansas on a very long train ride over several days with the shades pulled so the public could not view us passing through.

When I was about to finish high school, my brothers inquired about the possibility of their little sister also coming there, which I was able to do. Never in our wildest dream did we dream of our going together to college, to Swarthmore, and overlapping there for one year. At college, one of the thoughts we siblings had was the need to forgive our government for its errors, to work harder to overcome racial discrimination and to work to enhance understanding among all people, including international relations. We were impressed how the student body wanted to reach out to the children in our camps, conducting drives to collect toys, soap, and books to send to them. We came to know more about the Quakers and we could hardly wait to tell our mother that here was just the religious community she had been searching for, a truly spiritually-based group reaching out to others in so many ways.

Students also made us feel part of them. George worked with the SN radio group, Bill was a member of the student council, and I had the opportunity to experience weekend work camps in Philadelphia with some students. Our financial situation required each of us to be employed and we managed to find enough work and funds to meet our needs. We all worked in the dining room at one time or another, one or another of us in the bookstore, the post office, the alumni office, the gym and the Friends Historical Library.

By this time, the government was eager to have more internees leave, relaxing the restrictions and enabling people to leave without firm sponsors or destinations. Hostels were established in larger cities like Chicago and Philadelphia to which internees could go to begin their new lives outside the camps. Knowing that the three of us in our family were in Swarthmore near Philadelphia, they asked my parents to come help with the one there. My parents were also warmly welcomed in the Philadelphia community, and they happily continued living in Philadelphia for the rest of their lives.

My own discovery and revelation about the Quaker community continued in my life and as I went through medical school. I wanted to be of some service and also to be enriched by service. I was fortunate enough to meet a lifetime partner, David Bassett, who thought as I did, and to be in one way or another connected with the American Friends Service Committee ever since. We worked for two years in the planned ten-year AFSC project in Orissa, India—two of the most valuable years in our youth. We were privileged to work with Gandhian workers in a rural area where a huge dam was being built. Each of the Western workers in this multipurpose community development project had a counterpart Indian worker, and we lived together as we helped train village health workers, agricultural extension workers, workers to build safe wells and latrines, and workers in education and village crafts—the weavers.

We lived five years in Hawaii, being a part of the Honolulu Friends Meeting community, for me also working in pediatrics at the Kauikeolani Children's Hospital and the East West Center. I was fortunate to be able to do general pediatrics in Honolulu, and to be a part of a working team helping children with developmental problems. The work at the East West Center introduced me to another culture, working with wonderful medical practitioners from the Pacific Islands coming to continue part time work with the AFSC.

We came here thirty-seven years ago to work at the University of Michigan Medical center, my husband as an internist and I as an instructor to medical students in their pediatric clinic rotations. Branching out, there has also been the involvement with the Friends School in Detroit and the Ecumenical Campus Center in Ann Arbor. The work with the Friends School in Detroit increased my outreach in another area with children—the setting in which the teaching about Quaker values was important. Parents of children who knew little about Quakerism came to appreciate that there was something special enhancing their children's learning at Friends School—that non-violence, fairness, respect for others, simplicity, and community are integrated into every day activity and thoughts. This year, in learning to write *haiku*, one 4th grader wrote the following:

> "Hearts are a symbol.
> A symbol of love and peace
> Use them every day."

The school was called a jewel in Detroit, and it is that indeed. The Ecumenical Center—now called the Ecumenical Center-International Residence—is one where students from many countries have the experience of interacting, learning, and living with each other. Lifelong friendships are formed, and many return home to carry on important work in their specially trained fields. One simple task I enjoyed and still continue is participating in taking the students grocery shopping one day a week. The first trip for a newly-arrived student may take two to three hours in the supermarket, but it is a well-spent time of orientation to our culture. What better way to bring peace and international friendship!

My mother was asked by some people whether she was bitter about the experience she had to go through, and her response was, "Bitter? How can I be bitter when so many people have been so good to us and to our children?" For her this was a blessing, a blessing out of adversity. This in essence has been our feeling about the internment. Yes, it was an error of the government, it should not have happened. The error was admitted, and publicly and personally apologized by the government. We each received a letter of apology signed by the President in 1988 as a result of the Civil Liberties Act signed that year. The congressional Commission on Wartime Relocation and Internment of Civilians investigating the internment concluded that the detention was not driven by military necessity but by war hysteria, racial prejudice and lack of political leadership.

In my work in Michigan, David and I have continued our interest in peace issues and human and civil rights issues and have been trying to do what we can to work toward a world with peace, justice, and equality for everyone. And in 1980 those of us who were helped by the Japanese Student Relocation Council started a *Nisei Student Relocation Commemorative Fund* to help the children of the Southeast Asian refugees to continue their education after high school. Each year a different community in the country is selected where scholarship aid is given to the students in that area. Recently the event occurred in Lansing, Michigan, where high school graduates of refugee families from Vietnam, Indonesia, Thailand, and the Philippines, were given scholarship aid at an enjoyable festive occasion. *"On"* another Japanese value, is the returning of a favor with gratitude, for the help we received at the time of our internment.

214

Enlisted
[Miyao]

Yuzuru Takeshita

This chapter was drawn from the following articles by Yuzuru Takeshita: "Re-Americanization of a Kibei at Tule Lake" in Trials and Triumphs: A Collection of 21 Memoirs *Written by Members of the Class of 1945 Tri-State High School, Tule Lake Segregation Center, Newell, California, edited by Terry Ishihara and Ben Hara, 2004; and "Executive Order 9066 and I: A Reflection After 60 Years." published in AGENDA, a Monthly Independent News and Culture around Ann Arbor, February 2002.*

I was born on March 27, 1925, the third son of immigrant parents from Yame County, Fukuoka Prefecture on the Island of Kyushu: Manzo Takeshita (1898-1953) and Hatsumi Ikeda (1902-1984). They had independently come from neighboring villages to the U.S. as teenagers to join their respective fathers who had originally come to Hawaii as contract laborers and who then moved to California as farmhands when freed from their contracts. My parents are thus "Yobi-yose" (brought over) Issei as distinguished from the original Issei immigrants, making my sibling and me technically "third generation," or Sansei. My birth certificate records that I was delivered by a Japanese midwife in Alameda while the family was living in San Leandro. By the time I was ready for school, the family had moved from San Leandro where my father was a tenant farmer to Alameda where he took up gardening.

In Alameda I started school at Haight Elementary School. I also attended a Japanese language school and a Buddhist Sunday school. In 1933, we moved across the bay to San Mateo since my father took over a gardening job from my maternal grandfather who decided to retire and return to Japan after twenty-eight years in the United States. I enrolled at Laurence Elementary School. In second grade I remember having to write, "I will never chew gum in class again," a hundred times when I was caught doing so. But then soon after that I was promoted to the third grade a half-year ahead of my classmates.

In the summer of 1934, I experienced an event that was to change my life forever. My mother chose to take me and my older brother, four years my senior, to Japan to live with our maternal grandfather who had returned there a year before.

Kibei—lit. "Go Home to America"

Grandfather, who was widowed in the United States, had married my step-grandmother soon after he returned to Japan. Years later I learned from my mother that the reason we were taken there was to get a head start in the job market there since many Nisei, who were forced to seek employment in Japan during the Depression years, were writing back to their parents how much difficulty there were having in adjusting to life in Japan due to language and cultural differences.

It was when I was in 4th grade when the war in China broke out in July 7, 1936. War continued in China as I advanced to the 6th grade. I was appointed class president, based on being by then the top student. In sports I was on the track team and competed successfully in countywide meets. Those of us who aspired to go on to middle school had daily cram sessions to prepare for the entrance examinations. Once at home, I got together at night to study with my closest friend, Inoue Tsugio, who lived in the neighborhood. He was one of the bullies who had taunted me as an *"Amerika-jin,"* but we became fast friends over the years as we played and studied together, sharing boyhood dreams, common among us then, of a career in the military.

It is ironic that I who was taunted as an *"Amerika-jin"* in 1934 had by 1940 become

so Japanese both in mind and spirit that I was reluctant to return to my country of birth even in the face of a threat of war in the Pacific. But return I did in November 1940.

On the ship we boarded at Yokohama destined for San Francisco, I befriended a Jewish boy who told me he was a refugee from Nazi Germany. I had no idea about the Jews in Western history, much less about what was happening to them under Hitler. In fact, Hitler was admired by us in Japan at that time as a leader who rebuilt Germany from the devastating effect of the severe economic sanctions imposed on her by the Allies after World War I.

My resolve to regain my lost English as quickly as possible was strong because I felt humiliated by having to go through lower grades—namely, 3rd and 5th grades—with my own younger brothers and in grades far lower than my younger sisters, one of whom was in the 7th grade and another a freshman in high school. What is more, my classmates whom I left in 1934 were already juniors in high school. Once again my self-esteem was at its lowest, much like it was when I first went to Japan in 1934. My parents revealed to me later in life that they felt so bad about my circumstance that they had intended to send me back to Japan had war not broken out on December 7, 1941.

I was aware, of course, that my re-entry into American life required as a first step that I relearn the language that I had lost. Apparently the teachers who helped me through the reading lessons in the lower grades felt that I was finally ready to handle all lessons offered in the 8th grade. Once in the 8th grade I took another step, albeit small, towards my re-Americanization effort during the lessons in civics. I memorized the Preamble to the Constitution along with the Bill of Rights and learned to recite Lincoln's Gettysburg Address. I must confess though that while I memorized the words, the true meaning of the concepts of democracy represented in the words eluded me as they were different from the political concepts of the imperialistic, militaristic, and totalitarian system under which I had lived in Japan.

In the morning of Sunday, December 7, 1941, my brother drove several friends and me to a basketball game in Alameda where our team from San Mateo was playing. We chose to go by way of the San Francisco Oakland Bay Bridge since we wanted to stop by Oakland's Chinatown to buy some roast pork for our father. On our way we saw sailors hitchhiking back to the Treasure Island Naval Base, located on the island that connects the two spans of the Bay Bridge. We thought it strange that they should be going back to their base on a Sunday morning. When we stopped in Chinatown, the Chinese merchants, who were usually friendly, greeted us in a rather cold manner. We did not learn of the reason for these strange happenings until midway into the basketball game when someone came running into the gymnasium with copies of newspapers with huge headlines about Pearl Harbor. Stunned, we all looked at each other and asked, "Where is Pearl Harbor?"

The news was shocking. We didn't know how to react. All the way home, taking the San Mateo-Hayward Bridge to the south of Alameda, we anxiously wondered what might happen to those of us of Japanese ancestry. On Monday morning we were all assembled in the school auditorium to listen to President Roosevelt's "Day of Infamy" speech in which declaration of war with Japan was announced. In class and on the playground, steely eyes of our non-Japanese classmates intimidated us.

I suffered one of the most humiliating experiences of my life a few days after Pearl Harbor when my 8th grade teacher asked those of us of Japanese descent who were Boy Scouts to turn in our flashlight, compass, and scout knife presumably because she thought less of us as American citizens, influenced by the negative rhetoric of the time. To this day, my voice breaks when I relate this ugly episode to those who seek to hear about our wartime internment experience. Soon FBI agents started arresting leaders of our community such as officers of Japanese associations, Buddhist priests, Japanese language school teachers, and the like. Rumors were rampant that, lest we be charged with intent to engage in espionage, we should get rid of anything that could be construed as suggesting pro-Japan sentiments such as any family photos containing anyone in Japanese military uniform, books, magazines, and records that had any martial flavor to them and, of course, any equipment such as a shortwave radio, torch light, or arms—whether operational or not—that may be construed as potential weapons for use in any subversive acts. We hastily burned those things we could burn, not without tears, and buried in our backyard those that could not be burned. (It is likely that those things we buried are still there since we never went back to the house we had rented.) What I did not burn or bury were several dictionaries I needed in my desperate effort to relearn the English that I lost while spending my childhood in Japan. In the one suitcase that each of us was allowed to carry into camp I made sure these instruments of language support were packed. However, soon after entering the temporary assembly center set up on the grounds of the Tanforan Race Track near the San Francisco International Airport, the authorities announced that any Japanese books and records still in our possession would be subject to confiscation on a designated date when troops would come through the barracks. Desperate as I was, the night before the designated date, I sneaked out of the barracks at around 2:00 AM and hid my dictionaries under one of the buildings I could crawl under and retrieved them again at around 2:00 AM the next day. I was not going to let the authorities deny me my right to study the two languages, English and Japanese, that represent my dual heritage. Such defiance, I believe, had nothing to do with loyalty or disloyalty. For me it was a question of survival.

In September we were ordered to board an old dilapidated train and headed for Topaz in Central Utah. En route to the more permanent camp in Central Utah, I experienced another humiliation that still rankles. As our train pulled into Salt Lake City, recently the site of the Winter Olympics promoting international friendship, and as we waited for a change of tracks to head southward to our final destination, a troop train pulled up right next to us. We knew where the troops were headed and so quietly prayed for their safety only to be greeted with abusive catcalls and obscene gestures. To this day, I wonder how many of those soldiers whose safety we prayed for survived the war in the Pacific where they were headed. I hope many did.

At Topaz, located in ever-so-dusty Whirlwind Valley, I graduated from junior high

school and started my three-year enrollment in senior high school—all three years to be spent behind barbed wire. I was asked to deliver a speech at my junior high school graduation. Still relying heavily on my dictionaries, I gave a speech on being optimistic about our future in spite of the setback we had suffered by our internment. To my surprise, the speech caught the attention of Sgt. Ben Kuroki, one of the first Nisei war heroes of World War II, who happened to be in the audience. He was quoted in the camp newspaper the next day that he was impressed with the expression of loyalty by the speaker (me) in spite of being held behind barbed wire with our civil rights in abeyance.

Ironically, soon thereafter, our "loyalty" was to be severely tested. The authorities, having decided to tap the "idle" manpower behind barbed wire for military service and for farm work, initiated for all those who were seventeen or older a registration program which included a "loyalty test" as a way of establishing eligibility for both needs. This event split the community and caused unprecedented anguish in each individual who had to make a choice. While I attended a large number of mass meetings where the pros and cons were heatedly discussed. I did not have to register until I became seventeen in March, 1943. Called into register upon reaching seventeen, I had an opportunity to weigh the pros and cons quietly without the pressure of an aroused public. I chose to answer NO-NO to the twin questions (#27 and #28) that supposedly tested one's loyalty. I like to think that my decision was based on my understanding then of our rights as citizens. Admittedly, however, this belief is based on post factum reinterpretation of the decision process. The fact that I was a *Kibei* with all the conflicts such a marginal status in our community at the time entailed and the presence in the family of a strong-willed older brother who took a public stand as chairman of the committee that protested the loyalty questions obviously influenced my ultimate decision.

I was in my junior year when I was transferred to Tule Lake in September 1943. The family members were allowed to join us in this transfer, a decision we welcomed so that all ten of us could stay together. There was talk that the so-called "disloyals" would be deported to Japan. Japanese language schools sprang up to prepare the children who might be affected by such an eventuality. I was asked by my barrack mates as well as my brother to join them in teaching Japanese at their school they named, *Daitoa-juku* (Greater East Asia Private School). I declined and chose instead to attend Tri-State High School, motivated primarily by my desire to improve my English as much as possible before being deported. I had in mind by then that perhaps once back in Japan I could become a diplomat and contribute in some ways to reestablishing peace among nations. The time behind barbed wire as a prisoner in my own country by virtue of my ancestry could have been the worst four years (1942-46) of my life but for one redeeming experience.

I entered high school in camp and graduated from high school in camp. Ironically, as a high school student behind barbed wire, I had the good fortune to meet a teacher who taught me the true meaning of citizenship in a democracy: Margaret Crosby Gunderson. She and her husband had abandoned their teaching posts in Alameda County, California in protest of our internment and joined the faculty at a camp in Northern California where my family and I were transferred from Utah. A towering redhead, she insisted on the first day of school that our internment was something that should not have happened in America. Paraphrasing as best as I can remember, she challenged us as American citizens to fight injustice against any group of people among us when it happens, insisting that injustice anywhere is a threat to justice everywhere. She went on and argued that our internment was not a failure of the Constitution but a failure of the leadership on the West Coast and in Washington, D.C., and the public that supported their decisions. I saw in her deeds and words what democracy means in terms of what responsibility it requires of its citizens. Any ambivalence I may have had about my NO-NO responses to the two loyalty questions that brought me to Tule Lake disappeared quickly. In fact I felt vindicated for having taken that position and glad that I was transferred to Tule Lake where I found my salvation in the person of Margaret Gunderson. I say this with no intention of denigrating those who made other decisions based on their convictions regarding this issue.

Clearly by this time, four years after my return to the land of my birth, my re-Americanization was ostensibly well on its way—thanks to my dear teacher's tutelage of all places at Tule Lake. But to be truthful, at that time mine was a schizophrenic existence. By day, I went to school to learn about the true meaning of being an American and by day's end I was back in the barracks of an internment camp, exposed to all the forces and events that led Dorothy Swayne Thomas, after the war, to characterize Tule Lake as "the spoilage." With hundreds of others, I renounced my U.S. citizenship by convincing my action as justified and an expression of anger and defiance against the way we were treated in spite of our citizenship.

The war ended on August 15, 1945, when Japan surrendered just nine days after the first-ever atomic bomb was dropped on Hiroshima. Release from camp for some of us, however, did not immediately follow the end of the war. Those of us who renounced our citizenship had to await official clearance from the Justice Department. It was not until March 1946 that I was freed, long after the rest of our family had left in the fall of 1945. I left Tule Lake alone, boarding a bus to Klamath Falls and a train to San Francisco. A mixture of euphoria on being free again and anxiety as to the immediate future filled my mind even as I rejoiced viewing majestic snow-capped Mt. Shasta that

I was not going to let the authorities deny me my right to study the two languages, English and Japanese, that represent my dual heritage.

we used to see longingly in the distance from Tule Lake. Finally I felt at home as we approached San Francisco with the awesome Bay Bridge in sight. Reunion with the family, especially my mother who was ill, was a tearful event that lingers in my memory to this day.

I immediately enrolled in San Mateo Community College. In the meantime, to relieve that congestion in our family's temporary quarters in the basement of one of our relatives and the financial burden our father had to bear as he tried to recoup the family's losses brought on by the internment, my sisters and I found employment as "school girls" and a "school boy" in homes of affluent white families in the community. By then my draft classification was changed to 1-A and I was informed that I might be drafted at anytime. Upon consultation with my employer who happened to be on the draft board, I applied

for voluntary induction to circumvent the uncertainty of the situation.

I was sent to Fort Lewis, Washington, for my basic training. There was a sizeable number of Japanese Americans in our company, all draftees called after reclassification of their draft status after release from their respective camps. Military Intelligence Service was seeking Japanese language students from among us to be trained for service in the Occupation Forces in Japan and had us take a qualifying examination. Those who passed were then sent to Monterey, California, to start their studies upon completion of basic training. Being a *Kibei*, of course I qualified.

I was delighted that I found an appropriate niche in the service of my country and could eventually go to Japan and help her people—in particular, my relatives and friends I had left in 1940—recover from the war's devastation that my brother described in his first letter from Japan. Unfortunately, my stay at Monterey was short-lived. One day about a month or two after my enrollment, I was called in by the commandant and told that he had learned I had renounced my citizenship and that disqualified me to remain in the Intelligence Service. Together with a few others in a similar situation, I was sent back to Fort Lewis to serve with the Second Infantry Division as a foot soldier. Disillusioned, I chose to leave the army after serving only 8 months when I was given the option to leave, following the discontinuation of the draft. I hasten to add that through a federal court action, aided by ACLU, the renunciation of my citizenship was declared "null and void" soon after my discharge. This decision meant legally that "renunciation" did not take place and that I had never lost my citizenship.

Even with the limited service in the Armed Forces, I was eligible for the G.I. Bill which allowed me to afford enrollment in a four-year college. In September 1947, I went off to Park College (now Park University) near Kansas City, Missouri, a private college affiliated then with the Presbyterian Church.

I chose to major in sociology since I saw in the discipline a way to understand all that happened to us Japanese Americans during WWII in a society that valued liberty and justice for all its members. I had hoped that once I understood the underlying dynamics of how and why of what happened to us happened, I could find the means to avoid such a thing happening again to any group of people among us within nations or across nations. It was a great challenge I imposed on myself and found my study of sociology at Park College and subsequent graduate studies at the University of Michigan to be exciting.

At the invitation of my sociology professor I gave a talk at a Kansas City Chamber of Commerce luncheon meeting about my internment experience and how I felt it was an injustice that should not have happened in America. To my surprise, the talk evoked a strong negative reaction from the audience, many of whom I surmised were veterans of WWII. They accused me of being disloyal to question the government's decision for the internment that they insisted was based on national security concerns. Not being able to handle the rebuff at the time, I clammed up for nearly forty years before I spoke or wrote about my internment experience again.

Upon graduation from Park College in 1951, I went on to graduate school at the university of Michigan, earning an MA in 1952 and a PhD in 1962 in sociology. For my PhD dissertation research, I went to Japan in 1955 on a Fulbright Scholarship and conducted a survey on fertility and family planning among married women in the Osaka Metropolitan Area. The aim was to understand how Japan was able to reduce its birth rate in just a decade after WWII, following an unprecedented baby boom and an extremely high rate of population growth that threatened to undermine the postwar effort at economic recovery. The choice of this topic for my dissertation research turned out to be very important for my subsequent professional life since it served to establish my identity in academia as a specialist in population-based research.

My life since the end of WWII has been a series of attempts at redemption for what happened in my life prior to and during WWII. Long after WWII, however, I used to curse my parents for having sent me to Japan to live there during my childhood as I felt it was the source of all the difficulties and internal conflicts I faced in my life during and after WWII. But then when I was in graduate school in the 1960s, an exchange student from Japan pointed out that my bilingual and bicultural background could be an asset in bringing people together across the Pacific Ocean. Indeed, awakened by his comment, in much of what I have done since then to heal the wounds of war in the Pacific and Asia I have taken full advantage of my ability to speak, read, and write Japanese.

Walter Miyao & Elyse Miyao (née Yamaji)
[Miyao]

Walter Miyao

interviewed by Emily Lawsin & Scott Kurashige
Detroit, Michigan, October 27, 2002

WM: Florin had, by 1920, about two thousand Japanese. Because of that influx of Japanese immigrants into Florin... Florin is about seven miles south of Sacramento. There no longer Florin, now, Florin became Sacramento. But anyway, Florin's influx of Japanese became so great, the Caucasians of Florin thought that they'd been pushed out from Florin. Thus, Florin East Grammar School was for Japanese only. Florin West Grammar School was built after World War I, for white families only. So, you saw that picture, that graduation picture of 8th grade? I was the president of the class then.

WM: So... white families built their own grammar school, Florin West Grammar School, which is about a mile apart. East and West. So most of us went to exclusive, segregated grammar school. That is the only, in the whole USA, segregated school for nationality. Japanese only. There are a lot of them in the South, black-only school, but not for Japanese only in any part of the United States.

So, I graduated from Florin East Grammar School in 1932. Now, I'm going to tell you the history about 1932, before that... It's amazing that among the Japanese, there was politics involved in this. What I mean is this: Japanese felt, because we are speaking Japanese and talk in Japanese and live as Japanese, that is one of the reasons why we are being segregated and excluded. So many of the Japanese families in Florin were either Shinto or Buddhist in Japan, there were no Christian natives from Japan living in the United States. Then they converted themselves to Christian. They said, "The only way to be accepted by Americans is to change our religion." So some of these people who lived in Florin converted to Christianity, Methodist... Even among the Christian Japanese, we had problems politically. Christians felt that we had to change our thinking from Japanese religion to American religion. Being Buddhist was over as far as politically concerned. Some of those Christians felt that certain people dominated Florin by politics. About 1930, I don't know the exact year, there was arson. I can't say it was done by Christian faction, but there—Mr. and Mrs. Tanikawa were the [moralist?]. He had the general store in Florin, who was politically strong—what he said in Florin went his way. One night, the fire started from garage [in the] back end of the store. Most unusual part of the fire is this: there was a fire hydrant behind the garage—turned off. Someone bribed the water department. And so the whole building was burned. Tanikawa's store and Kato's. Kato was a fish and meat store. And Tanikawa general merchandise. They burned down completely. That did not decrease the political problem of [river side?]. Tanikawa, fortunately had insurance; instead of a wooden general merchandise store, the insurance company built a concrete store, so that building still exists, fortunately. Mr.

and Mrs. Tanikawa had one child, whose son was Howard Roger. Before the war, this son Tanikawa went back... not went back... went to Tokyo and later on he became mayor of Tokyo. If you ever study the mayors of Tokyo, Tanikawa's name... he's American educated at Harvard, but lived in Tokyo.

SK: *He was a Nisei?*

WM: He was a Nisei, yeah... I don't know.

SK: *Was he older than you, or younger than you?*

WM: I hadn't met him, although my brother did, in Tokyo. Under MacArthur's regime. So anyway, Tanikawa was politically strong. So the arson... well, there was no evidence to prove it was done by them, but it's more or less my assumption.

SK: *But it was the Japanese Christians.*

WM: Yeah. Oh, yeah. Methodist Japanese and Buddhist Japanese. Buddhist was stronger. See, in Japan, if there were any Christians, it was very rare. Actually, they converted. Any Christian you find in the United States, Japanese, is converted or family member became whatever the church they belong to. Although the most interesting part of the whole thing was that Florin had Methodist Church and Buddhist Church. And the Buddhist Church was built during World War I. People in Florin made money during the war, and contributed to build the Florin Buddhist Church. Most interesting part of the whole thing is this: that church (see, we don't call it church—temple) temple still exists. It's the historical monument for [Cedar?] California has taken over the building. So that will be there as long as California historical commission holds.

I'm a Florin Buddhist, okay? We have a property of about seventy acres, bought during WWI, so Florin Buddhist Church had a church, and later on—in the 20's—they built a city community center for a meeting place. Then, about 1940, before evacuation, we young people (then) decided we had to have a bigger community center for young people. So we built a gymnasium, basketball-sized. It's still there. And that property has Florin Buddhist temple… or, there is no temple… new temple, gymnasium, school… we had—before the war—Florin Buddhist group built a Japanese school house.

SK: *Did you go to Japanese school there? Is that where you learned to speak Japanese?*

WM: That's exactly what I did. Although I went to UC and took Japanese language. Yes, I did. This is one of the reasons why the Christian faction was there again, we became "too Japanese-y", that's why you were discriminated.

SK: *Were your parents leading members in the temple? In the church, did they play a leading role?*

WM: No, Miyao… financially, but politically: zero. Because my father was uneducated.

SK: *Oh, okay… interesting… Did they go to service every Sunday?*

WM: Oh, yeah. I did, Sunday School; but my parents only went to the special services.

SK: *Like Higan, Hana-matsuri… That's right. Exactly.*

Dedication of gymnasium, 1940

SK: *How about the school, how often would you go to the Japanese school there?*

WM: Well now, every afternoon, after grammar school.

SK: *Every day.*

WM: Every day, five days a week.

SK: *And what would you study in Japanese school?*

WM: Basic Japanese... basic Japanese.

SK: *Did they teach anything else, Japanese history, or culture?*

WM: Whatever was in the book. But I used to read books, anyway, on Japanese history and culture.

SK: *And how about your parents, did your parents speak English?*

WM: This is the most interesting part of the whole thing. How did Japanese, from Japan, come to the United States, ever exist without knowing one word? Not a single word. My father came in 1890... no, 1895... '99... He spoke zero English. But he came to the United States. How did he survive? You ever thought about it?

SK: *A little bit, yeah.*

WM: I mean, with no knowledge of American culture, come out here and work.

SK: *So, did he learn English, over time, at all? No... none?*

WM: Well, by time they had their own community, so they didn't need to. We did the translation. So they had absolutely no reason to learn English after we were born. And besides... getting older... So they didn't. The other interesting fact about the history of Japanese in Florin—or any part of the United States—You know the entire Japanese Land Act? How did they buy the land? Until about 1930, they didn't buy the land. They leased it. How did they buy, then? Under children's names. When my brother became twenty-one, we bought the land.

SK: *How big?*

WM: Seventy acres.

SK: *Seventy acres!*

WM: Worth over a million dollars right now.

SK: *Uh-huh!*

WM: My brother-in-law's family, in another part, not in Florin, his island (?) had five thousand acres. Over $15 million. So those who went back after WWII did well. And my brother went back, whereas...

Well, let's go back to history again. Like I said to you, I'm a UC graduate. Berkeley. I took the school of public health. In senior year, twenty of us were accepted to the school of public health. Only twenty, in senior year, two semesters. In order for us student graduate to practice public health in the State of California requires an internship—one year. After graduation. I was of the twenty students graduating from the school of public health. Only Japanese. One of the classmates, his name was John, John said, "Walter, where are you going to have an internship?"

I said, "I don't know. I have no idea."

"Why don't you go see Dr. Lucas, she makes the assignments."

"Naw, that's a waste of time."

"Go ahead!" So he pushed me into it.

"Dr. Lucas, you going to assign me an internship?"

She said, "Mr. Miyao, you're Japanese. I can't."

After four years' schooling, what happened to my residency? *Zero.* So, that's how bad it was, discrimination against Japanese before the war. I went to segregated school, and then when I graduated from college, no one assigned me internship. What am I going to do? I have no job. I worked for Sacramento

Tokumatsu Miyao [Miyao]

county hospital for one month, for $30 a month. *A dollar a day.* With a degree. In the same group, a student who graduated same time as me, making $175 a month. I was $30. And that frustrated me. She was almost a failure in school, gets $175. Here I was, standard graduate, getting almost zero. Now, we're talking about before WWII. For me to get some sort of a medical practice, well, I said, I wonder what I can do. October... no, May... no, July 1941 I signed for three years, U.S. army, medical corps. So I could get some sort of job. In signing up, I was sent to medical training section of the army, medical corps. In the meanwhile, war had started anyway. So I would've been taken in the army. So here, I got the training in public health, more or less, by joining medical corps in the U.S. army. From Texas, training, to Arkansas, Little Rock Arkansas, Camp Robinson. I was assigned a medical hospital. I tell you this much, I think school did me a favor by not sending me to medical school... I mean, internship. I tell you why: after I finished army training, I came to city of Detroit, and asked the civil service for a job. They gave me a job, city health department. With that public health training, eventually I was assigned as assistant director of the laboratory. In California, it was zero—even though you had an internship. I would never become that level, as assistant director. Whereas here, they had no idea of the history of Japanese, they took me as if I was a part of the society.

She said, "Mr. Miyao, you're Japanese. I can't give you an internship."

SK: *So did you feel different, did you feel like people in Detroit treated Japanese differently than people in California did?*

WM: Differently? They think we were part of them. In California, they're separated.

SK: *Even during the war?*

WM: During the war, they even segregated... I'll tell you this: are you familiar with 442?

SK: *Yes.*

WM: After I got two years in the hospital corps, they took us to the 442.

SK: *In Europe? So you went to Europe.*

WM: They sent me to Europe. But because of my physical, disqualified. They discharged me from army, 1944. 1944, they discharged me from army. I went into the Amache. Are you familiar with Amache?

SK: *Yes.*

WM: With uniform, now, from the Presidio in Monterey, I was discharged. From there, I went into Amache. Then in my home in Florin—we were restricted in travel in California. Even with uniform. I had a special ticket, card, given by General DeWitt, that I could travel when I need to after I was discharged from army.

SK: *So how long did you spend in Europe?*

WM: I didn't stay any time.

SK: *No.*

WM: They discharged me while in training.

SK: *Oh, so did you ever go, were you ever sent?*

WM: No.

SK: *You were never sent.*

WM: No, I was given permission... They discharged me, period.

SK: *What was their reason for discharging you?*

WM: Physically unfit.

SK: *What was it about your health that made you unfit?*

WM: I get the compensation from the U.S. army, even now. My back was the problem. Actually, not only that, but I had a problem with my ears before I went in service. I had perforated eardrums. Before the army, before WWI… No, II. And they took me anyway, because that's how much discriminated against us. They needed a number of us included in the army, so regardless of my eardrum, they took me anyway. By 1944, my eardrum was bad, so finally they said, well, we don't want you.

I'll tell you how bad it was, discrimination. I got discharged in '44, okay? My brother George, the oldest one, was in camp and from camp he went to Chicago. And from Chicago went home to Florin. As soon as I got discharged, and as soon as my brother George got to Florin, they took him in place of me. But the most unusual thing about this is this: he had only one eye. He had crystal ball in one side. Now, they took him with one eye in place of me. But there was this army regulation, if any individual who got hurt during the training or after the training, 90 days, he would get compensation, full compensation. They discharged him after 99 days, so they wouldn't give him compensation. That's how bad it was. Now, they knew; he took it out and showed them, the crystal ball. See how bad it was? How badly they treated Japanese in California.

SK: *So, while you were in the army, your family was in Amache?*

WM: Amache, Jerome, Tule Lake… Tule Lake, Jerome, and now Amache.

SK: *Oh, they went to Tule Lake first.*

WM: Oh, yeah. In 1941. From Little Rock, Arkansas, where I was at Camp Robinson, I took a tour, a trip to Tule Lake. And that's where I met my wife, at Tule Lake.

SK: *Where was your wife from? She was also a Nisei?*

WM: Elyse Yamaji.

SK: *How did you meet her?*

WM: At the camp?

SK: *Uh-huh.*

WM: Block ten, you know the block? Block ten. My sister, Maxine, and her friend said, let's have a reception for these young people who made a trip to Tule Lake. So they organized a dance party at Block ten for me and three others. My sister Maxine said, "Walter, I want you to meet this young lady, a friend of mine."

"Okay."

"This is Elyse Yamaji, she lives in Block ten so-and-so." "Oh yeah, okay. Okay, thank you." Now, I stayed in Tule Lake for about seven days. And there, I went to meet her every day for seven days. At the end of seven days, I had to go back, I said to her, would you marry me? Period! Just like that! She said… She looked at me…

From Tule Lake, they were transferred to Jerome, Arkansas. They were going to close up Tule Lake. As you know, they had

At the end of seven days, I had to go back, I said to her, would you marry me? Period! Just like that!

political problems in Tule Lake, those who wished to be sent back to Japan were sent to Tule Lake. And my father and mother didn't want to do that because we were from a family of ten; eight of us. And they didn't want to send us. So they took a chance with Jerome, Arkansas. The reason they picked Jerome, Arkansas is because I was there, and my brother was there, too. So they said, well, let's go to Jerome, Arkansas. So that's where they came, and while she was there, we got married, in '43. And then, from Jerome—they were going to close that place, so they went to Amache. So that's the history.

SK: *But your wife left the camp to join you, when you got married. Where did you get married? In the camp? Where was your wedding?*

WM: Well, a Buddhist minister performed, unofficially, before she was out. And then she and I came to Little Rock, Arkansas. I went to Justice of the Peace in courthouse in Little Rock, and he performed the official marriage. So in '43, we got married. October 10, 1943. That's how it is. All the history's in there.

SK: *Okay. What happened to your parents' farm in Florin, during the war?*

WM: They were occupied by somebody responsible, but I understand from my brother George... Most of the things were stolen. The farm was retaken by George, my oldest brother. After the war, he farmed

it, but it became very difficult for farmers in California to get help. It was almost impossible, because most of the people worked in industry. They'd get better pay than the farm, so it was almost impossible for George to run the farm. Number two: the property tax keeps on going up, because property is getting more expensive. So by 1970 or '75—I've forgotten which—he had to sell, because the taxes became so steep. But he didn't lose money! He made money, but he was a farmer to start with.

SK: *What did they grow on the farm, before the war?*

WM: Strawberries and grapes. Where are you from, by the way?

SK: *I'm from Los Angeles.*

WM: Oh. You know, we grew grapes and strawberries, and we did well.

SK: *Did you work in the field?*

WM: Well, I was working as much as I can, while I was going to school. But after the war, no, because I was in Detroit. By the time they went back, I was here.

SK: *When you were a child, what type of work would you do in the fields?*

WM: I worked the farm in strawberries and grapes.

SK: *Doing what—planting, picking, weeding?*

WM: Everything.

SK: *Everything. So, all your brothers and sisters worked in the fields. Did they hire other workers?*

WM: Oh, yeah. We used to hire, total, about twenty people. Local people. Although we had transient Issei. We had a place for them.

SK: *So the workers were mostly Issei, or were they Mexicans, Filipinos?*

WM: We had Filipinos, too, yeah. In the 30's. So, they were as much as, total, as a whole, about twenty. Although the hired hands... maybe six or seven. And then my oldest brother got married and had two kids—makes fourteen in the whole house.

SK: *So what kind of house did you live in?*

WM: Shack. Not house—shack. I don't think Issei appreciated modern facilities. They never encountered the problem. But anyway, they were able to exist in the shack.

SK: *Did you have electricity?*

WM: Oh, yeah, we had electricity early. Very early, during the '20s we had electricity.

SK: *Running water?*

WM: Yes, we always had running water, ourselves. We had 2,000 gallon tank for that purpose.

SK: *Okay... So, better than your average shack.*

WM: Well, that's average. I don't think any Japanese lived in shacks without running water, or they have one of these pumps. But they didn't have running... toilets, though. That's a common thing. But otherwise—we had running water.

SK: *Was the work in the fields, was that hard work?*

WM: Oh, depends on whom you talk to. To us, it was routine. It's hand-and-knee, I tell you, this is what...

SK: *Let me make sure I can see you on this.*

WM: It's hand-and knee. Picking strawberries. Whereas the grapes, of course, has vines so... City folks won't know how to pick strawberries. They couldn't stand ten minutes.

SK: *How many of your siblings went to college?*

WM: None of my sisters went. Three of five boys went to college. They all had a chance to go to college, but they didn't want it. Whereas three was... Five, four, three... all went to college. And I was determined to go to college. My oldest one, older than I was... Let's put it this way: he was somewhat crippled. He had a car accident in the '20s. Broke his leg. While those days, medically they did a very poor of mending, so he couldn't run. About this much. And this here, because of the cast, this here — about two inches in like this. So he couldn't do this. So mother and father said he had to go to college. He wouldn't be able to exist. So this pushed him to college, while I said, "If he's going to college, I'm going to college, too." Which I did.

SK: *How did you choose your field of study?*

WM: What do you mean?

Children in the block #10 aTule Lake ca. 1943 [Miyao]

SK: *How did you choose your major and your career, public health? Why did you choose that job, that career?*

WM: Back to history, then. Florin Buddhist Church sponsored movies once a month, the Young Buddhists' Association. They had one of the historical movies, "Dr. Noguchi." He's a Johns Hopkins—no, no, Rockefeller Institute employee. He was a microbiologist from Harvard. Although he was a Japanese national, went to Rockefeller Institute and worked there. That kind of gave me something to look for, "I could be like him." Noguchi. You'll find that in anyplace, a biography of Noguchi.

Anyway, I saw a movie of Noguchi, said, "I'm going to be like him." That was the start of my going to—not public health, but microbiology. But I'll tell you this much, the reason I didn't choose microbiology as a major... I forgot her name now, darn it... She had a PhD from UC Berkeley, before the war. She couldn't be hired by anybody, with a PhD in microbiology!

WM: So I was taking microbiology in school, public health, so I could be there. So that's why I went into public health. Because to become public health, you had to have microbiology to start with. And then, statistics is the other thing. Those are two things that you go after for public health. So I took both. So that's how I got into public health.

SK: *Where did you live, while you were going to Berkeley?*

WM: I forgot the name of the street now, darn it... There were seven of us. Seven of us, all Japanese. There were two chemistry majors, two engineer majors, myself, and two political science—*Kibei*. So we batched and we were assigned by order of students what I was supposed to do. First I went there, and I was making lunches for seven of us, every day. And then, later on, you get better, you become dinner once a week. Well, anyway, that's how we lived. You know how much you needed? Less than $25 a month. That includes room and board. That's how much we paid. I used to ask my brother for $35 a month to subside, and that paid for everything.

SK: *Did you belong to any organizations when you were in college?*

235

WM: No. One semester I worked with WPA. Within the school. Washed dishes. In microbiology, you know, Petri dishes and so forth. That's just spending money.

SK: *Now, what is your date of birth?*

WM: It's in there… Everything's in there. Bring that, show it to me…

SK: *Okay. We'd like to get it on the tape, too. January 10, 1917. Now, among your ten in your family, the ten children, where do you fall?*

WM: I'm number three. That means that, out of five boys, I'm the only living soul. And three sisters still living. So, one, two, three… and five passed away. Four, me; and then six, seven, eight — the girls — they're all still living.

SK: *Okay. So you're the fourth in the family.*

WM: Yeah, fourth. I said three, but four.

SK: *But everyone was born in California?*

WM: That's right.

SK: *And your parents came… 1907?*

WM: Yeah… got married.

SK: *They got married in 1907.*

WM: Father left when he was nineteen. He was born in 1899. He left Japan.

SK: *And he always worked as a farm laborer? Now when did they first settle the land in Florin?*

WM: Before… about 1931, '30. We bought the land. George was twenty.

SK: *Were they working a different land before that?*

WM: Oh, yeah, we leased it.

SK: *The same one?*

WM: No, just about a quarter-mile away, they have another — Jackson family, forty acres of grapes — father leased it. They were able to lease, but they couldn't buy it, until my brother became age twenty-one.

SK: *So who did they buy the land from? Was it* hakujin?

WM: Yeah, oh yeah. See, they were already depressed. They were depressed. That would be prime land. If you bought that right now, it would cost a million dollars. That same property.

SK: *So let's see. You spent about three years in the army? What type of work were you doing in the army?*

WM: Hospital.

SK: *Hospital? Were you working with patients, or were you doing research, administrative work?*

WM: It's unusual, because Camp Robinson, they more or less sent all Japanese there. So there was one UC graduate from Berkeley I was working with, Nishida, he's from Marysville. And then… we used to call Tojo. He's a high school graduate as a helper. And then… I've kind of forgotten… another Japanese, Dr. Matsura, a dentist, graduated from U of

Yamaji Family and workers [Miyao]

D dental school here; he was with us. So there was: Matsura, Nishida, Tojo, myself... four Japanese among ten *hakujin*. Because Camp Robinson was a nucleus of Japanese during the war. Until they start sending to Europe, for 442 Regiment.

SK: *So what was your job there?*

WM: Later on, I became more in charge of the whole lab, under *[inaudible]*.

SK: *What was the lab's function?*

WM: We did general public health, uh, general laboratory, like bacteriology, chemistry, hematology, pathology...

SK: *So you lived on the base, at Camp Robinson?*

WM: What do you mean?

SK: *You lived on the army base?*

WM: Yeah, except before they tried to send me to 442 Regiment, from there they send me to Fort McClelland, Alabama for training for 442 Regiment. From 442 Regiment training center in Fort McClelland, they discharged me and they didn't send me back to Camp Robinson, but they sent me back to Presidio, Cal... Monterey for a discharge.

SK: *Was your wife living with you at that time?*

WM: Oh, no. She was in Jerome.

SK: *So even after you got married, she stayed in Jerome.*

WM: Well, no, she was in Little Rock with me. And then after I got discharged, I called her from Little Rock to Amache, and from Amache... I got bored doing nothing, so I wrote a letter to various cities in the United States, for employment. I received affirmative note the city of Detroit, so I came here.

SK: *How many different cities did you write to, do you remember?*

WM: At least half a dozen.

SK: *All in the Midwest and East Coast?*

WM: No, all over the United States. I wasn't interested in certain places, but Detroit more or less gave me encouragement.

SK: *Did they interview you? How did you get the job?*

WM: Oh, yeah, after I applied for the civil service, they interviewed me, my background.

SK: *So you got clearance from the WRA to leave Amache.*

WM: I only stayed one month.

SK: *Only one month. Where were you living in the camp?*

WM: In the camp, by myself. My wife wasn't there yet, until the last week before my departure of Amache.

SK: *So what type of barrack did you have in Amache?*

WM: One bedroom.

SK: *And you lived by yourself there.*

WM: By myself.

SK: *So then you sent your resume?*

WM: My mother and father lived in Amache then... they lived in Jerome and they came to Amache, so that's why I picked Amache. Because her mother... my wife's mother and father, and my father and mother and sister were in Amache.

SK: *One month, though... Did you qualify for redress, from the government?*

WM: One day... as long as you sign the... well, it wasn't my idea. They wouldn't let me go back to my home in California. Where else am I supposed to go?

SK: *So you wrote the letters to these cities... Did anybody else write back to you, besides Detroit?*

WM: Uh-uh.

SK: *No? Hmm. What did they tell you, did they tell you to come and take the civil service exam?*

WM: No, they said there is an opening, period.

SK: *Oh, wow; so they offered you the job.*

WM: Well, you see, they wouldn't know that I'm qualified or not. And take the civil service exam. So they couldn't say, "Sure, we've got a job for you." They couldn't say that.

SK: *But they told you to come and take the exam.*

WM: Yeah.

SK: *So you left Amache, straight to Detroit?*

WM: That's right.

SK: *How did you get there?*

WM: I think I took a Greyhound bus... no, was a train... I forgot now. Going from Fort McClelland, I took a train to Amache. And then... no... Amache, I took a train. From Presidio, Monterey, I took a train to Amache.

SK: *So then, from Amache, you went to...*

238

Yae, George, Walter, & Martin Miyao, c.1917
[Miyao]

WM: Here.

SK: *...here. By bus.*

WM: I kind of forgotten, which way, bus or train.

SK: *What did you know about Detroit, before you came here? Did you know anything about Detroit?*

WM: Zero. Zero. I know... my brother and sister were already in Chicago by that time, '43, '44. But Chicago didn't answer my inquiry. So, Detroit, and here I am, since 1944.

SK: *So were you worried about coming to a place that you didn't know anything about?*

WM: No, I wasn't worried at all. But I'll tell you, this was how bad it was, when I first came here in Detroit, I stayed at the Y. And then I looked through the newspaper for housing. Oh, here's one opening... I used to either walk or take a streetcar — in those days, they didn't have buses you know — and then, *knock, knock.* The landlord would say, "Sorry, it's taken." From one after another. No place to live, except the Y.

SK: *The downtown Y? Which one was that?*

WM: Downtown. And then, when my wife stayed at the hotel, I tell you it was almost impossible for us to find a place to live. Even though there were apartments available. Or rooms available. So my wife said, "I know what I'll do," she said. "I'm going to apply for a maid job in Grosse Pointe." She looked at it and said, "Here's one." She applied; the family name is Kelly, Mr. and Mrs. Kelly. She said, "Sure. The husband could live on the third floor with you." I said, okay, as long as I have a place to live. That's how bad it was, to have to go to maid job to find a place to live.

SK: *So how long did you stay there?*

WM: Well, let's see now, Lloyd was born in 1945... and my wife said, "Mrs. Kelly, I'm pregnant." She said, "What? Pregnant? You can't stay here." "Well we're staying here right now", as if... So you know what they did? They found a place for us. Kelly did, because they didn't want a pregnant woman living with them. That's our first apartment, on East Grand Boulevard and Gratiot, she found a place for us.

SK: *Small place.*

239

WM: Well, one room. But I had a hell of a time taking the civil service… I wasn't taking the civil service exam yet. I have a picture, I don't know, I gave it to somebody else, Ishino, you know him?

SK: *No.*

WM: He's from Michigan State, just like you. He was there, at the party.

SK: *Oh, okay. Yes, yes.*

WM: I gave to him the picture of where I was studying for the civil service.

SK: *So you didn't have a job at first?*

WM: No, well see, I wasn't sure… I never knew there was such a thing as civil service until I came here. That's the way it was.

SK: *But they didn't hire right away, when you got here, or they did? Did you have a job when you arrived?*

WM: When they hired me, yes, but until I applied for it… let's see, what year was that? I was working… '45? I must have gotten… found a job at civil service.

SK: *'45. What were you doing for that period?*

WM: I'll tell you, I was freelancing. But anyway, these two fellows, two policemen, ex-policemen, opened up a health center in the Penobscot building. They know, to open, they need someone like me. Take exam for them, which I did. And I worked for so much per day. About a month later, they folded up and I lost money. And then I started work for another company. A company, I think. They actually hired me.

SK: *So you moved to the Eastside of Detroit. Do you remember what street you were living on there?*

WM: Well, the first street, like I said, East Grand Boulevard and Gratiot. That's where I used to live.

SK: *What was the name of the street you were living on?*

WM: I can't… I forgot.

SK: *What was that area like, at that time?*

WM: It's pretty nice. It's near Sears Roebuck out there.

SK: *Near Belle Isle, too, right? Not too far from Belle Isle?*

WM: Oh, yeah, I could walk to Belle Isle. That's right. And there was a hostel for Japanese on East Grand Boulevard.

SK: *There was? Close by… do you remember where that was located?*

WM: I've kind of forgotten, but it was about half a mile from Belle Isle.

SK: *On East Grand?*

WM: Yeah, on East Grand. Going north on East Grand.

SK: *Who was running that, a church or something?*

WM: I have no idea. I've forgotten the name… it's a Nisei.

SK: *A Nisei was running a hostel there. And you knew some of the people that lived there?*

WM: Well, my brother and sister-in-law came from Chicago to visit me, I sent them there.

SK: *To stay there. That's interesting; I never knew anything about it. Who was living in the neighborhood at that time, it was mostly* hakujin?

WM: All *hakujin*. I don't think they'd ever seen a Japanese.

SK: *How long did you live in that apartment?*

WM: Oh, less than a year. And then I started buying a house. Okay, the neighborhood along East Grand Boulevard? I put down $100 to buy a house. I waited one month… two months… no response. So I went back to the real estate. The real estate agent said, "I'm sorry, the community wouldn't accept you in their neighborhood." They wouldn't sell it to me. So I came to West Side, Monica and Livernois area. There was a house for sale. And that was unusual, too.

I said to the real estate, "I put down payment, how come you put on For Sale sign in newspaper?" "I did?" As if they didn't know about it. So as soon as I went back and complained, they took it off and gave me the house on Monica St. And then, what happened there, in the '50s, a black family tried to buy a house, just about two or three blocks from where I used to live. Arson. I said, "My God, we can't stay here. This is a bad place to live." They burned the house down, because a black family owns it. So, I saw in the newspaper, for sale, on Glendale, on the West Side near Telegraph, just about a mile from here; two miles from where I used to live, a house on sale. Housing project, about fifty homes were built there. And I went there, to the real estate,

"Before I put money down, do you sell to Japanese Americans?" They were kind of flabbergasted, "What are you talking about?" "I just want to know, yes or no?" "Sure, we will." So I bought it.

SK: *That was a new house?*

WM: Since 1956 until I came here three years ago. That's the history.

SK: *Over forty years you lived in that house.*

WM: Oh yeah, over forty years.

SK: *So you only lived about, maybe, 8-9 years in the Monica house?*

WM: 1956… Yeah, about 7-8 years.

SK: *Did you ever meet that black family, that had their house… ?*

WM: Uh-uh.

SK: *No. How did the neighbors treat you, there? How did they feel about your moving in there?*

WM: Very nice. I had— we had no problem. Ask my Carolyn. She was born there. No… was she? No, she was born on… I had the street, I've kind of forgotten.

SK: *She was born in the Eastside house, you're saying.*

WM: Westside. I used to live on… I bought myself a two-family flat.

SK: *In addition to the other house.*

WM: Before. From Gratiot, came to the Eastside, near Fenkell and… oh, they had royal-sounding…

241

SK: *Oh, uh-huh, near 12th Street.*

WM: Yeah, on 12th Street, that's right.

SK: *Victoria Park?*

WM: Yeah.

SK: *So you lived there for awhile, too.*

WM: I only lived... one year. I made money, though.

SK: *And you sold that, and then you moved.*

WM: And then, to Monica.

SK: *Now why do you think they were more accepting of a Japanese family than a black family, in that neighborhood?*

WM: What do you mean?

SK: *Well, you said that you never had problems in that neighborhood, right?*

WM: I wasn't looking for yes or no, I just wanted to buy a house, period. It didn't make any difference who lived in the neighborhood.

SK: *But why do you think they were so hostile, people in that neighborhood were so hostile towards a black family moving in?*

WM: No, no blacks. Those days, very few blacks lived in our side of the boulevard.

SK: *So people in that neighborhood were more tolerant though, of Japanese, of Nisei?*

WM: Well, you'd have to ask Carolyn. She knows more than I do. But they were well-treated. They were invited for birthdays and so forth. So, no problems whatsoever.

SK: *Now, who were your friends in Detroit? Were they mostly other Nisei, or were they people from work?*

WM: Let's see now. Friends? Friends are Japanese. There are a few *hakujin*, but we didn't do too much socializing.

SK: *But you were involved in...*

WM: JACL. I was president twice. So I know most of the Japanese in the community for fifty years. Over fifty. I know he was there at the party, but I knew him for... fifty? Fifty, fifty-two years, fifty-five years? I don't know. I became chairman of JACL during, between '50 and '56, the first time. And ten years earlier, I volunteered service again. So I used to know most of the people, Japanese people, in the whole community.

SK: *What was the main activity of the JACL in that time?*

WM: Thinking of kids. Thinking of kids. So we had a Halloween party, Easter party and so forth. And then, we were talking about discrimination, politically. But the get together was more or less for children. That was the main concern.

SK: *What were some of the political issues that you worked on?*

WM: I suppose, discrimination, I think that's the most... concern with the Nisei.

SK: *Was it... finding a job, buying a house?*

Miyao Family c.1950. Elyse, Lloyd, Walter, Carolyn and Charlotte.

WM: I don't think so, although like I said, during the early '50s, you couldn't find a house for Japanese outside of Evergreen, within the center area. '56 I came outside of Southfield, but that's rare. But I think that was the main concern for Nisei, where they want to live. For children's sake, education. Nisei are, just like Issei, very concerned with education.

SK: *What was the Calendar Club? Was that something you were a part of?*

WM: The Calendar Club, I formed that.

SK: *You were the founder of that? What was it, why did you start it?*

WM: Social group.

SK: *Oh, I heard people talking about... you used to do mochi-tsuki, right?*

WM: Yeah, I formed it. Because the wife hadn't had a chance to meet the other people. They're confined to house, so Calendar Club had a party once a month and the man and wife and children attend. So they have a chance to meet each other, together, rather than... JACL is a political outfit, whereas Calendar Club was a social club.

SK: *How big was it?*

WM: About ten families. Limited. Discrimination, but we had to have a more social-fitted group, rather than just any Japanese. You had to have a family with children because we were interested in meeting each other with the family. So you had to have children, one. Number two, social level equal. So, out of that, educated ones, so I was the only one.

SK: *So you used to do a mochi-tsuki with the Calendar Club?*

WM: Oh, yeah.

SK: *How about Obon? Would you do anything for Obon?*

WM: I don't know.

SK: *How long did that club last?*

WM: See, we had *Mr/Mrs Club*, and we had Calendar Club. *Mr/Mrs Club,* this is what we did. Are you familiar with *Mr/Mrs?*

SK: *No, tell me.*

WM: That's another social group. Anybody could join that. It's a social group. And then, that became too big, and idea became more or less distressed. Didn't work out. So I said, well, let's have Calendar Club. Eleven meetings, eleven families; twelfth one in Calendar is, we go out night-clubbing. We went to Canada, we went to different nightclubs, twelfth month. It could be theatre, it could be a trip to some place; whereas eleven families... we would meet. It's your turn; your turn; so forth. That's how I decided to give a chance to my wife to meet other people.

SK: *How long did that group continue to meet?*

WM: We still have members!

SK: *It still exists!*

WM: I'm one, Otsuji's, two, Higo's three, Oda's four, Takemoto's five... there's still five out of eleven.

SK: *Since the 1950s.*

WM: I don't know what year it was. Is that what you said?

SK: *I don't know, you said you were the founder, so... But you still meet?*

WM: I've kind of forgotten. We still have Calendar Club members.

SK: *And the Buddhist congregation, you helped to start that, too?*

WM: I'm a chairperson for [the] Buddhist congregation.

SK: *Did you help found that one, too? When did you start that?*

WM: Well, let's see now... in '40s... No, I didn't... Isao Sunamato did. Because Sunamato is very close to the minister, then. They used to live nearby, there. He was the nucleus of the Buddhist temple.

SK: *So at one time you actually had a Buddhist minister in Detroit?*

WM: We used to go to that center... Anyway, we go to that as a main place to meet. It's the... [Brightmoor] Community Center.

SK: *Community Center in Detroit?*

WM: Detroit.

SK: *Do you remember who your minister was?*

WM: I can't... Oh, minister? We had Cleveland and Chicago come.

SK: *So they always came from out of town?*

Studying for the Civil Service Exam
[Miyao]

You never had a minister in Detroit.

WM: We originally had, in '40 and '50, but they went back to California.

SK: *Oh, you did have one here, originally. But you never, there was never...*

WM: Never the church, so we used the family home as a meeting place. And then I took over, the Community Center became the center for church service, once a month.

WM: No, we didn't have enough members. No, there was talk about a church... you know we're talking about $100,000.

SK: *So what was the biggest that the Buddhist congregation ever got?*

WM: We used to have about 150.

SK: *That's pretty big.*

WM: Yeah, but there was the transit. They're from... Half of them were from Japan. Workers have wives... No, we couldn't afford to do that.

SK: *What were the biggest occasions for the Buddhist congregation? Was it Obon, or New Year...*

WM: New year service, I think.

SK: *Did you ever have a festival? An Obon festival?*

WM: We did, early '50s–'60s but since then, no.

EL: *Where did you have those?*

WM: We had *bon odori*... Kelly was in there, I think she practiced with them, but, no, since then... We're talking about Sansei, their friends are Caucasian. There was zero after they left. I used to hear Carolyn say, "I don't understand that minister speaking Japanese!" No, we had no intention of converting. Whatever they want, they can. But like I said, Calendar Club was mainly for wives, the other social group. JACL was a political group.

SK: *In terms of the social life in Detroit, where were some of the popular places for the Nisei? The bars and the restaurants and the stores...*

WM: We don't go to bars. No, we go night-clubbing. I've kind of forgotten. That was fancy outfit, you know, dress? Would give them a chance to dress.

SK: *So is it some of the fancy clubs downtown, people would go dancing.*

245

WM: I don't know. But we were thinking of [the] wives. Very much so. More than us men only. We want the children to grow with this type of existence rather than "men's only" type of existence.

SK: *How long did your wife continue to work for the Kelly family?*

WM: About a year.

SK: *Just about a year.*

WM: Not even a year. She was already pregnant then.

SK: *So after she had your first child, did she work somewhere else?*

WM: No, she didn't work. Well, she worked with the school board. At the school as an assistant to the luncheon club for the school. She got paid for that. But, no, there was no reason for her to work. She just occupied her time.

SK: *Raising the kids mostly?*

WM: During school period, hours, she goes around 11:00 and comes back around 2:00-3:00 in the afternoon, after lunch is finished.

SK: *So you first started working for the city in 1946?*

WM: Something like that. Is that what it says?

SK: *That's what it says. What was your job with the city? How did you get hired? What was your job?*

WM: First, I was junior med-tech. Junior med-tech. For people with degrees, it was junior med-tech. And then, within a year, I was promoted to senior med-tech. And a few years later, principal med-tech. And a few years later, head med-tech. And then, finally, assistant med-tech. And so forth. So anyway, if you wish to come and see the picture, that cabinet picture is very nice.

EL: *Can I show you some, and you tell us about them?*

WM: You can borrow from her. Not me!

SK: *Okay.*

WM: And then if you want to see more, you come and see me. My house—I don't know what I have...

Testimonial Dinner
May 15, 1955

Japanese American Resettlement in Detroit

Greg Robinson

World War II completely reshaped ethnic Japanese communities in the United States. On February 19, 1942, President Franklin Roosevelt signed Executive Order 9066. Under authority of the order, Army commanders, acting on the basis of a blanket (and unsupported) claim of military necessity, rounded up all West Coast Japanese Americans, Issei and Nisei alike, during Spring 1942. The Japanese Americans were confined en masse in holding centers established in abandoned fairgrounds and racetracks on the West Coast. Over the following months, military authorities transported the Japanese Americans to ten large-scale camps constructed in desolate areas of the Western States and Arkansas, where they lived under armed guard.

Most Japanese Americans remained confined in these camps throughout the war, even after government leaders realized that there was no necessity for their continued confinement. West Coast military commanders long refused to permit any people of Japanese ancestry to return to their home region, and the government's own action in approving mass removal convinced important elements of public opinion that the Japanese Americans represented a danger. However, approximately one-fourth of the confined Issei and Nisei were able to gain official permission to leave camp during the war years, and others followed after West Coast exclusion was lifted and the camps opened in 1945. The first group of inmates to resettle, starting in mid-1942, was composed of college students who were offered scholarships at colleges outside the West Coast through the efforts of a private operated social welfare organization, the National Japanese American Student Relocation Council. Soon after, the War Relocation Authority, the government agency created to operate the camps, established a system of "indefinite leave permits" to enable those Japanese Americans who were able to obtain offers of employment through outside sponsors to leave the camps and resettle outside the West Coast. However, fearing a backlash against resettlement by anti-Japanese American public opinion, WRA officials designed a leave system that was both extremely restrictive and little publicized among the camp population. As a result, only a few hundred people were able to resettle during the following months.

In early 1943, hoping to boost both manpower and morale, the War Department decided to create a segregated all-Nisei combat unit, the 442nd Regimental Combat team, and military commanders appointed a Joint Board under the direction of the Army Provost Marshal General's Office to determine the "loyalty" to the United States of the volunteers. Seizing on the chance to provide political cover for resettlement by associating the Army with the plan, the WRA commissioned the Joint Board to examine the "loyalty" of all adult inmates to determine their eligibility for "leave permits." The procedure the government developed to test the loyalty of Japanese Americans was composed of a "loyalty questionnaire" combined with information from intelligence agencies and character references by outside whites. The procedure, designed primarily to placate public hostility by giving the appearance of objective inquiry, was in fact random and haphazard, reflecting the impossibility of determining or judging individual opinion. Japanese Americans were adjudged loyal or disloyal on the basis of a series of shifting and largely irrelevant criteria. Moreover, the questionnaire itself, hastily constructed and forced on the inmates without explanation or consideration of how the information could be used, led to much confusion and divisiveness among Japanese Americans. Most notably, Question 27, which asked the inmates whether they would be willing to join the Armed forces, was widely perceived as a ruse to force Japanese Americans to enlist. Question 28, which inquired whether the inmates were prepared to swear unqualified allegiance to the United States and foreswear all allegiance to Japan, was even more troublesome. Issei, barred from American citizenship on racial grounds, could not take such an oath without losing the only citizenship they possessed. Meanwhile, the Nisei, already reluctant to swear unqualified loyalty to a government that had violated their citizenship rights, were offended by the requirement that they foreswear allegiance to Japan, since such an act implied that they had previously held such allegiance. Some 15 percent of inmates, driven by anger, confusion, protest, support for Japan or other reasons, answered "no" or refused to answer these questions.

Still, the vast majority of inmates conquered their misgivings and answered "yes" to the two questions and were adjudged loyal. They were then eligible to apply for "leave permits" to resettle outside the West Coast excluded area. Most of the first wave of resettlers were Nisei in their late teens or twenties who left camp to join the Army, enroll in college or take up outside employment. [1] As these pioneers put down roots in their new communities, they were joined by siblings and friends, and in some cases parents and other relatives. Once the army lifted its West Coast exclusion orders in January 1945, most inmates from the camps began to return to the West Coast. Although resettlement east of the Rockies continued at a slower pace, the Japanese populations of the Midwest and East Coast began to decline as those who had first moved there out of camp returned to their former homes. By the end of 1946, the majority of the mainland ethnic Japanese population was once again settled on the Pacific Coast, although significant pockets of Japanese American settlement remained in other parts of the country.

The resettlers attempted to rebuild their lives under difficult and trying circumstances. Despoiled of most of their property during removal and psychologically scarred by their unjust confinement, they entered their new communities with little in the way of resources or contacts. Very often they represented the first sizable population of Japanese ancestry in these areas, and they were sometimes exposed to ethnic-based hostility and exclusion by whites. Despite the wartime economic boom, the resettlers faced widespread economic hardship and were forced to take whatever jobs they could get, which generally meant that even those with high educational or professional experience were forced to accept jobs doing low-status domestic, clerical, or menial labor. [2] Although the resettlers were warned by the War Relocation Authority and the FBI to fit in as much as possible and to promise to stay away from other Japanese Americans as a condition of their "leave" from the camps, they were brought together into Japanese enclaves both by internal factors such as religious observance and the need for community and by external factors such as racial prejudice and housing discrimination. [3]

The resettlement of Japanese Americans to the Detroit area mostly followed these larger patterns. [4] Just over three thousand Japanese Americans moved to Michigan directly from camp during the war years, of whom a large majority settled in the greater Detroit area. (In addition, 534 Japanese Americans moved to Ann Arbor.) More specifically, 1,007 Japanese Americans took up residence within Detroit's city limits during 1943-1944, making it the fifth largest center of resettlement nationwide, behind Chicago, Denver, New York, and Cleveland. Of this total, almost 90 percent (899) were Nisei. Once West Coast exclusion was lifted, individual Issei and family groups predominated among new arrivals — Issei accounted for 186 of the 456 newcomers to the city between January 1, 1945 and Spring 1946. [5] The city's ethnic Japanese population was further swelled by the arrival of former camp inmates who had initially resettled elsewhere, as well as by Japanese Americans who had never been confined in camp. For example, Fred Korematsu, who unsuccessfully challenged the constitutionality of mass "evacuation" before the Supreme Court in the notorious case of Korematsu v. United States, originally resettled in Salt Lake City, then moved to Detroit in 1944. The architect Minoru Yamasaki, future designer of the World Trade Center, spent the war years in New York, but then was hired in 1945 as chief of design for the architectural firm of Smith Hinchman & Grylls, and took up residence in

Detroit. Another transplanted New Yorker, Sociologist T. Scott Miyakawa, entered the area after he was hired as a visiting lecturer at University of Michigan.

In the vast majority of cases, the Japanese Americans newcomers had never previously lived in or even visited Detroit. Those who settled in rural areas were almost exclusively employed in farm labor. Inside Detroit, the newcomers took up all sorts of jobs. A large percentage of Issei of both sexes worked as domestics or gardeners. Nisei women found work as stenographers, secretaries, and in domestic service. Nisei men were employed as dishwashers in city restaurants, as domestic workers, and as blue-collar workers, particularly in the city's dominant automobile industry. The Ford Motor Company, traditionally known for employing African American labor (albeit sometimes as a union-busting tool), was a major employer of Nisei, as was the Chrysler Corporation. In addition, Kustu Ishimaru and Gilbert Kurihara worked as auto mechanics in garages, while Bill Kitamura was employed by the Detroit Street Railway. Other big employers of Nisei labor included the Briggs Manufacturing Company, the Hoskins Manufacturing Company, the Essex Wire Company, Gar Wood industries, and the Ex-Cell-O company. Groups of younger Nisei attended college or studied in trade schools. Wayne University welcomed a number of Nisei students—including a class of fifteen cadet nurses preparing for military duty. In 1946, Yoshikazu Morita graduated at the head of his class at Wayne's medical school.[6] Grace Hospital engaged a pair of Nisei physicians as residents. A half-dozen Nisei beauticians were graduated from the Dermaway University of Hair and Beauty Culture in mid-1945![7]

As time passed, a wider spectrum of skilled and sales jobs opened up. By 1945, Frank Doi was hired as a dental lab technician, Grace Fujii was employed as a hospital social worker, George Kawamoto ran a photography studio, and Roy Setsuda was hired as an interior decorator. A number of Nisei women were hired as sales clerks by the Johnson Milk Company. Others found public sector positions: Marie Doi was employed as a relocation officer by the WRA's Detroit office (opened in April 1943), while Roku Yasui worked for the city's Postwar Planning Division, and Jane Togasaki worked for the Michigan State Health Department. A few Japanese Americans went into business for themselves. Mr. and Mrs. Masujiro Ishioka, an Issei couple, operated an apartment house on Cass Avenue. Mr. and Mrs. Anthony Yasutake started a dry goods store in the suburb of Royal Oak. A Japanese American family operated the Oriental Restaurant. The most popular Nisei small business (capitalizing on popular stereotypes of Asian labor) was the laundry. George Akamine, Mas Hashimoto, and Tom and Jimmie Tagami and their families each opened cleaning establishments in Detroit. Few resettlers were able to establish themselves in management or white-collar positions, although the community was served by a group of medical professionals such as dentists Kiyoshi Sonoda and Mark Kanda and optometrist John Koyama.

As in other cities, the task of aiding the absorption and adjustment of the resettlers was taken up by a coalition of the local WRA office and private church and welfare groups. As early as mid-1942, WRA resettlement director Thomas Holland and George Rundquist of the Protestant Council of Churches organized a Detroit Resettlement Committee under the lead of the Reverend Father James McCormick to help locate housing and jobs for the resettlers. In September 1943, (following the lead of Reverend T. T. Brumbaugh, a former missionary in Japan) the Detroit Council of Churches established its own United Ministry to Resettlers.

The Council invited Reverend Shigeo Tanabe, a Nisei pastor from Washington, to operate the ministry. In 1945, after the War Relocation Authority announced plans to wind up its operations, local civil leaders formed the Detroit Committee to Aid Resettlers of Japanese Ancestry, which operated approximately through the end of 1947. In Summer 1946 Virginia Swanson, who had previously worked with Japanese Americans with the Terminal Island Baptist Church, was engaged by the Detroit Council of Churches to aid resettlers. The Detroit chapter of the JACL, formed in 1946 with Peter Fujioka as founding president, also contributed to supporting resettlement.

Housing remained the most important item on the resettlement aid agenda, as it was by far the most difficult commodity for the newcomers to acquire — as a report of the Detroit Relocation Committee put it, "Housing was the 'nightmare' of all newcomers to the city."[8] The wartime economic boom had brought such a huge influx of war workers, primarily African Americans and white Southerners, that local housing stock was completely inadequate to contain them (so explosive was the housing shortage that the opening of a public housing project for Blacks, the Sojourner Truth Homes, in Spring 1942 touched off mass demonstrations and threats of violence by local whites who insisted that they should be assigned the homes). A number of new resettlers obtained long-term housing at the city's Y.M.C.A (which also hired a cadre of Nisei workers). WRA officials attempted to steer newcomers, especially single Nisei, into taking domestic service positions, since they would thereby be provided lodging.

The housing proble was relieved in part by community efforts. Those with the means to buy homes opened space for lodgers. Jack Shimoda, a Japanese American businessmen who had lived in Detroit during the prewar era, purchased a boarding house on Forest Avenue which was filled with new arrivals. Under the auspices of the United Ministry to resettlers, Reverend Tanabe established Fellowship House, a Nisei hostel, at 130 East Grand Boulevard. The WRA subsequently opened a family hostel at 3915 Trumbull in July 1945 under the auspices of the Buddhist Church of Detroit. Reverend and Mrs. Shawshew Sakow were the hostel's managers. In addition to serving as temporary housing for the resettlers, the hostels served as recreational centers, providing libraries and game rooms where the newcomers joined together for social events. In addition, a Nisei committee formed at the International Institute in 1944. It arranged biweekly dances and ping-pong nights to encourage sociability. Young Nisei joined baseball teams, and a Nisei basketball club participated in an interstate tournament. As in other places, the most popular Nisei sport was bowling — in 1945 an entire Detroit area Nisei Bowling League was formed.

The question of discrimination is a complex one. Detroit was notorious in prewar years as a center of Ku Klux Klan and white supremacist activity, with right-wing leader Gerald L.K. Smith and the anti-Semitic "radio priest" Father Charles Coughlin as the movement's most visible figures. During the war, existing racial tensions were exacerbated by rapid population shifts, which led to overcrowding and shortages of transportation, schools, and housing. These tensions exploded into violent confrontation in June 1943, when fights at the city's Belle Isle resort area ignited a large-scale racial riot. The riot lasted thre days and claimed thirty-four lives (twenty-five of them African Americans).

Nevertheless, Japanese Americans had an easier time in Detroit than they had known on the West Coast, let alone the camps.

According to various accounts, Nisei in Detroit felt welcomed. Columnist Dale Oka, who resettled in Detroit in June 1943, stated that he was initially wary of how he would be accepted, but was soon put at ease:

> "The reception accorded me since my advent to this area has surpassed my most optimistic hopes. Perhaps I belong to that fortunate few who found their relocation paths strewn with flowers of welcome instead of thorns. But I prefer to believe that the great majority of us have discovered their new lives to be similarly pleasant and encouraging."[9]

Liberal and religious groups in the city mobilized to aid Japanese Americans. As mentioned, the Detroit Council of Churches (which as early as Spring 1942 had voted an official resolution deploring mass evacuation and calling for rapid loyalty hearings for Japanese Americans) took a leading role in aiding resettlers and in advocating for their rights. Public opinion, as reflected in media accounts, was overwhelmingly positive. The *Detroit News* editorialized in 1944 that "There are now numbers of Japanese here, migrants from the Pacific Coast, whose records have been sifted and who should be regarded and treated as loyal friends in the war against Japan."[10] The following year, the *Detroit Free Press* ran a positive article on the approximately two thousand Japanese Americans, "all American citizens who speak our own language," living in Detroit. The article featured an interview with Mrs. Terry Koyama, who praised the treatment she had received in Detroit and expressed optimism about her future:

> "The dispersal was good because we used to live too close together on the West Coast, anyway. Now we're more spread out and we have a better chance—without the old prejudices."[11]

Still, both anecdotal evidence and the records of the WRA's Detroit office, which was responsible for finding jobs and advocating for the newcomers, testify to widespread patterns of discrimination in the region. In mid-1942, Reverend Owen Geer, pastor of the Mt. Olivet Baptist Church in Dearborn, proposed bringing in a Nisei resettler, Kenji Murase. The Dearborn Safety Commission vetoed the plan, and when Reverend Geer requested an open hearing on the matter, three hundred local residents attended the meeting to protest the idea.[12] When the Yoshiki family left camp for Detroit in 1944, one family member travelled ahead to find housing. Before arriving in Detroit, he called a local hotel to reserve a room. When he appeared at the hotel, however, the hotel's owners—shocked to discover that Yoshiki was Japanese and not Polish, as they had assumed from his name—refused him lodging.[13] Educational discrimination was also palpable in the Detroit area. Administrators at the University of Michigan made a confidential decision to limit admission of Nisei students to a quota of twenty-seven per year, spread among the university's different faculties. When challenged on its discriminatory policy, the university denied that it had established any quota, and defended its policy on the pretext that the FBI and Army refused to grant clearances (a transparent falsehood in view of the fact that the Army's Japanese language school was on campus, and that the University simultaneously hired over two hundred Nisei employees to take up menial labor jobs on its grounds). Even after all government controls over Nisei students were abandoned in fall 1944, the university maintained its discriminatory policy.[14]

Employers and labor unionists also were mixed in their reactions to Japanese Americans. The local chapter of the AFL-affiliated Teamster's Union (following national policy) was extremely hostile to Nisei and refused to allow them to join the union or to support their employment in the industry. The leadership of the Congress of Industrial Organizations (CIO) was supportive—United Auto Workers leader Walter Reuther even joined a delegation to ask the Detroit Housing Commission to open public housing to Japanese Americans— but local activists were often recalcitrant. In Ann Arbor, the CIO refused to accept Japanese Americans in a factory producing defense material. Similarly, in April 1944, Tom Nakamura, a resettler from Jerome, was hired by the Palmer Company, a Detroit war plant. When he appeared for work, employees staged a walkout to protest the hiring of a Japanese American. Although swift action by the local Fair Employment Practices Committee and the local CIO officials limited the action to a single day and assured Nakamura's continued employment, the incident revealed the existence of widespread, if subtle, currents of anti-Nisei sentiment.[15]

In the years following their initial resettlement, Japanese Americans in Detroit began to put down roots. Ironically, because Nisei tended to stay out of jobs in war industries, which they needed special permission from the Army Provost Marshal General's office to take, they were relatively well-insulated from cutbacks. There were several notable achievers. Dr. James Mimura, a veteran of the 442nd Regimental Combat Team, moved to Oakland County after medical school, established his practice, and taught at Wayne State University's medical school.[16] Another physician, Dr. Ted Kokubo, settled in Birmingham. Curt Sugiyama, who had been confined in Gila River as a child, became an honors student and president of his

class at Chadsey High School in 1951, and was awarded a scholarship by the national JACL. Reverend Minoru Mochizuki became pastor at Dearborn's First Presbyterian Church. After the 1952 McCarran-Walter Act opened naturalization to Issei for the first time, Taizo Kokubo organized citizenship classes, and seventy-three local Issei rushed to apply.[17]

1   U.S. Department of the Interior. War Relocation Authority, *The Evacuated People: A Quantitative Description*, New York, AMS Press, 1975 [1946]. Slightly more men than women left camp, but since those joining the Army were virtually all male, the majority of those who relocated for residence were female.

2   U.S. Department of the Interior. War Relocation Authority, *The Relocation Program*, New York, AMS Press, 1975 [1946].

3   For resettlement generally, see U.S. Department of the Interior, War Agency Liquidation Unit, *People in Motion: The Postwar Adjustment of the Evacuated Japanese Americans*, Washington D.C., U.S.. Government Printing Office, 1947; Allan W. Austin, "Eastward Pioneers: Japanese American Resettlement during World War II and the Contested Meaning of Exile and Incarceration," Journal of American Ethnic History 26:2 (2007): 58-84. On housing discrimination and concentration, see Charlotte Brooks, "In the Twilight Zone Between Black and White: Japanese American Resettlement and Community in Chicago, 1942-1945," *Journal of American History* 86.4 (Fall 2000), 1655-1687.

4   For a comparison between the condition of resettlers in Detroit and in other cities, see Greg Robinson, Japantown Born and Reborn: Comparing the Resettlement Experience of Issei and Nisei in Detroit, New York, and

Los Angeles," in *After Camp: Portraits in Mid-century Japanese American Life and Politics*, Berkeley, University of California Press, 2012, pp. 43-65.

5   War Relocation Authority, *The Evacuated People,* p.43.

6   "Japanese Ranks at Top of Class," *Reno Evening Gazette,* April 16, 1946, p. 7.

7   U.S. Department of the Interior, War Agency Liquidation Unit, *People in Motion: The Postwar Adjustment of the Evacuated Japanese Americans,* Washington, D.C., Government Printing Office, 1947, pp.159-162.

8   Report of Detroit Resettlement Committee, July 1945, papers of Detroit District Relocation Office, War Relocation Authority, Japanese Evacuation and Resettlement Survey Records, Reel 10, Bancroft Library.

9   Dale Oka, "Just Incidentally," *Pacific Citizen*, April 15, 1944.

10 Cited in Dale Oka, "Just Incidentally," *Pacific Citizen*, April 22, 1944. Ironically, the editorial came in response to an incident where a Filipino immigrant was struck by a white man who mistook him for Japanese.

11 Arthur Juntunen, "2,000 Jap-Americans 'Adopt' Detroit, More are Expected to Come," *Detroit Free Press*, clipping in War Relocation Authority Papers, RG 210, National Archives, Washington D.C..

12 "Michigan City Approves Hitler's Race Theories: Refuses to Admit U.S.-Born Japanese to Residence," *Pacific Citizen,* July 3, 1942, p. 1.

13 Author interview, Marian Yoshiki-Kovanick, San Marino, California, January 2004.

14 Letter, T. Scott Miyakawa to Roger Baldwin, October 31, 1944. ACLU papers, Princeton University (microfilm copy in Library of Congress)

15 "CIO, FEPC Action Ends Walkout Over Nisei Worker," Pacific Citizen, May 6, 1944, 3.

16 Frank Beckmann, "Hero Overcame Germans, Racial Bias to Heal Detroiters," The Detroit News, March 6, 2009. According to the article, when Mimura arrived in the Detroit area, a Birmingham real estate agent informed him, "We don't sell to Japanese people"

17 Kay Miyaya, "73 Detroit Issei Citizens Feted by Chapter; Late Mr. Kokubo Cited," Pacific Citizen, May 27, 1955.

Passport photo: female - 15 years and 5 months old, 1924
[Yamamoto]

Asae Shichi

interviewed by Mikaru Lasher

AS: My name is Asae Shichi. The person who is interviewing me is my daughter. I am a Japanese born in Japan — born in Japan and came here and naturalized, so I am a Japanese American now.

ML: *So I'd like to start by asking you to tell me. What made you come to the United States?*

AS: I was selected to become the representative of the student organization called the International Student Association. In 1954 I was a senior in college and I was very much interested in exchanging ideas about the Japanese Americans to Asians. And at the time, we were very much interested in the issue of atomic bomb testing in the Pacific — people who died being exposed to that. And so I think the whole country was boiling over this kind of a thing — that the United States was still experimenting on the atomic bomb and that there were some casualties resulting from that. And what to do about it and what kind of relationship Japan is going to have with America and things like that. And so this conference sponsored by the ISA — the International Student Association — focused on having discussions one year in the United States and the next three years or so in Japan. We were doing it interchangeably and that happens to be the year we were having it in the United States. I was selected to be the representative of the Japanese students and about ten delegates came, and so I came to have this debate and discussions in six major universities here in the United States.

ML: *How did you get selected to come as part of the group?*

AS: There were some kinds of tests, and they were testing us to see if we can actually speak *[laughs]* and then how we would present our faults and so forth. And they made sure we were not the second generation or something, you know. And have to make sure that we were just so-called quote-unquote "pure Japanese" Somehow I was selected, and it was very exciting to get the notice that I was selected. And then I will be away for a good month or so traveling, so I had to get the okay from the University. And of course that was fine.

ML: *Were you worried about coming here at all or afraid, since it had been after World War II?*

AS: No. There was no fear like that and especially when we're at the student level. You know we really do not know enough about the fact there are some hatred or, you know, biases or anything of that sort. But then we'll find out when we come here *[laughs]*, you know.

ML: *And how was your experience when you came here?*

AS: It was just wonderful. It was the students that we talked to. They were all very open and frank. They seemed to be so much interested in their internal issues like campus issues. And they have never heard of these concerns the Japanese students had—such as the experiment that goes on at the Bikini Atoll in the Pacific or anything of that sort. The Japanese students were also concerned about the Red China that we used to call in those days. And Red China's participation in the United Nations and things like that. We couldn't really have any talks like that seriously because our point of view—what we were thinking and what our concerns were totally different. So that's interesting. I also had the chance to wear kimono and like show how to do flower arrangements and things like that. So that was kind of fun.

ML: *So you have a positive experience coming here the first time. Then you went back to Japan and you returned clearly because you are living here now. How did you come to return here again?*

AS: Well I think from the beginning—there is something about this dream of coming to the United States. And this dream really has to do with something very concrete that took place in my childhood. And when I was five, my father was appointed to come to the United States to observe the facilities that were making airplanes—both military airplanes and non-military airplanes. So he was here for one year, traveling all over the United States. And when we went to see him off at Yokohama and he was leaving for this task, we actually got to get on the ship, and it was such an exciting kind of experience just being on something so big. *[laughs]* I think being a part of this just made a tremendous impact on me. I was just very adventurous as a five year old. Somehow I was getting escorted by this young man who worked for my father's company. And then when my family realized I was not seen anywhere, I was totally lost on the ship. And so they were very much worried, and then eventually they found me. My cousin spotted me, and here is the picture of that. And this picture of me with this handsome escort, and I was five years old in this. All dressed up and my cousin is worried. But I had the best time on this ship.

Whenever I think of this, I think it was really a defining moment in my life, and I thought, "Just what a wonderful thing to be able to go away like that." My sister who is two years older than me was more worried—the surroundings. Look at me I'm just, you know, very happy and pulling my grandmother's hand—and then just ready for an adventure. I sort of told myself that someday—someday I am going to go there and do what my father did without really knowing what it was that my father did. *[laughs]* It was this grand dream that somehow I could always like refer to. It's an interesting kind of a thing you know, what motivates you. But anyway,

being exposed in 1954 to this land where things were just so clean, so vast, and the campuses were just wonderful, so alive. Somehow, I just set my mind that okay I am coming back here. Then I applied to this grant that the Fulbright Commission had set out. It actually pays for the travel expenses, and we have to find out the scholarships in this country that take care of everything. Because the Japanese are from Japan, we could not take out any money in those days because it was the government's policy to keep the dollar reserve to certain amount. And so even if I got the Fulbright grant after many examinations and so forth to come here, I was allowed to take out only twenty dollars to come and stay here for three years. Was I worried about it? No *[laughs]*, somehow, because I didn't know to what to expect. I was interested in pursuing the Christian studies.

I was looking at this academic institution called Pendle Hill, which is a Quaker institution in Wallingford, Pennsylvania. The Friends' people, the American Friends Service Committee was very active in Japan, and I attended many of their seminars during summer time. So I got to know some of the leaders and talked about my hopes and that overall would be a very good place because it is an international kind of a place. It does leadership training, but it is more of a community living. So while my English is not so good, I can sort of learn more to get adjusted to the life here, which was a great idea so that is what I did. So I got scholarship from Pendle Hill to study for one year and then see if I can get more scholarships to study further.

ML: *Was there a close community?*

AS: There were always weekend seminars, and people would come from all over the United States to interact, so often we would be exposed to many people from outside, as well. Yes it was a close community because it is a Quaker community. And you start the day with the worship service and then have your study and you can attend lectures—usually in the evenings. And very open and the whole requirement for the semester was to write one paper. And it could be a book or it could be a few pages. But whatever you can produce would be accepted. And I studied there more than anywhere else I have ever studied because I could spend all my time in the library and then go to the mentors and have discussions. And it was just a wonderful eye opening experience for me.

ML: *Since you mention going to study about Christian studies. Maybe you could tell us a little about how you being Christian in Japan might be different from here and sort of how that has affected you.*

AS: I think that was really the starting point and as well as this defining moment I talked about coming here. The Christianity is such a small existence in Japan. It is a total minority. Usually only half of one percent of the population would be Christian, including the Catholics and Protestants and everything else. And so especially, we went through this war experience, which just about covered the whole of my experience like a dark, dark cloud. Christianity was considered American. Anybody who believed in Christianity would be like anti-Japanese. So the teachers at school would—let's say there were six hundred students there and

we were about five or six of us who were Christian or who were from a Christian family. So we really represented a small minority, and the fact that I was more outspoken than other people, I was kind of like targeted. So they really made it really hard for me—like throwing stones at me on my way to school and so forth. It was hard, but still I didn't think there was anything wrong with Christianity itself. So my deduction was that they were wrong *[laughs]* to judge that Christians were anti-Japanese. So it made it very clear to me that, okay, I am a Christian. There must be something in here. My parents were Christians, and my grandparents were Christian, which was a really rare thing in Japan. And so it was my deepest identity and it sort of led me to seek more and to find out more about my identity and to seek what Christianity was all about. I was quite serious.

ML: *How did your grandparents become Christians, since it was so rare?*

AS: Yeah, that is really rare, and I did not hear much about the grandparents—this is the grandparents on the mother's side. The grandparents on the father's side—they all died quite young so we did not have any anecdotes and stories that are with us, but the grandparents on the mother's side are very much closer. I don't know much about the grandfather because he also died very young, and in fact I never met him because he died before I was born. But my grandmother came to live with us after her husband died, and so she was there all the time. She told us that she was born in Kumamoto in the southern part of Japan, and when she was born her mother was divorced because the mother could not bring a son to the family. So at the earliest time my grandmother had a traumatic experience—well, probably she didn't realize that.

ML: *So she stayed with her father?*

AS: Right, oh yes, and also my grandmother's father was an alcoholic, I think. He had a very bad habit when he got drunk, and so my grandmother had a very bad time. She had to go out and buy the liquor and do that kind of errand, and then maybe he abused the family as well. So when she went to elementary school and graduated from elementary school she stayed on in that school almost like a janitor because she wanted to be there with the school somehow.

ML: *Rather than go home.*

AS: She sort of studied by listening to the lessons that were given there. Like in the eighth grade level, she learned everything by listening to it from outside the door of the classroom. And so she was hired later to become a teacher there. She was a math teacher. Then around that time, I think she discovered a translation of the Ecclesiastes, the Old Testament, and she was profoundly influenced by that and she was converted to Christianity. So all this sad experiences in childhood and so forth, I think became the cornerstone or became the foundation for her to build her life to cope with it, to deal with it, or to overcome it. So she became a Christian, and she worked in a Christian school. Then she got married to this man who was a government-run, city high school foreman in Kumamoto. The government-run high schools are very high quality. It is almost at the college or university level today. He was an English teacher there, and later he

became the headmaster of this women's Christian school, which is small like a junior high now, Kasui in Nagasaki. My mother was born around that time in Nagasaki. Later he was transferred to Nippon Women's University in Tokyo, professor of English and Christian ethics.

The fact that I was more outspoken than other people, I was kind of like targeted. So they really made it really hard for me—like throwing stones at me on my way to school and so forth.

ML: *And how old was your mother at that time?*

AS: She was just starting college. This one that my grandfather worked was the Nippon Women's University and there's another university called Tokyo Woman's Christian University today. I think since my mother was the only child, the parents couldn't just stand her studying in Tokyo all by herself, so in a way they were very happy to accept this offer to be working at Nippon Women's University, which was in Tokyo. So then they could live together. You see so I think that was more like what was in the background.

ML: *She had already gone onto school and they followed her.*

AS: Right. Right. Very unusual case, isn't it?

ML: *And what did she study?*

AS: She studied English and English literature, and she was just a graduate of a four-year senior high school, which is like one or two years less than what some other students had gone through. And so my mother had a very difficult time trying to follow with the studies—that's what she said. But she had never experienced snow because she had lived in the warm part of the country all this time, and then for the first time she was exposed to snow. And also she also lived in a very strict home, which banned reading of the novels and literature and so forth.

So my mother was so excited that she could read anything under the sun and all the books in the library—the school library that is. So she had tremendous experience of freedom or so she was very much influenced by this one headmaster of the dormitory who was also like the dean of the students then, Mrs. *[inaudible]*, who influenced just hundreds and thousands of students at the time with our special kind of style or, should I say, philosophy of thinking or of doing. That was more like today I think that instead of trying to convert students, her approach was more like making aware, making it more of a question for those students who have never been exposed to Christianity that there is something beyond. There is that value that is beyond the ordinary values. And also in that dormitory at the college, students were given individual rooms, which was very unique in those days because regularly they shared rooms in those days. Four or six students used to share one room, but this was an individual room. And it was like a confinement to many people who never have been

exposed to that kind of life, but this way of life forcing yourself to be alone and forcing yourself to think independently. I think it made a tremendous affect on my mother and she was determined to raise me that way. So I was very much brought up with that kind of idea that each person is unique and different and you can become independent and you can have your own thought and not necessarily follow the authority or the head of the family and so forth.

ML: *How is it different from the more traditional…*

AS: You don't count, individuals don't count in the traditional way. You are just a member of the household and especially girls don't matter much. Whatever you think doesn't matter much and whatever the person in authority decides is what you have to follow. And you are not even supposed to doubt or have any questions about that. So it's a very different kind of thinking and philosophy and of course I had no trouble living in the United States because that's how things are done.

ML: *But was it hard for you living in Japan?*

AS: Yeah, it makes it harder to live in Japan because you want to speak up your mind and you want to say your opinions and you want to think independently and you really have to be tactful in trying to tell them that your thought is different from others and it's okay to think differently—especially when you don't act diplomatically then you become the troublemaker within the group.

ML: *Where do you find yourself in that position?*

AS: I learned to be more diplomatic and so I was always somehow in the leader position within the class or group. I learned to be very careful how to present myself, but I will not be quiet. *[laughs]*

ML: *That's good for when you are living here. [laughs]*

AS: Right.

ML: *Now your experience coming here it sounds like the way you were raised kind of influenced the way you were being able to adapt to living here. Since you said that most people aren't raised that way, how do you think it compares with the people who come here now and just come and stay for a while and go back to Japan. How does your experience differ from that?*

AS: I think it is very difficult for Japanese who have not been exposed to this way of thinking or trained to live this way. Number one: be able to even form your opinions because you are always checking who is the authority within the group. And as you locate who the authority is you ask that person to see if it's okay to do such and such or just wait for the order to come and it's really like not taking initiative at all. And so that is certainly a problem here. And then since in Japan we are not supposed to have our own individual opinions, it is difficult to have our own individual study. This is talking about the college campus for instance. The assignment may be that you write your own project or think of your own project, and the Japanese students always fail that course because they cannot come up with this creative kind of a theme or topic or how to develop it on her own or on his own. So I think

that are the two major problems there. Usually people from Japan are very gentle and nice, and very easy to get along with, and usually don't cause problems. But then sometimes, since they cannot communicate very well how they feel themselves, there is like pent up energy there and frustration and so one day sort of explodes. That usually separates the people around them—"that is how you've been feeling, then why don't you say that." And they are not trained to say that. And also I think the total thinking pattern is different in America and Japan. So here the logical thinking pattern is appreciated, and there are certain ways of Western thinking that is based upon the Greek way of thinking and so forth. Which is just totally Western logical thinking, which is totally different from the Eastern thinking, which doesn't divide things up that clearly and we don't come out with the how things should be.

No, let me put it this way. Here we say we come up with this theme or thesis and we'll say that it should be *A* and if it is not that, then it should be *non-A* or *B*. If it's neither then it should be *C* or so forth. But in the Orient the thinking pattern is not that defining so we'll say it's neither *A* nor *B* nor *C*. It's just all they're asking. It is just all grey. No black and white. And so it's very ambiguous and we just tolerate ambiguity, and we love ambiguity. And that's just how things are, so nobody is clear about where things stand.

ML: *How do feel? Do you feel your way of thinking is more of the Western way of thinking versus the more Japanese way of thinking? And as a result do you think that's why you continue to stay here versus trying to go back to stay in Japan?*

AS: I think I would rather be unhappy staying in Japan and trying to get along with the people around me. Still, I am a mix of the two cultures I feel. Whatever the percentage is, I don't know, but there is just still all this Asiatic way or Japanese way of thinking in me. It's a mix.

ML: *You think it would be harder living in Japan?*

AS: I think so because I have become very much aware of how different I am. And today it is less so, but in those days growing up in Japan. Number one is there is just no job for woman other than being a school teacher—that one is okay, but other things you just get married and have children. That is a way of relating so...

ML: *So when you came here and you pursued graduate studies—showing really that you are very different I guess than most young women at that time? Maybe you can tell us more about that. Because traditionally you were saying that women usually get married and have kids, and it was probably true here too at the time, yet you didn't do that.*

AS: Right. The Fifties. I think that by the time I was in the graduate school, those were all the people that have the same kind of desires and so forth. But these are the American kids with different kind of background and *[laughs]* it was interesting because I was in Christian education, and you interact with children and you have field work and all that. In working there, I was very quick to sense what's happening within the group.

I could see how the relationship was going among the children, and I could see what happened in that case when some teachers were being trained to become teachers—how some teachers' words, actions, and such influence the students and so forth. I could just see those things. Right away! All others were totally oblivious of that sort of thing, and they were not even noticing that whatever somebody said was affecting the children, for instance. So our teacher, who would have the review session after this practicum, was interested that I could observe so much. And then I realize that this was the family training, and it is the "Japanese-ness" in me. And that is the to be very sensitive to the number of virtues and to be able to understand what goes on when nothing is said. We were really raised very consciously to become sensitive to each other within a group. So I think that's a very Japanese kind of thing that other students didn't have.

ML: *Did you have any kind of pressure? Did you feel social pressure? Family pressure for continuing your education?*

AS: Well, I don't know. I think my parents are very proud of me, and they also have my older sister who was two years older than me and she was more typically Japanese. She sort of satisfied their desire to have the grandchildren and so forth.

ML: *There wasn't any pressure on you? You could do anything that you wanted to do?*

AS: That is right.

ML: *So what was it like living in Tokyo during the war?*

AS: Actually the war started with China when I was much younger. World War II was 1941, so I was eight by then, but Japan's invasion of China and this fighting was already going on. So we were kind of used to seeing army soldiers around. We didn't have television in those days but still the newspapers would carry the pictures of bombing and so forth. So we are used to this concept of war and what it is like. And when the war started in Tokyo, actually it was a far away thing. Things were not really affecting us so much. But pretty soon things were getting bad and then the air raid started. Tokyo was heavily bombed, in fact the city of Tokyo itself was completely devastated—nothing left around Tokyo station. The first American air raid targeted the military facilities in Japan.

ML: *So that didn't affect you at all.*

AS: Right. Later there was bombing of the residential areas, so everywhere like the suburbs were not exempt from that, but that started getting serious in the fall of 1944.

ML: *And you were how old?*

AS: I was eleven by then, I think. The daytime air raid is scary but there is always warning. The siren goes on or the radio—we always have to have it on—start to tell you any reconnaissance plane or anything comes in over Japan and so we know just whereabout the size of the attack and where it was coming.

ML: *Did you do anything for safety? Was there any procedure or anything that you followed?*

AS: Yeah, when it seems like the airplane was coming closer then they would alert us, and there is a different type of siren going on. And so we may have to go under the desk, for instance, if we are studying in a classroom. *[laughs]* We'll go like a tornado here.

ML: *If they dropped a bomb would it actually protect you if you went under a desk?*

AS: Well, it at least helps a little bit I think.

ML: *But there were no bomb shelters?*

AS: Oh yes, there are plenty of those. And each house has to have a bomb shelter. So we'll go under there. If we are at home, then we can go there.

ML: *Underground?*

AS: Underground. Oh yes! It's quite a deep one that we'll like have dug by some professional. So it was like well structured and we would carry some of our precious things and have them there, and some rich people would have more fancy kind of shelter built and so forth. It's all covered with dirt so nothing shows from above, and then we were growing pumpkins on that. *[laughs]* So pumpkins were hanging on top of the shelter, you know.

ML: *How frequently did you have to go down there?*

AS: Well, first it's more like twice a week or so, but then it was like every other night. Soon the night air raids started. It was quite scary because things from far away look quite close at night. And so if something is burning it looks very close.

ML: *So you could see the planes and the bombs dropping?*

AS: Very much so. By the time you can see if it is coming your way, then you're done. We learn to distinguish the different airplanes. The B-29 and how it sounds and if it is in a certain angle, it is really dangerous. Or if you are seeing it sideways then you know then it is not…

ML: *Heading towards you.*

AS: *[laughs]* Heading towards you. So you are safe and so forth. And then the lighter planes, they can, you know, really do more of the damage. But heavier ones, the B-29 and 31 and so forth and so on, we just learn to detect by just hearing the sounds of the…

ML: *Because they would drop the bigger bombs or…*

AS: Oh yeah, right, right.

ML: *The smaller planes just shooting.*

AS: Yeah, they are shooting. Sometimes we can see the faces of the pilots but if you can do that and you can see them sideways, you are safe because they are not shooting at you. They can get down real low, but the sound of it was scarier then the actual sight of it. But they were all very silver, and they are surrounded usually at night time by the anti-aircraft guns. So you see the airplanes surrounded by all the search lights and fire and smoke and all that. But just beautiful! Beautiful in the night sky. And it doesn't look like enemy planes. Nothing personal. It's scary, but it may be our own anti-aircraft bombshell that comes down to hit you also. Very often people get hurt from that, so that the enemy up there is more so like firecrackers than just a simple airplane flying there. Yes it's scary, but the unpredictable elements of that—you never know which way it's coming or which would be the target that night.

ML: *But once you went in the shelter, you couldn't see that anymore, right?*

AS: All you do is just hope that—you listen on the radio and then see it will be all over soon. That's all you could hope for.

ML: *How long would you stay down there?*

AS: Sometimes half an hour, sometimes longer. And usually they are up in the sky and they don't stay there too long. They just pass and then if they pass, that's it. So you can come out and do your own stuff again. But night time we are already dressed—always dressed. We would change into pajamas, but we would have to wear something on top of that because you would be awakened in the middle of the night and in two minutes you would have to be out, carrying all these things that you have prepared. Number one, you have to wear this hood—the padded hood. It looks like the winter coat, you know. And so it's a longer kind of a hood, and it's all padded and stuffed heavily with cotton so that it would at least protect your head. It should have your name and your blood type. So that if you are dead or if you are injured, somebody could take care of you and notify the family. So you are always carrying those things and you are also wearing that name tag with the blood type on yourself all the time as well. So even if you are sleeping at night, you are always wondering you know can we sleep tonight.

And then just automatically do these things and get into the shelter. My grandmother always said that she's too tired to go into the shelter. She would just go into like a closet and that was fine with her. And she just refused to go there, and you know nothing happened anyway.

ML: *So did your house get bombed?*

AS: No, no. It was safe, but like, you know, after I married your father, he would tell us about his wartime experience. Just about the same generation, so he went through the whole thing, but he lived in Nagoya. Nagoya has the heavy manufacturing industry. They were bombed completely and heavily, and so he kept moving from the house. Because the first house he used to live got all burned down, and they would move into another house, which got burned down. Then the third one got burned down. So by then, they didn't have anything with them. Just like a bundle of something they were using every day. So they had to leave Nagoya to go out into the suburb. But in some cases like Kobe and Osaka, they were just completely bombed. The carpet bombing is really something else. They first drop bombs by the mountain ridge and they also drop bombs by the seas, so there is no way that people could run out. It was such a complete bombing I hear that a lot of people really perished in the fire and smoke. So it is a scary thing, but the whole school — all the schools, all the children had to evacuate, big towns.

ML: *In Tokyo or in general?*

AS: In general. You can either evacuate personally by either going to your relatives home in the outskirt of anywhere. Or you could join the school evacuation and move with the school. So the school set up like a temple in some suburb.

ML: *Was it safe?*

AS: Hopefully safe environment. Sometimes it so happens it is not so safe. We only lived less than half a year in the temple,.

ML: *And your sister went there too...*

AS: No, she was already in the junior high school.

ML: *So you were separated from your whole family?*

AS: Oh yeah, right, right. You know what the scary part is you don't very get much information. You can see in the Tokyo sky, you know. We were in the west of Tokyo and would look east and see the whole city burning you know. And then, you know, the whole area get so red and then you just worry so much. That's the worst part.

ML: *Well, your family, your parents and grandmother were still in the house.*

AS: Still in the house. Oh yeah... and my father was still working at this manufacturing company which was doing the production of the military airplanes. So they were working very hard. Sometimes there were no trains, so you had to use a bicycle and commute to this company. Yeah everybody had to work or do whatever. My sister's case, the whole school was doing this kind of war-related industry. They were doing something to do with the light bulbs. They were making or doing something, and then they were all employed to do that kind of work for the factory.

ML: *So rather than going to classes they were having to work.*

AS: Oh yes.

ML: *And then for yourself because you were younger, you...*

AS: Right, we really had the best time I think. It's like a picnic all the time. You were away from your parents and...

ML: *So you were continuing with your...*

AS: We could study and could play and you know we had no problem finding friends. *[laughs]* You know they were there, all together. So if we were adults in wartime, we would be of aware all these tragic things that were going on around us, but since we were children we are a little bit more innocent. I think we are, we didn't know what was going on or when the war was going to end or anything.

ML: *I think it was about six months you said. Did you see your sister or your family during that time at all?*

AS: My mother was the only one that was allowed to come visit and so she visited about once or twice.

ML: *That's still really hard at such a young age.*

AS: For us, you know, we were already sixth grade, so we were okay then. Nobody cried or anything like that, but the younger ones you know, they were 3rd grade, 4th grade, they were just awfully homesick, so we had to sort of take care of them too.

ML: *And so did you experience firsthand any of your friends or anything like that, that have gotten bombed or have really suffered badly?*

AS: No, the suburb where we lived away from Tokyo was not really any target so we didn't lose anybody. Some of my relatives went as kamikaze pilots, and they died. And we just felt our individual loss. Like your father's case, he witnessed many of such shooting right in front of his face. It was like his friends getting shot at, because his friend was stupid enough to run when the airplane came down, you know, trying to shoot at the students and so you just have to hide, you know.

ML: *I can't even believe they would shoot at children.*

AS: Oh, anybody really. Anything moving would be the target. In your father's case, the whole school got burned down. Then there was a pool beside the school, and many students jumped into the pool and they all died in there. Like your father has to help get the bodies out of the water and so forth. This was around the time of graduation from elementary school. So things were really, really bad. I think the worst for the students was that we were always hungry. I think transportation wasn't good then, so the rice wasn't really coming to the cities anymore. We didn't have any butter or sugar or flour or anything that is part of the every day food.

So in most homes, we had a family garden where we had to produce anything edible, like the pumpkins I talked about and corn or the potatoes and tomatoes. Any vegetables would just help. So most people had in those days like a broth, fish kind of a base with lots of vegetables in it.

If you had any flour, you could dilute the flour and then cook that inside this vegetable soup. It's nothing that is very nutritious.

ML: *So no rice, right?*

AS: No rice.

ML: *But you could get fish.*

AS: Yes, sometimes. We pretty much lived on dried fish. It was then that some people thought of catching locust and roast them and then make them into this fine powder. It was a great protein source. So we were eating locust like that.

ML: *You didn't eat them cold.*

AS: You don't want to see the whole thing. By the time it is roasted, it's you know...

ML: *Rather powdery?*

AS: Right. So unless you belong to some farming class, people didn't have food. So unfair. After this evacuation, we came home to attend to junior high school. Around that time, we would go out on our bicycles and then go to the nearby farms to see if they would sell us anything like milk and eggs.

ML: *So you had money.*

AS: Yes, but the farmers didn't want any money. Again in Japan, it's a different kind of a thing than here; they have their own lifestyle. They would never have some of the things that city people had, and so the farmers would ask for kimonos. So the mothers had to give away many of their beautiful kimonos to get some rice and some farmers asked for pianos. Some things that they could never...

ML: *They couldn't get in those days.*

AS: Right! There was much resentment among the city people that the farmers were not helping out.

ML: *Taking advantage.*

AS: Right! Exactly! We were doing quite alright, but some people were so hungry. Some people did not have lunch to bring to school. You had to guard your lunch box because some people might want to steal them because they are so hungry. And, you know, what can you do? You yourself don't have a very good lunch because it's mostly sweet potato or something.

ML: *How long did this go on for?*

AS: Well the actual first chill lasted for quite some time, but when Japan surrendered, occupation forces came in. And there was this big move for the occupation forces to supply food, but they brought the stale corn that they couldn't even use for feeding animals here. What do we do with stale corn? They may be more dead or something and then in some areas they gave out butter and people were not even used to using butter. There was this complete misconception—so we learned to do, we knew what to do with the corn. My resourceful great-grandmother knew how to cook Western ways by associating with the missionaries in those days, who knew how to make corn bread. She would make this wonderful cornbread using the stale corn. You would grind it and that was the task you had to have — every day after you came back from school. No more air raid, but you have to grind the corn. And then make all this wonderful corn bread.

ML: *At least you had something to eat.*

AS: Oh yes, right, right. The area where my father worked, before the military had this large airfield, that immediately became the headquarters for the Air Force.

ML: *The American?*

AS: The American Air Force base. So it became the material supply area. So my father had to work with all these American officers and none of them, I was told, spoke to my father. "Oh and I remember you, You came long ago to my factory in America." There was some person my father met.

ML: *When you came in the 1930s?*

AS: Right, 1938 trip to the United States so that was interesting. But they were like my father — officials from the Air Force. They also are very curious about Japanese families, and so they would come visit our home and in those fancy American cars of the '40s, you know. With the entire blue car with the fins and so forth, the fancy ones.

ML: *Wow! They had them there?*

AS: They had them there and they would come driving up to our house and all the neighbors would run up to look at the car, and it was really something. They were not really supposed to spend too much time with natives and so forth. They enjoy knowing the family, and they also showered us with gifts. Whatever they used every day would be a total treasure for us like soap, shampoo, or a nice wool yarn, or cakes, and chocolates, and things like that. So I think we were really lucky. It was just being spoiled I think. I remember it was what a surprise to us to use this fancy American shampoo because the Japanese shampoo in those days was just hideous. I don't know what it was made of. It was more like this clay something, and you needed a whole half a cup full of that on your hair. Also, in those days we didn't have hot water inside the house, and so there was a well outside and so we'll draw the water from the well and burn wood outside to make hot water. Then you'll just be by the well and then do your hair thing. I was just using this beautiful shampoo that was given to me, one of the Christmas presents. Then I didn't know how much to put on so I just assumed I would need quite a bit and this shampoo became like a whole cloud of fragrant thing all over me, and it was just so amazing. *[laughs]* It was my first encounter with this American shampoo. But it was all very positive.

ML: *So your father made friends with Americans, but was there any fear in after the war since he worked for the military sort of indirectly?*

AS: Anybody who was above him had to quit the official jobs and so they had to tell the GHQ—the general headquarters—which really handled everything in those days, that they had worked for the Japanese government or the military and you know held just ranks and did such and such. Then GHQ had to decide to purge you or not. So "purge" was the one word we kept hearing. Many people couldn't get back to their job. They'd get some other jobs, but then nothing in this kind of official category. A whole lot of people couldn't. In relation to that—how GHQ was handling those things and also the re-education of the Japanese people—they were examining all the school textbooks and any literature and everything else, the drama, anything that was available.

ML: *Is this a Japanese, like the GHQ was...*

AS: American.

ML: *American, okay.*

AS: The Japanese had nothing to say about that. It says everywhere in the city that under the GHQ control or by the law of the GHQ, such and such. We were told to bring all our textbooks to school and some of the textbooks that were totally inappropriate, like Japanese history, had to be burned.

ML: *Why? What was inappropriate about that?*

AS: Because it praised militarism.

ML: *Oh okay.*

AS: And so those were taken home, and we were to burn them. So we had a bonfire and burned all those books. And then some of the textbooks were irrelevant or not good, so we were to take our ink and erase all those lines that were supposed to be bad. They would say, "Okay, open page such and such and erase the first five lines," and so every [body] erases that.

ML: *But didn't you read them while you were erasing them?*

AS: Of course! And then the funniest one was that the GHQ also banned like *Kabuki* stories.

ML: *Why did they?*

AS: Because that's like using sword and it's like everything in praise of militarism that goes too far. They didn't know where to stop. Even some children's games couldn't show or use certain things because that's military.

ML: *So anything that had a sword or something would be considered military, it was more of a cultural...*

AS: Oh yeah, totally cultural, but then it was funny. How much authority the GHQ have to actually censor all these things. Isn't it amazing?

ML: *I know that a lot of American soldiers had sort of returned home with the souvenirs like the swords. Could you tell me a bit about that?*

AS: I think that by the end of the war, everybody had to surrender any-thing that looked like a weapon, especially the Japanese sword. Anybody who had any sword had to turn it in. We thought that it would be dealt with accordingly, but then many of those swords were taken home by those soldiers. So we can find good swords here *[laughs]* in America.

ML: *Did your family have any swords?*

AS: No, we didn't have any. No, no. But during the war time, they needed every little metal, precious stones, everything, so my mother had to donate or give the rings that she had with all these gold or platinum or silver on it to the Japanese government or military. So I think of the Gone With the Wind story you know. You had to give all these things.

ML: *Do you remember what it felt like? It seems like in increments you had to keep on giving up and giving up more and more. You had no control over that. First of all, you didn't have things, available resources, and then the Japanese government is requiring you to give up personal possessions and then the American government comes in and makes you give up. Do you remember your feelings about that or did you have any?*

AS: I wasn't really giving up anything other than something more spiritual I think many people who had possessions they really had their gripes about that or you could always hide them, but then of course you are fearing that the retribution would be great if you hide them. I guess the more you had, then the more trouble you had probably. I think by then people are so depressed anyways. Most people are just depressed and then because there is inflation going on, and then there is just a whole lot more than what's going on so this was just a very minor sort of thing.

ML: *When the war started, did you remember when you first found out when this war was starting, and what it was like?*

AS: It was the morning of December 8th and it was 1941. I must have been eight years old. I was having breakfast with my sister. I remember just how beautiful and calm everything was because my father came in as he was tying his necktie and he was smiling as he said, "So finally Japan finally started war on America." Since he was smiling, I thought this was okay. It was a war, but like you know after this incident with China still going on, then "so that's another war" kind of a thing. We didn't really know the scale of this thing, but then pretty soon, we heard about this Pearl Harbor attack and everything.

ML: *What was your reaction to that Pearl Harbor attack? Did you feel if it was a positive feeling like "oh we were able to strike"? Or was it more of a...*

AS: We didn't of course know the whole story. We thought that of course they must have declared it and then did it. It was like a clever attack rather than a sneak attack. And yet I think in the history of wars in Japan, inside Japan from many hundreds of years, there are certain like clever tactics, always a tricky one and the unfair one. They should be clever at the same time have to be fair in letting others know of the intentions. There is always this sudden attack, especially when the number of soldiers and horses or arms and so forth are deficient. If they didn't have enough, they really had to be clever in planning out this kind of surprise attack I guess. So it didn't really strike us since we didn't know the full story at the time. It didn't seem to be unfair.

ML: *It seemed like "oh one for our team." Plus because you were just getting the point of view they wanted to tell you in the media.*

AS: Right. Exactly, you were never told that there were some problems or defeat or some people got lost in the defeat. Nothing, nothing. It's mostly lies.

ML: *So as a child during the war, did you feel the Americans were the enemy and did you feel any real kind of hatred or feelings towards the Americans?*

AS: No, it's not really like that. It's all about your head, so to speak. Nothing really personal about that. Even if at school, they tried to run a propaganda that the enemy is such and such or that Westerners are crude or cruel. I already knew some American people by then personally. I know them to be good and with great humor, wonderful people! So rather than going along with what the teachers were saying, I thought that the American people are great! I had this very fixed memory in my head of my father going there, and then of course when he came back of all the stories he told me about America—this wonderful land, the wonderful souvenirs that he brought: the little bears, the books, and things like that. America was just always like shining in this beautiful kind of rainbow.

ML: *Even throughout the war?*

AS: Even throughout the war. It was so unfortunate. We felt a more devious kind of fear about the Chinese and the Russians because Japan already had had the Russo-Japan war by that time.

ML: *And they were the neighbors.*

AS: Right. They were much closer, and the culture is closer. You feel like they were like much sneakier. You don't really know much about them. That was a kind of a feeling.

ML: *Do you think your feelings were pretty different from most Japanese people during the war?*

AS: I should think so because I knew those missionaries and I knew those friends of my parents made a completely different impression. Most people had just no idea what Americans were really like; they didn't really show us or tell us, so we had no idea who we were fighting against.

ML: *It wasn't like what they said here about the Japanese?*

AS: No, no, no. *[laughs]*

ML: *I want to get ahead again to when you had to come here later. You had mentioned you had got to Pendle Hill and then you kind of continued your studies. If you could talk about when you had come here again?*

AS: I think after going back from my studies in New York and after the Fulbright studies you were obliged to spend at least the same amount of time in Japan. Because they fear that the Japanese won't continue living here. *[laughs]* Of course the whole point is to train us to work productively in Japan, so I worked for three years in Japan doing the church-related kind of work. I really wanted to do more study in leadership training, which I started to get my hands on while I was studying opinion.

So I came to study again at the University of California. It seemed like instead of going into psychology, I was to choose the Ed.D. program in education, but still taking most courses in psychology. So that was the study that I did. I was supposed to spend at least three or four years to finish my doctorate there, but after my first year, I finished a master's equivalent there.

ML: *You already had a master's though.*

AS: I already did, but this is another one in another field. And I met your father, and we decided to get married here in America. Then my husband wanted to go back to Japan.

ML: *He was finishing his studies right?*

AS: He was finishing his studies and he just took his PhD there. And after he had spent five years in America, he was ready to go home. So I said okay, so I am going to continue my studies back in Japan. And so we went back to Japan.

ML: *Could he have stayed here because he was also on a student visa?*

AS: He was also on the Fulbright. He stayed beyond the ordinary three years of their requirement, so he had to go home.

ML: *And you would have to separate in order for you to stay.*

AS: Yeah, I wouldn't think of that. *[laughs]* That was my failed attempt to do my doctorate.

ML: *Were you able to keep studying in Japan?*

AS: No way! *[laughs]* Especially in the Nagoya area. It's a very traditional society, and we lived about one hour away from the city of Nagoya which is close to Toyota city that manufactures all these Toyota cars. So I looked for certain like university-level studies there, but it didn't seem like it was appropriate. Also I'm just a housewife, and I am just going to really explore the life of countryside in Japan, which was so totally different from Tokyo. I thought that the difference between Tokyo and New York is much less than the difference between Tokyo and Nagoya. It's a totally traditional kind of society with all this group pressure. About a dozen neighbors, they form a group. This is all officially assigned since the time of Tokugawa I guess. For many hundreds of years, they had this kind of a system mainly

from the 17th century actually, mainly to watch over the banned Christians, the banned Christian activities.

ML: *Oh really?*

AS: Yes. That was the original, this neighborhood association.

ML: *So you were probably the only Christian?*

AS: But in those days, they just had to make sure that in any nook and cranny of this whole of Japan, there should be no Christian. There was a great big persecution. They really wanted to get rid of all the missionaries and Christians in the 17th century. They kept this particular way of like watching over, the big brothers watching over. They still have that system alive and well. In Tokyo they have that. It's just more convenience.

ML: *That was in Okazaki?*

AS: That was in Okazaki, yes. It's an old town of Okazaki. It's a farm town. I was surprised one morning by the voice of all the neighbors and it was very early in the morning, like eight o'clock. They came to welcome us to this city and to this organization. And they brought some special kind of welcome gift, probably for our wedding. Early in the morning, just like that, without appointment. You don't call. People don't have telephones, you know. You are surprised, and you get up and deal with it. But one day, there was this representative of this neighborhood association came and wanted to collect money for the mending of the roof of the shrine that was destroyed during some kind of storm. So I said, "Well, I am a Christian so I cannot donate money for your cause because that is Shinto shrine." The big Ieyasu shrine in that area, which is like the mother shrine of Japan. And of course my communication didn't go very well with this representative because she thought I was just misunderstanding what she was asking. I knew exactly what she was asking for, and then I was taking my stand, you know. There is something called religious freedom. You are not supposed to donate money for the cause that you don't support. You shouldn't, but of course they don't understand it that way.

So they were very—the representatives, two of them I think, tried to convince me that this is like a neighborhood project. And if we don't pay, somebody else has to pay for that amount, but I wasn't going to give up you know. This is where the Christians had to take stand in Japan, you see, because these things are done everywhere, every day. And in little ways, they just let you know there is no such thing as religious freedom. Anyway, fortunately, your grandmother, your father's mother came back from an errand, and she said, "What's this all about?" And I told her, and she said, of course, she would pay. That's no problem. She can support a Shinto shrine. She's not a Christian.

ML: *But she's also not Shinto.*

AS: She's also more like a Buddhist, but still okay. It's still a neighborhood thing, you know. If we were living there, if we are going to live there for ten years or fifteen years, raising children there, boy, I think we would have invited some trouble because you don't do such things in Japan. But it's like that. So I was already working for the YWCA in Nagoya because

I just couldn't sit at home and do nothing. A couple of days after I arrived there, yes, I was going to look for work, and I immediately got work and so I was working. So every day I was commuting for an hour on this train, going to Nagoya city to work at this place, and it was very, very rewarding. But being exposed to this kind of a country life and more traditional Japanese life was very, very helpful much later when I was writing a book about Japanese communication system because this is more Japan rather than Tokyo life which is not really representative of all of Japan. It isn't.

ML: *So then you stayed in Okazaki and you stayed for some time and then you had children and moved or you moved first?*

AS: Yeah, around that time your father had the appointment to move to Tokyo University on a different project, so that is what we did. We were happy to come back to Tokyo. With your father's salary we couldn't afford a home or something like that, so we decided to live with my parents in the suburb of Tokyo. That's where you were born and your sister was born.

ML: *And so you weren't able to go back to school at that point either because you had children.*

AS: Two babies, yes.

ML: *Now what point did you decide to come back here?*

AS: I think by the time, we were moving back to Tokyo, we were very much determined to come back here because of the work situation, especially for your father. The

Japanese system *[laughs]* was not really what he could put up with. He was so totally trained in the United States.

ML: *So he was really wanting to come back here to work?*

AS: So he applied for the green card there, and we were waiting for that. The issuance got delayed because the green card was lost within the United States some-where, and so we had to wait for another year. So we actually waited for four years in Tokyo for that.

ML: *So you tried to come back before you had children and everything, but it took so long to get all the papers in order?*

AS: Right.

ML: *And so you came back here finally?*

AS: Finally came back to Maryland and your father was working for the National Institute of Health, and he was pursuing the study he had wanted to do. I was learning a lot about American society through rearing children because that's the very good way to get to know what America was all about. Already there in Washington, Maryland area, the racial tension was very high and then there was the Martin Luther King assassination.

ML: *So the racial tension meaning...*

AS: Meaning black and white.

ML: *And what year was this?*

AS: It was '67.

ML: *So across the country. So how did that affect you in terms of the racial tension issues?*

AS: Well, it didn't really affect me personally, but we just learned to be very careful speaking about even what coffee we were ordering. You couldn't say black. *[laughs]* Like that. It was that kind of atmosphere. We still lived in an apartment. It was an independent home environment that we had after so many years, so that was just great.

ML: *And were you working?*

AS: I started work after all the children started going full time at school. So after then, I was doing the volunteer work for the church like being the director of Christian education and things like that. So it was usually volunteer work, and so I got to teach at the Tokyo Washington's Women's club. They needed some teacher there as a volunteer. I was teaching Japanese.

ML: *Oh! And who were you teaching?*

AS: Some of the American wives who were in Japan before and they were the members of this Washington Tokyo Women's Club. So we're having all these classes for the Japanese to learn English and some of us were teaching Japanese to Americans.

ML: *Did you have a lot of Japanese friends?*

AS: We had quite a bit. There were different groups. The scientists who were all poor, but they were having a great time and then the journalists. Since this was Washington, we had the top journalists, so we got to know many of those journalists and then the diplomats. It was a very different type of friends than in Detroit. So not very many business people there.

Even a whole image of a Japanese from Japan just evoked so much pain in those people. I had never realized that this was so...

ML: *So these were all Japanese people from Japan and were they sort of temporarily here?*

AS: Yes they were all temporary and some stayed on and some were Nikkei people. The Japan American society became very active later, but at that time the Japan American Society wasn't so active. I attended some of the JACL's regional *mochi* meeting or something, the January meeting. They pound the mochi. That is done everywhere. Some people asked me which camp did you go to? It kind of struck me you know because I wasn't a Nikkei person, I came from Japan. By the time I explained it, the Nikkei people who had to go to these camps, they sort of lost interest in me. For the first time, I saw this great big gap between the Nikkei people and the Japanese from Japan. It was good to realize that.

ML: *Did you know about how there had been internees in the camp?*

AS: I didn't realize just how deep that experience affected them. I encountered some Japanese American scientists and one of them, upon learning that we are Japanese from Japan, he wouldn't even look at us. He just turned around and walked away. Even a whole image of a Japanese from Japan just evoked so much pain in those people. I had never realized that this was so...

ML: *How did it make you feel that there was sort of negative feeling or maybe hostility towards you? I mean, you weren't causing the war. You were too young to even be involved.*

AS: Right, but I just realized that is just what it is here. That is a learning opportunity for me at the personal level. But there are many great Nisei people. In fact, your father's friend was a Nisei person, and another friend of his was a Nisei who went to the Italian battleground. We associated very closely, and yet there is this kind of a line we couldn't cross, so to speak.

ML: *It sounds like pretty much they didn't want to know about your side of the story. They just sort of didn't want to hear about it or anything like that. Was that how it was or was there some people who were interested in seeing what it was like from your perspective?*

AS: No, I didn't think so. That was just that. I think we were more involved with some projects that were trying to show what Japan is to the Americans. I think immediately such questions were put down and forgotten I guess.

ML: *How about today? Do you feel that things have changed today?*

AS: I think so. I really think so, and we had to go through Japan-bashing you know. But then with Japan's presence in the United States through this kind of industry and technology people in general are seeing Japan with a more positive kind of an eye, and I think that probably contributed somewhat to ease this kind of tension between the Nikkei and the Japanese. I hope.

ML: *How was your experience different when you moved to the Detroit area?*

AS: Coming to Detroit had to do with your father's job again. He decided to leave the National Institute of Health and accept an offer to teach at Oakland University. And so we came here. As we were looking for a house, everybody that we encountered or talked with would say, "Oh, so you are not in business." *[laughs]* "School?" I realize we are totally a minority so to speak. So it was a big change to see everybody who was working here for Ford or GM or Chrysler. And if you are not, then who are you? *[laughs]*

ML: *And this was what year?*

AS: This was '81.

ML: *How about the climate, especially the Detroit area?*

AS: It was very bad. Yeah. We were going through the first wave of the Japan-bashing and we would go through another wave of Japan-bashing. Of course each time, it was getting more and more severe. So very soon after we arrived here, somehow my name was in the newspaper or something or somebody gave my name. So I was interviewed by the newspaper about things here, and I really haven't had time to see just what things were like. Japan-bashing and also the Vincent Chin case which was the following year, '82 — they were trying to ask what my reactions were. "What? Why are they calling me?"

was my first reaction. Because I didn't realize that Vincent Chin was targeted as a Japanese, and I didn't know the whole story then for some reason and so I was wondering why they wanted to even say that and wanted to hear my reaction. Anyway, I think most of the Japanese industry here, which was represented in this association called the JBSD, The Japan Business Society of Detroit. They told everybody just to lay flat, lay low and don't say anything because the storm would go away again. You were not supposed to speak about it or say your opinion.

ML: *Very Japanese.*

AS: Very Japanese *[laughs]* and I told myself this was the time to tell the story and stand up and say that things are not good and that Japan-bashing is just wrong and so forth and so on. At the Oakland University where I started to work, it immediately started this cross-culture Japan kind of a thing and bring our system to different American businesses so that we could talk more about the differences, the cultural differences, or what Japan is like, why Japanese people think the way they do, or why do they do things the way they do in a more academic way. This was really more than anything else for fundraising because the universities had funding cut from the state and they had to close down many departments. This was a worse time for the universities then, and so they needed to raise money on their own. So we had to immediately start working on these projects, and this cross-culture thing with Japan was more successful. They had some Latin and German and some other programs, but Japan was very much in demand. So we would go to Ford, Chrysler,

GM, and many other organizations and then present just about Japan—what Japan is all about, and its land and resources, and so forth. So that was a great study for me and a great chance to like encounter this Japan-bashing kind of a trend full force.

ML: *It sounds like this is a kind of a positive way to counteract that.*

AS: Right, rather than lay low and hiding. When the worst Japan-bashing was going on, the television wanted to have a special program. That was a scary encounter because when I went there, we were surrounded by all these GM people, who lost their jobs. They were surrounding the TV station building, and I had just a hard time getting inside. And they would look at me like this, and I almost thought, well, would I come out alive? That was the feeling, you know.

So all these kinds of bashing things, they were expressing the feelings of hatred and so forth in the program, and at the same time, you have to take your stand. I would tell them, the America that I know is much friendlier. It is a gentleman country. We have had such great time here, and these are my hopes. By the end of the program, the table was just completely turned around because some people who are already working for the Japanese company, they raised their voice. The Americans who worked in Japanese companies, manufacturing companies making cars, they said just how America has been lacking in education and precision and so forth and so on. They have to blame themselves. That was a conclusion of this program. We didn't really intend it that way, but it was

just amazing that we could still find hope in the middle of all this kind of a fearful storm.

ML: *And kind of confront and diffuse the situation that could have gone worse.*

AS: Could have been dangerous. Yes.

ML: *So then you continued to do this work with this kind of cross-cultural...*

AS: Which kind of crystallized into this book that I published in Japan. It's called *The Foreign Culture Syndrome.* It was '88. After that, I wrote some more about the business relationship and business English and so forth. You are helping me with that.

ML: *Could you tell us a little bit about the book? How did you come to write that?*

AS: I was encouraged to express the kind of the things that I found in all these seminars. Through all these seminars it was really clear to me that nothing was really wrong with the Japanese system of thinking or the American system of thinking, but the very fact that we are unaware of how we are thinking or how we are communicating is the source of this conflict. And so how to ease this conflict or just to become aware of how we are thinking or how we are doing things and how things are done in this country or what the basis of thinking and so forth, how these things are done: that was the basis of the book. I just needed to tell my Japanese friends and people that I have never met in Japan that these are the things that people have to be aware of when they are coming to America or when they are meeting with Americans.

So there were lots of applicable findings I have made through child-rearing and just how people form relationships here, how people are brought up, meaning more for independence and clearer communication. I think those really spoke more than anything else. I hate the theoretical approach. There are many books like that, but these are the striking differences that we find in every day life.

ML: *So it seems like you kind of covered both areas. You were teaching the Americans about the Japanese and then teaching the Japanese about the Americans.*

AS: Right, exactly. I always wanted to play a role as a bridge, and I was just very happy that I could do that. So the book was published in Japan and people say you know, "Why don't you write the second book or the sequel to it?" But then I was thinking more of, well, if I could not just translate it, but write something like that in English, explaining more about Japan, that would be very nice. That's a future project.

ML: *Now your husband, when he came here he worked for the government, so he needed to become a citizen immediately, correct?*

AS: Yes, right. That was correct, because any government organization would require the naturalization right away, so yeah, right.

ML: *But he alone did that. The rest of the family didn't do that, but why was that?*

AS: I think that for a time, we were not clear that we were going to be staying here, but taking a citizenship was then to me, was such a stride. I couldn't quite make myself do that and then I was very ready to do that.

ML: *Why?*

AS: Well, I think there was this element of betrayal, you know, of leaving Japanese nationality? What would my family in Japan think? What would my parents think? Of course, they didn't think of that as betrayal. It's a step forward. It was no problem as we talked about it later.

ML: *Were you worried that they would feel like they were being rejected?*

AS: Or left, I think. Many people still today, those people who come from Japan and live here, they haven't made the decision to become citizens for various reasons, and I think that usually this was the concern for their own families back in Japan. How can you console them? How can you tell them that you have, you know, jumped? You have jumped ship and you have become like somebody else. It's just a totally legal procedure for me.

ML: *It's so different from many other cultures or people coming from other countries. They want to get citizenship as soon as possible, often for practical reasons. So it is interesting that many Japanese people don't feel that way. They want to hold on to their Japanese citizenship.*

AS: Yes, right, right. They can always go back there, they feel. That's where their identity is and their ancestors are and so forth. The practical side of it is that their life is not that different whether they live here or in Japan, and probably in Japan that's better. So they go back and they don't want to lose that identity. They are here by choice, but at the same time there is always something that they have in their own personal life that would limit their activities if they lived in Japan and they are happier here. They are freer here, so they choose to stay on.

ML: *But they still feel like they might want to go back someday. Did you feel that way? Did you feel like you might want to go back?*

AS: No. No, I don't. I don't at all.

ML: *Well, you did obtain citizenship.*

AS: Yes. That was that.

ML: *1995? And what prompted you to do it, finally?*

AS: You know, I was ready. After all this researching and writing a book and everything, the more I thought about it, the more I thought I was ready. It won't be right if I haven't made the decision.

ML: *Do you think your identity kind of changed?*

AS: I think so. I have sort of been looking at the United States from outside, and now I am looking at it from inside. Although, I think it is still a legal step for me. So legally I am an American, but if you ask me my flesh and blood and myself, it is very, very Japanese. With all these elements we had talked about, my "Japanese-ness" is complete. Yet, I do not accept all the ways that the Japanese culture demands. I see many problems *[laughs]* with the Japanese culture, but still I am very much Japanese. So my identity is still very Japanese.

ML: *So it seems like, just looking at the timeline, it's about half and half, the amount of time you spent in Japan and the time you spent here. Much of your adult life has been here. It feels like although you still identify with being Japanese, at the same time you are kind of in a different category because you spent so much time here.*

Mary & Iwao Ishino [Ishino]

Iwao Ishino

Edited transcript of presentation to "History of Asian Americans" course at the University of Michigan taught by Scott Kurashige. February 22, 2006.

You know, United States' speakers usually begin with a joke, but I'm not beginning with a joke. In Japan, speakers begin with an apology, and I'm going to use the Japanese custom of beginning with a little apology. I was asked to not only talk about the internment but also something about my life before internment, before World War II, as well as after World War II. It's a big assignment. And when you're my age, eighty-five, you know something happens to your memory. You can't remember anything. You can't remember names. You can't remember events and so on.

We've broken down this big assignment into four questions. The first question is: How did the anti-Japanese sentiments of the 1930's and 1940's shape the decisions you made in your life?

I was born in 1921. So I was a teenager in the 1930's, okay. Let's give you some time perspective. We had in San Diego an ice box, no refrigerator. It was my job as the older son to empty the water from the melted ice. Every day we had milk delivered, and they would deliver it by a horse-drawn cart. We had a radio. How many of you know what a crystal set is? *[laughs]* One, good for you! A crystal set is a little earphone radio with a crystal that picks up radio waves and that was probably the fact that I made my crystal set that can pick up KFI, a station in Los Angeles, one hundred miles away.

I was a part of the Japanese American community formed before World War II as I said. My father was running a fruit and vegetable stand in San Diego, just outside of the barrio. How many of you know what a *barrio* is? Oh good! *[laughs]* Barrio is an area, at least in San Diego, where Mexican Americans lived in not a very wealthy place. Anyway, then the Great Depression came along—not a psychological depression, but economic depression came along, and my father lost the vegetable stand. I can tell you as a result of growing up in the vegetable stand, I have to do all the vegetable and fruit shopping for my wife and me [audience laughs] 'cause I know how to tell a ripe watermelon, but when an avocado is ready. We've got freezing peaches and...

Anyway, my father lost his vegetable stand and he went to work as a janitor. So when World War II came along, we weren't very wealthy. We were poor as a matter of fact, and these were tough times to be growing up, especially in San Diego. I couldn't afford to ride the bus to go to high school. I walked two miles each way, up and down the hills in San Diego. There was also a very interesting feeling about San Diego. I was born with the help of a midwife who came to this place. Now this happened to be the first location of the Japanese American Christian Church, and my father was a member of the trustees of the First Congregational Church of San Diego, which sponsored a special church for Japanese living in San Diego. And eventually we became the church. And the reason why I bring the church up is that most of our social life

centered around the church. Now there's another church in town for Japanese and that was a Buddhist church. So we had in a town about two thousand Japanese Americans, two churches or temples, whatever you want to call it. And most of our social life circled around that particular site. And to raise funds for the church, they put on Japanese plays. *Kabuki*, some of you may have heard of Kabuki. The costumes were brought over from Japan and we put on shows like Kabuki plays. We also had movies from Japan which we showed and people, you know, paid to come to those movies. And that's how the church sponsored those activities.

Well, it was a tough time when I was going to college. I started college in 1939. Because I had experience in the fruit and vegetable stand, I got weekend jobs at a vegetable stand in San Diego. And a very interesting thing at the time, farmers were dumping milk into rivers because they couldn't sell the milk. The owner of my vegetable stand used to go to hotel market place, first time to get real good stuff and second time to pick up stuff that wasn't selling that day. And I remember to my horror, one day he brings back a pile, a box of carrots. Now carrots in those days were sold in bunches, you know five or six to a bunch, and we sold our whole bunch of carrots that would probably sell for, what, thirty-five to forty cents per day. Another interesting thing about this particular market that I worked in was that it was open 24 hours a day. Now, in your time, you know like Meijers would be open 24 hours a day, but in my days there was hardly any place that was open 24 hours a day, much less to stay open on Sundays. This place was open 24 hours a day, 7 days a week. Why? Come on *[claps his hands]*. Why would it be open 24 hours a day?

[Student] "To be able to make the most profit?"

Alright, that's one reason. Well, in the evening hours to the morning up, there would be a couple of guys working on, and they were sold out of rude vegetables, rude tomatoes, and so on. And they put them in small baskets, and sell them for a penny a piece and poor people would come along to buy those. So what do you know? So you look at it, you know, good stuff, medium stuff, and lousy stuff. And we made that pay because we let people work overnight, and I guess it was a very good idea. Meijers does the same thing.

Okay, so much for the depression. The second question is: What was your emotional reaction to racial discrimination? I didn't say very much about racial discrimination, but I implied that. Most of our social life centered around the church because although we went to school with African Americans, Mexicans, Italians, whites, and so on, our social life again seemed to be more or less centered around the church. In fact, I can remember only one or two white kids growing up in San Diego that I knew real well as a friend. That's how segregated we were, okay? So, on the other hand, I developed a philosophy that this was a situation that I didn't create. It was a situation that was handed down from the past. I couldn't do anything about the law, U.S. law that says

further immigration from Japan will be stopped in 1924. Or that my parent's generation was ineligible to become naturalized citizens. Or because our parents were ineligible to become citizens, they couldn't own land. While we were in the 1940's only one percent of the population in California, we produced ten percent of the value of the farm crops.

I developed a kind of fatalistic attitude towards discrimination. The Japanese word for it is shikata ga nai... "It can't be helped."

Why? How did that happen? *[bangs the table]* Come on, this is history class! *[laughs and bangs the table again]* Since Japanese or Chinese were ineligible to become citizens they were not able to own land. Well, the children of that generation were born in California, the United States, and they became citizens. So what did our parents' generation do? Raise the land in the name of their children. My wife's father ran a five-acre poultry farm and guess who owned the land legally? *[laughs]* It was hers, not her father's, okay?

Alright! So there was discrimination but the point: I developed a sense that these things happened in the past and there was nothing I could do about it. None of us. I developed a kind of fatalism: this is the way it is. This is the way the cookie crumbles, okay. So the answer to the question: I said that I developed a kind of fatalistic attitude towards discrimination. The Japanese word for it is *shikata ga nai*. It stands for more, in liberal terms, "It can't be helped." That's what it is *shikata ga nai*. So that's my emotional reaction to discrimination.

The third question: How did the internment impact your family? Oh, this is a tough one. This is a long story. Well, my first reaction was that I couldn't believe it, you know. I thought we were not going to—we were still citizens and there were certain laws that were available. So, you know, it took a long time for that to sink in.

I said to myself, "We've got to demonstrate that we are patriotic—that we are loyal and so on." We did whatever we could to demonstrate that, and so I said that if the army ordered us to go in, we'll go in peacefully and not engage in strikes or sit downs. We could've done all that, you know? We could've sat down, you know, and complaints and put on strikes and so on and demonstrations. But we didn't. Most of us and our leaders said, "Okay, that's the way it is, huh. Let's show our loyalty. Let's go peacefully, and do what they want us to do."

I was the oldest son in my family. After me came two brothers, one sister. The youngest of the brothers was born in January of 1942, just a month after Pearl Harbor. And the San Diego bunch was put into incarceration, into camps, into internment, April Fools' Day 1942. And so you can see my mother had a baby two months old. And in those days, there was no diapers, disposable diapers. You can't imagine when orders came up, you can take only what you can carry in a suitcase. What a job it was for my family to care for all that stuff. And furthermore, we were put into these kinds of beds, and we were divided into six parts with one wall separating us. And my mother had had a hard time being with a baby crying all the time and made it very annoying.

What was the result? Eventually, my mother had a breakdown, a nervous breakdown. And she was put in the hospital. They put her in the camp hospital, and she was making too much noise, nagging, and so on, when they finally had to take her to the Arizona State Mental Hospital. That's one of the impacts on my family.

My parents' generation was an interesting property. They made gardens and they went out carving and started making all kinds of things like artificial flowers and stuff, interesting things. That parents' generation didn't have to work anymore in terms of a steady job, but my generation primarily got involved in various jobs in janitorial work, working in the kitchens, you know, cleaning up, and so on. There were lots of other jobs. Then there was a project in which an army networking subcommittee made camouflage for military persons, and they do that kind of work. There was lots of jobs for us, maintaining the camp situation under these permanent conditions.

When the war came along and we were interned, as I said, my wife's family had five acres of land and poultry farm with poultry in it. I don't know how many of you know that strawberries are available all-year round. At one time strawberries were only available in certain parts of time and because they came from California; her brother was one of the early ones that took strawberries and went to Mexico to grow strawberries off-season and ship to the United States. You know, so he played a very interesting role.

My family was so poor, we didn't have any problems of that kind. The only thing *[laughs]* I remember is that we had a very fancy lav that my father got as a gift from the local nursery. One of these fancy lavs that you see on the Antiques Roadshow.

And that was put into the church, and I don't know what happened to it afterwards. We lost it eventually. There wasn't much that we could talk about in terms of losing property. We didn't have any property to deal with. I lost my car. [laughs] It was a '39 Ford that I used to ride to the state college.

I don't know if you realize it or not; the orders for evacuation leaving California or leaving Oregon or Washington was not done at one time. There was sequence over time, and we in San Diego were one of the earlier ones. Why do you suppose we were one of the earlier ones to be interned?

[Student] "There were more Japanese in San Diego than in Washington."

Oh no! We were a very small population.

[Student] "You were closer to Hawaii?"

We were very close to there. We in San Diego had a big fishing business, and we had around five hundred boats and with radio communications and so on, and we were suspected of using these boats as espionage and so on. When we were sent to Santa Anita, we all bragged that we stepped in Seabiscuit's stall. It smelled a little bit when we were put there.

Anyway, coming back to San Diego, we had a very interesting community. One group that specialized in fishing. You know, during this period the Catholics did not eat meat or rice, and so there was a great demand for fish and the whole tuna fish industry developed during this period. And they brought specialists from Japan to introduce a new method of fishing of which the fathers of my friends brought these new techniques that eventually that became the pattern for all of the West Coast. There's a picture of one of the bigger boats the Japanese, my friend's father, had purchased, and when the war came along we had to give up those ships because those ships were used by the

Navy for other purposes. But anyway, the picture I want to bring out is a bunch of my friends here that I grew up with. All those people are living all over the place. The interesting part of my point of view is that I have never reconnected with them after the war. They went all over the place, and I went here and so on. And I lost my friendship buddies. And I don't know how many of you are here still in contact with friends you grew up with and it's a great loss to lose your friends because of this particular experience. Okay? Alright!

Now, let me emphasize [pauses] some of the positive consequences of being interned, and I told you the sad part. My mother suffering from her own illness, and I won't go in any detail after that [says in a slightly depressed tone]. Let me talk about the positive aspects—or what I think are the positive aspects—and often I give this talk in terms of what I call "unintended consequences." Okay? Let me give you an unintended consequence: Japanese Americans were put into these camps, interned, but one of the interesting unintended consequences is that Japanese Americans did think that they wanted to prove their loyalty to the United States. And I think you've all read about the 442nd, right? Or the Japanese Americans who played an important part in the Military Intelligence work in the Pacific Theater. Some six thousand of them served in that theater.

Let me tell you what some of the unintended consequences of me being in camp was. By the time I was interned in the camp I had three years of college, and the camp that I went to is Poston, Arizona. It was partially administered or managed by the Indian Bureau. We were on Indian Reservation, and the head of the Indian Bureau was looking at Poston as a way of developing that agricultural land. I told you that the Japanese were known for their agricultural work, so the chief of the

Indian Bureau was hoping that after camp was over that that land would be turned into rich agricultural land. And he was responsible for setting up research on the camp, and he appointed a couple of anthropologists to set up a bureau. They called it Bureau of Sociological Research. Since I was a student with three years of college behind me, I was one of fifteen that was recruited that served as interviewers and so on. I had my first University of Chicago course in camp to be trained as part of the Sociological Research. [laughs] Up to that time, I was going to be an architect. [laughs] And uh, I guess I won't tell you that story.

[Audience laughs]

I will then, alright! When I was in high school, I was recruited to put up a design for SDHS—San Diego High School— a big sign up in front. And I was proud of the fact that I worked on that project. For every time I would pass by, I says, "Look! I worked on that project!" [laughs] And that was made me thinking about working as an architect.

Anyway, the war came along and put me into something else. The war came along, and I was recruited for this job as a researcher, sociological researcher. And eventually, one thing led to another, and the research team wrote this book, *The Governing of Men*. And I was privileged to spend one month on Indian reservation helping to gather data to write this book. And then after that, they wanted to do some more research and decided two of us would spend a month at the University of Denver learning how to run a public working research center. Now in those days, public working research really became popular. Up to that time it was not scientifically based. The statisticians were not involved in it. With this new thing, they wanted to bring that idea into camp and do public working research.

Then, the head of our research unit, Alexander Leighton, who was a psychiatrist and anthropologist, got a grant to take five of us from the camp to go to Washington, D.C., and to work with the Pentagon. What did we do at the Pentagon? I told you about the two thousand Japanese Americans who were interviewing Japanese prisoners of war, and they wrote these reports of those prisoners. They came into the Pentagon, and we analyzed them for content. And we followed that process, and made recommendations to the Office of War Information about what we were learning. We, for example, predicted not the end of the war but the fact that the Japanese were ready to surrender three months before the atom bomb was dropped. No, we came across data such as Japanese soldiers were practicing cannibalism because their supplies were gone and so on. Okay?

The 442nd was doing very well; the Japanese American troops in Europe were doing very well. They had one of the highest rate of injuries and deaths and so on, and that changed the public opinion. And they changed the War Department attitude, so that at one time when we were reclassified at the beginning of the war from 1-A to 4-C. Your generation doesn't know anything about that. We were drafted, you know? We didn't volunteer for that. We were drafted. And when our classification changed from 4-C [back] to 1-A, we were drafted. I got my draft notice. In those days, we got about three weeks. You had to actually sign up for the army. The first week I proposed to my wife. The second week I got married with all of the arrangements. The third week we went on our honeymoon.

When the war started, there were about three thousand of us Japanese Americans in the army already and because of the suspicions, many of us were reassigned to non-dangerous areas or even honorably discharged. And so at the same time those of us who were of age, we were classified 1-A but reclassified to 4-C because 4-C included enemy aliens. So those of us who were not yet in the army didn't have to serve because we were classified as enemy alien. When the soldiers in Europe were doing so well, the army changes mine and now we say we changed back to 1-A and that's how I got my draft notice. So I proposed to my wife, as I just told you, and we got married, June 18, 1944, and we still remember that! Almost sixty-two years ago.

I appeared before the sergeant on the day I was supposed to report. "This is Fort Meade, Jap! Fort Meade, Maryland." And I said, "Sergeant, my name is Ishino! I-S-H-I-N-O." He looks at me slickly, and he says, "Oh!" He says, "Here, you're to report to your office." I says, "Okay." So I reported back to my office at the Pentagon, and everybody at the office is laughing away. Why? I got a presidential deferment because I was doing such an important job. *[laughs]* Anyway, that experience is written up in this book.

[Mary Ishino] "You didn't tell them what you said."

Oh! They're laughing, and my comment was "Oh hell! I didn't have to get married." *[Audience laughs]* I can't believe I'm still married. *[chuckles]*

I'll have to summarize the good things after internment camp. The co-director of this unit at the Pentagon was Clyde Kluckhohn; he's a Harvard professor. So, when the war ended, I had to go into the army. They put me in Military Intelligence, here, and I had to serve eighteen months. And Clyde Kluckhohn says, "Okay, when you're finished with your army duty, write to me and we'll see if we can get you into Harvard." And I did write to him, and I did get

into Harvard. And by the time I was there for two years, a job opened up in the occupation of Japan. A Harvard professor who was working the Bureau of Sociological Research and Public Opinion was coming back to Harvard in the positional, so through Kluckhohn, I got this job in the occupation of Japan.

Can you believe that? "Wow!" I says to myself. I was there as a simulated major, and we had a very fancy accommodation appropriate to a major stay. My wife—we had one child by that time—and my wife had nothing to do because she was given a maid and a houseboy to run this place. So what did she do? She did lots of things, but one of the things that she took up was flowering arrangement, Japanese ikebana. And she's been doing this for twenty years now at the University Club at East Lansing. Anyway, one unintended consequence.

Back to me. The occupation ended, and the Bureau of Sociological Research and Public Opinion was asked to help the occupying forces research whether to return Okinawa to Japan or to become an independent state or to become a trustee territory. So since I had the so-called expertise in public opinion, they asked me to go to Okinawa and do a survey on what the future of Okinawa should be according to the public opinion. And I did that and finished. And then I got a job at Ohio State because the co-director of the public opinion and sociological research division had a job at Ohio State. So after my Okinawa survey, I went to Ohio State, and did that for a couple of years.

And then Michigan State by this time had a project in Okinawa. They were beginning a new university in Okinawa. And they were looking for people with various backgrounds, and they asked would I be interested in coming to Michigan State. And I said "yes" because I wanted to be in Okinawa where I was three months ago.

So that experience then eventually led to the fact that I got a two-year stay in Okinawa with my family. That experience also led to the fact that I was one year on Fulbright in Japan at the University of Tokyo. And eventually a whole series of other things came across, but I won't go into all the details.

I was very privileged to be, you know, educated and had these contacts with these jobs. But two brothers went into the army and did so-so, but not very much. You know, they had mediocre jobs and so on. They didn't, they didn't finish college the way I did and so on. So I don't know; maybe I should've encouraged them to do more, but I didn't. I wasn't a good big brother to them.

But the point is, the internment situation gave me a chance not in architecture, but in social science research, and I taught social science research since 1956, retired fourteen years ago. Living in Michigan was wonderful because this was in the postwar period, and things were going very well—at least in our academic community. We were a town about fifty thousand people, and our four girls grew up there and enjoyed the good life. Of course, we also spent a couple of years away for living in Japan for the Fulbright and two years in Okinawa and so on. Also, we spent two years in Washington, D.C., because I had a National Science Foundation project in anthropology for two years, so all that kind of thing. And we had a fairly interesting experience living in East Lansing. Our girls grew up in a fairly nice small community and no overt kind of discrimination that we found in California, growing up.

About six months ago, I sent some materials to my granddaughter who was writing about the internment. Actually my generation actually blanked out the camp experience. You know there's a term called... what's the term?

Something stress syndrome. Post-traumatic stress syndrome. And most of our generation blanked out on that, and it wasn't until our grandchildren—our daughter's generation, next generation—came along and started reading about and asking their parents, you know, what went on.

296

The picture bride
[Ishino]

Iwao and Mary Ishino

interviewed by Soh Suzuki
September 20, 2003

ss: *Now, the first question I have is your family background.*

II: *[To MI]* Why don't you start it? Or, do you want me to start it?

MI: Yes.

II: These past few days, I've been going through my photographs and organizing them because I want to see what kind of materials have I got on my family background, and so I've been doing some readings in the materials. Let's start with my father, who came over in 1906 and landed in San Francisco and they had an earthquake. I don't know if you know about that. Eventually, he worked as a farmhand and he had gone down to Mexico for work. He spoke a little Spanish. *[To MI]* Did you know he spoke Spanish? Yeah? Eventually, his first job coming to San Diego was working for Iwata Shokai, that's the Japanese company down in Japantown. I have pictures to show you. You should have a camera and take all the pictures. Anyway. That and eventually, you know, the Japanese Issei, like Koreans in America, formed a kind of credit accumulation organization. My father started a fruit and vegetable stand. And, then in the 1929 Depression. I don't know if you know about that. He had to give that up and went to work at Barcelona Hotel as a janitor, "custodians" these days. So that gives you some idea of the level of income. We were very poor. We had—before the war came around— five children in the family and for my mother and father to keep the family going. I guess that's enough for the time being.

I should say something about that, huh? My dad had a fruit and vegetable stand that the Japanese family had established and we were rather unique because the stand was open 24 hours a day. That's unusual. Nowadays, we see a lot of stores open 24 hours. The reason why they kept it open 24 hours was two reasons. One was that it was too much trouble to move the vegetables back and fourth every night to close up. Second was that during the Depression, we used the evenings, the night hours, to sort out vegetables and fruits. And, they slightly marked up the vegetables or fruit. They also did something, I think that was, rather interesting. At eleven 'clock when the wholesale markets are about to close, we used to wait for the wholesale managers and got things cheap because they had to get rid of the vegetables… Like, I can remember, for example, a whole bunch of carrots was selling for one cent. The ordinal price was ten cents—but, also reminds you what neighborhood we were living in and all that store was… poor people coming around and low income people coming around. Anyway, through high school and through three years of college, I worked on the weekends at this 24-hour store and another store in the another side of town, I was making around ten dollars a week?

SS: *Now, do you have a sibling?*

II: Do I have what?

SS: *Do you have a brother or a sister?*

II: Yes, I had two brothers and two sisters. And, they are all younger than I. I'll tell you more about it later on.

MI: My name is Mary Kobayashi Ishino, and my father came in 1915 to the United States and went to work at—what did they call it?—working hospital. And, he went to Arizona and he worked at a hospital and went to high school and he graduated from high school, and he went back to Goyojima, Ehime-ken, and went to find a bride. He knew my mother because they are from the same island. He must have took her because we went to visit my mother's place and talked about visiting my aunt's later. He came back to the United States in 1916 and worked hard and my mother did too. She—my brother Joe was born in 1916… 1917… and they went down to Southern California because they knew someone down there and they worked. My brother Roy was born in 1918, and they were there in Santa Ana. They moved to Gardena, and my brother Fred was born there in 1919. And, 1920 Bill was born and, 1921, my brother Jim was born.

At that time, my father was a little ill too, from a social problem. He tried to become a poultry farmer himself and he found a place in Southern California and that's when I was born, in 1922. They decided to buy a bigger ranch. We had a lot of fun growing up. We all played football with my brothers and all kind of other sports.

II: We have some very nice pictures of those poultry farms. And, some very nice pictures of her playing tennis and things like that.

MI: Well, anyway…

II: We gotta make some reproduction of the images.

MI: One day, we tried to have a eggfight, because the eggs didn't hatch and we had to throw them away. So we put up barricades of sacks on a frame and we threw eggs at each other. A few days later, my father comes in and says, "Who threw eggs out in the backyard?" We all were guilty. That was so much fun. And one of the things we did a lot was we camped at each others' house and spent the night. We used to go the Pacific Ocean to go swimming and talking about swimming. A lot of other things… going to movie…

We, in our town, we went to the movies. We had to sit way upstairs. And we couldn't sit downstairs. And those were some of the drawbacks.

II: I don't remember any of that kind of stuff in San Diego. Most likely that… we in San Diego kept pretty much to ourselves and our social lives depends on the church. We had a Buddhist church and a Christian church, and my dad belonged to the Christian church. So we were very active in there. There's some pictures of the church, in 1926. And one of the very interesting things about this San Diego community was that it sat around the church to raise funds for the church activities. We had movies from Japan so I saw a lot of early movies from 1920s. Also, we had plays. My dad, this is the picture of my dad here in a kabuki play. I have a picture of myself in one of the kabuki plays. *Chushingura* and all that kind of stuff. Anyway, the important part I'm trying to make is that it was a good deal of networking within the Japanese community. And, for example, we had picnics, you know, in the summertime.

Tennis Team
[Ishino]

And we had *Kenjin-kais* and people from *Kenjin-ken,* got together. Then, in terms of Christian churches, young people from San Diego got together and so on. Here is an example of that kind of meetings. And we had Boy scouts, one of the important features of my growing up. Boy Scout activities and Girl Scout activities, as well.

SS: *So, San Diego had a high concentration of Japanese?*

II: Oh, about 2,000, 2,500, something like that. I don't know if we can call it a high concentration.

MI: Most of the people were farmers in the Orange County.

II: Well, in San Diego, we had two major industries. One was the fishing industry and the Japanese fathers of my friends introduced me to fishing techniques, and my friend still continues that. And they introduced tuna fishing in a highly systematic way. They brought in abalone.

MI: *Awabi.*

II: Awabi. And then, what's that... *katsuo.* They produced...

MI: Tuna?

II: No... katsuo. Bonito.

MI: Oh, yes, katsuo.

II: All that industry started in San Diego area by Isseis... an amazing industry. And the other side was farming. A major winter production. They produced celery for the rest of the country. Anyway, what I am leading up to is that my mother would get fish from the fisherman, and when farmers came into town, she would give fish and they would give her vegetables in return. She helped a lot in getting food for us.

SS: *You already shared a little about your growing... Is there something you would like to add?*

MI: We grew up in farms. Most of the people in that area were farmers. They grow strawberries, celeries. Anyway, mostly produce.

II: It was a kind of interesting thing that Japanese Isseis came in and got into the business of vegetable farming. And that led to establishment of wholesale markets. And that led to the establishment of retail market. And all of this was linkage. And, in one sense, although we were in California, less than one percent of the California population, we made about ten percent of all income from agriculture because of high concentration. And as a result of this, to give you a little historical background, the Chinese first came and worked on the railroads and that made it possible for refrigerated cars and that made it possible to transport to the Midwest and East Coast. All that is a part of history.

We had a midwife, Kobayashi by the name, and she was a midwife for every one of my brothers and sisters. And she lived here. I don't know why. You should also mention that you are the last.

MI: I'm the last of the family.

II: They were all boys until she came on. That gives you some idea of sense of community of Japanese American community at that time.

MI: Where we lived had a Japanese community too, but very small.

II: Yours was much smaller.

MI: Yeah. Because they had farming, and had a lot of acreage.

The egg farm
[Ishino-3]

II: Spread out.

MI: Yeah, we were spread out.

II: Did you have a Buddhist church?

MI: No. We had a Christian church. The First Baptist Church. Old Japanese minister came one night, and we had young people's group too.

II: Like us. But, you didn't have a Japanese school. After regular school, we went to a Japanese school. The church was sponsoring that.

MI: There was a Japanese school.

II: Where?

MI: Oh...

II: But, you didn't go there. Huh?

MI: I went to for a year or so. I cannot remember.

II: Never mind.

MI: Anyway, uh, we were the first people that supplied the Knott's Berry Farm with chicken. And, you know, the Knott's Berry Farm in California? They have Knott's Berry jam.

II: Was that competition to Disneyland?

MI: Before it grew. Before the Knott's Berry Farm grew. They asked us at least to give them three dozen a month. We thought we had to refer them to another Japanese family that had a bigger poultry farm.

II: The question was where your parents came from. My parents came from Fukuoka, a district in Kyushu. One of my father's brother was a Buddhist priest so during the occupation when we were in Japan, I visited the temple there. The last visit, we also visited there.

MI: Oh, yeah, we have to tell him what the situation is.

SS: *You mentioned your parents were from Ehime.*

MI: Yes. Goyojima. We went, instead of going to Hong Kong, we went visiting our relatives in Ehime-ken and then went to Goyojima. When we went, I looked up my family, my father's Kobayashi, but so many of them that, a series of a family came, Sakiichiro, Toru, Susumu, and that's my family.

MI: And, when we went there we saw an older man and wanted to know where the...

II: *Yakuba* (town hall).

MI: Yakuba. We went there and they told us it's just two blocks down the road, so we just went there. When we went to the place, I wanted to asked for Kobayashi and Kitaya.

II: Kitaya's father's name?

MI: My mother's name. And, my brother... my uncle was deceased then. They said that your aunt is still alive and so the other clerk says she lives only a block away so went down asking for my mother's side and my father's side. And then, they took us there and went to the door and the clerk knocked on the door and said Mrs. Kitaya, her mother, and they came from the United States because of my mother. And three of us were there and, you know, some strangers coming from the United States. So they said I'll ask my mother, and she said by all means and she opens the sliding door and says "come on over." So we talked to her for a good hour, huh? And we got reacquainted but she had Alzheimer's and repeated... but, good to see her.

SS: *Is there anything else you would like to share about your experience? Such as going to school.*

II: You know when I was in high school, the Japanese war in Manchuria began and was a very interesting period. I began to sense tensions in the Japanese in high school. One of the incidents I remember was that I was in the ROTC, and there was a Chinese Nisei who was also in the ROTC so two of us were interviewed by the San Diego

303

union about what we thought about the war in China.

MI: I think I had quite a happy life. We were never without things, but I still remember going to the store, and some people got nickels to buy candy bars and we couldn't afford it with six children, you know. But, other than that, we were happy.

II: Oh, I remember another thing. In 1935-36, San Diego had an Exposition and a lot of people came to San Diego for the Exposition. And the hotel in which my father worked in was very busy and I got a job as an elevator boy and also helped out with janitorial work, occasionally.

MI: That's why he is good at cleaning our house.

II: When we married I was the one who had to clean the house. And, then, when we go to shopping, because I know vegetables and fruits, I end up picking up those. I know when avocados are ripe.

SS: *I'd like to ask both of you about the World War II experience.*

II: Well, they said the San Diego group was incarcerated early because we had a great fishing fleet and was concerned about us acting as espionage agents and so on. So, we were called in on April 1st to register for the evacuation and on April 8th, we were all put on the train and put into Santa Anita racetrack. Temporarily, until August of that 1942, we were in this racetrack area living in these horse stalls. I used to talk about the World War II days and write about the fact that we, my family, stayed in Seabiscuit's stall. There is a movie out now called *Seabiscuit*.

People who I talked to before the movie became famous, these kids never understood who or what Seabiscuit was. Anyway, um, we stayed in those stalls until August of 1942, and this was very hard on my mother because my youngest brother, Thomas, was born in January of that year so only a few months old and had diapers and all those other things to do. So my mother really had a hard time. Eventually, when we moved to Poston internment camp, she had a mental breakdown. Eventually, she was put into a hospital. My life was very busy in that period. And then a major connection I had to this was... A long story, I'm going to make it short. I had three years of college by this time and so I was one of fifteen or so college educated people to act as Bureau of Sociological Research and thisparticular camp was run by people who... Indian Service... the Bureau of Indian... then, the idea they had was that to bring people together, the problem of governing camp. Eighteen thousand people were put into one camp. How would you administer that? How would you feed them? What would you do to school them and what would you do with young people and all those other kind of stuff? That was what the Bureau of Sociological Research had to do. Anyway, the head of Bureau of Sociological Research was a psychiatrist who was at the same time a lieutenant in the medical corps, and he was very helpful in helping my mother find a hospital outside the camp. I had my first course in Anthropology at the camp with graduate students, Tommy Tsuchiyama and another person, Richard Crawson. Both graduate students at the University of California and they were parttime instructors in training us college people for interviewing and carrying on

First Japanese Congregational Church, 1927 [Ishino]

ethnographic research. Eventually, Crawson became chairperson of Anthropology Department and Tommy Tsuchiyama and I spoke with him about the job. Anyway, that was kind of an interesting experience. I manage to spend—I forgot how long— a month or so on the Indian Reservations to write up a research report, and then when that was finished, the head of this unit took five of us to Washington, D.C. to work with the Pentagon. That was the beginning of my career in anthropology. I won't go into all the details at this point.

MI: The Pentagon: you should say the office of…

II: The Office of War Information, working for the Pentagon. The idea there was to interview Japanese soldiers who were captured. And those interview materials then were analyzed by us in the Pentagon. The good deal of the interviews were done by Nisei or *Kibei*, who were trained. And so, we traced the decline of morals in the Pacific War. And the three months before the atom bomb was dropped, our unit put out the report saying that the Japanese are ready to surrender because of all kinds of moral problems. Even cases of cannibalism were observed. Anyway, Ruth Benedict who wrote *Kiku to Katana, The Chrysanthimum and the Sword…*

What else? We went to Washington, D.C. and married after the week in Washington, D.C. She'll tell you about her story. Anyway, eventually, we got together, and we got married in Washington, D.C. June 18, 1944.

MI: Oh, you remember!

II: Well, it's almost the sixtieth anniversary—

MI: —anniversary, next year.

II: That's enough for the time. Well, go ahead.

MI: Well, when my father got property in California; he put it in my two brothers' names because the Japanese couldn't own a property. And so we had to rent our property before we were incarcerated into the camp. And, they came, they emptied our and searched the place and took my brothers' Boy Scout knives, camera, radio... I think that's it. There was my father who was with an interpreter. And they said, "Well, wait a minute" and "let me check the list." and the man checked the list and my father's name was on the list. We found out later that he went to a prisoner of war camp in Montana. And the man who collected the money collected on false pretense. So they let all those people on the list go, and they came and joined us in Poston, Arizona. We, at that time, we were also, we were sent to camps on April 8, 1942. And my mother unfortunately got a metaphase and had a hard time, and fortunately my father came home in about three months. I worked, since I had one year of a junior college, and I worked there as an assistant to the teacher. I went out to Washington, D.C. to work in a Quakers' home. The Quaker homes housed the African Americans so they could get housing in Washington D.C.,—they were not allowed to stay at the hotel. And, I worked at a business college and met Iwao again. I met him in camp and met again in Washington, D.C.

MI: We should tell how we came to Michigan?

II: Okay, we should explain that her father ran a poultry farm and she has five brothers. Two of those brothers...

MI: Three.

II: Three of those brothers went to a poultry school in California. And, so, when they went to camp, they ran a poultry farm in the camp. And, then the Secretary of Interior and his wife had a poultry farm and so he asked the Nisei to come out there and happened to be her brothers to work in Maryland and on the poultry farm. That's the reason why she went out to Maryland and Washington, D.C.

MI: My parents were still in camp. They couldn't go out of the camp.

II: But, do you see? That's why, I guess, her father was thinking about his son taking over the farm and the war comes along and he becomes... selected for the farm. They didn't stay too long. Eventually, he went to a Military Intelligence school and went to Japan and worked for the occupation forces. That explains why she went out because her brothers were... and you understand why I went to Washington, D.C. So, we connected that way. We're still married. Okay, what else.

MI: Oh, why we came to Michigan.

II: Are you asking that question now? I thought we are ready for the post-World War II. When the war ended, my department stay ended, therefore I was eligible for the draft. At that time, U.S. Army was looking for people to work in Japan as translators and interpreters. And, of course, I was called and drafted for the Military Intelligence school at that time in Monterey, California. And I spent roughly eighteen months there. At that time, they figured that most people like me were poor in Japanese. I needed more time, more than a year's time. So, we wound up filing department papers for an extension for three years of training heading up to Japan. Well, because I worked in the Pentagon and a Harvard professor was one of the associate directors in that Pentagon job, he told me, "As soon as you get out of the Army, write me and maybe we can get you into Harvard." So, knowing that, I did not volunteer for an extension to work at the intelligence school. After eighteen months, I applied to Harvard and got into Harvard. I didn't have a degree but got into PhD program. After spending two years at Harvard, I passed my oral exam

We stayed in those stalls... and this was very hard on my mother. My youngest brother, Thomas, was born in January of that year Eventually, when we moved to Poston internment camp, she had a mental break down.

and so on and a job opened. I was going to Brazil to study Issei immigration in Brazil. But a Harvard Professor returned to Harvard; he was working in a unit called Public Opinion and Sociological Research Division. When he returned, a job opened and somehow I got that job. One of the reasons was that during the wartime experience in camp, I had two months training at the University of Denver on public opinion research paper, so having that background and Harvard training, they thought that I would be a good candidate for the Public Opinion and

Sociological Research division. That's how I got the job. Anyway, I had a the rank of a major and by this time, we had a daughter.

MI: Yeah, 1948.

II: We lived at fairly fancy quarters, military quarters near Washington Heights. This is the time, we were in Japan—another long story. Anyway, we had a houseboy and a maid to run a household, a way to get them employment. So Mary didn't have much to do, and one of her friends, no... her sister-in-law, recommended that she pick up *ikebana*. And, that's why she's been practicing ikebana. Another one of these unintended consequences of things. One of the interesting things about that was her two brothers by this time were working for the Army in Japan.

MI: They went to Military Intelligence.

II: They went to Military Intelligence. So, interesting. We connected up in Tokyo again. Anyway, interesting connection. You can see some of our furniture Mary collected and all the cooking she does and *ningyo* in the other room and so on.

MI: You know, I got the *tansu* and coffee table through his job. Other people were worst off and he could buy through his job, so I bought them furniture.

SS: *How long were you in Japan?*

II: 1949 to 1951. They had to come a little bit later. Our first daughter was a little baby at that time.

MI: She was a year and half.

II: Well, the unit—the Sociological Research and Public Opinion—was dissolving in the summer of 1951 and 1951 was the year in which the occupation ended. Okinawa was still a part of the occupation and there was the question of what the future of Okinawa should be. Should it become an independent country, should it be returned to Japan, or should it become a territory like Pacific Islands. And that was the big question before the administration. And a unit called Trust Territory of the Pacific in the Washington, D.C. wanted somebody to do a survey on the problem. So, when the other members of the Bureau of Sociological Research Division had to go back or wanted to go back to teaching positions or whatever, I didn't have a job. I was out of graduate school and had materials gathered for my PhD dissertation so I was invited to pick up this project. And I took three Japanese women and went down to Okinawa to do this survey from Okinawa to Amami Oshima, Ryukyu Islands.

And, we did that survey, and I finished around November and December. By that time, the director of that unit was at Ohio State and he got a grant from the Office of Naval Research to write up a report we did during the occupation periods, called Japan Studies, Japanese Studies. So, when I finished that Okinawa survey, we went to Ohio State, and worked on the book we wrote, writing up the material, language, foreign project. In 1956, five years later, by this time, I was an assistant professor at Ohio State. In 1956, Michigan State University, under President John Hannah, was expanding rapidly. And they were bringing a number of professors here. So I came here. I was interested in Michigan State because why? Michigan State by this time had started this project studying Okinawa at Okinawa University. And that was because I was in Okinawa in 1951, and I was interested in returning there as part of the Michigan State project. So, I accepted the job at Michigan State and came here in 1956 and stayed here for the rest of my academic career, except for the fact that I had occasionally left. I spent two years in Okinawa and a year of Fulbright in the University of Tokyo and we did a survey at Japanese Sociological Museum and so on. The point is it was that reason I came to Michigan State. The last year was fiftieth anniversary at the university.

MI: At Ohio State, we had two girls. Katherine and Susie were born in 1952 and 1954. And, 1962, Tomi was born. And I don't know what you wanna know. I just came along with you, Iwao. One thing I like to stress is I'm fortunate to have had my education before the war.

II: For twenty years, she's been doing the flower arrangement at the University Club. But, you've also done substitute teaching, and you've also been involved in… what is that called? … language learning?

MI: Helping class. It's not English as Second Language.

II: Literacy program… You should tell that earlier, when we came here, because you were working on ikebana, you started taking up pottery.

MI: I made… I took a pottery class because we had four children and in order to… pottery, I took up… ikebana and pottery. I took ceramics at MSU. I took three years of it.

On the Tennis Court [Ishino]

II: She has a collection now, over two hundred bowls now. I just want to make a point that this *ikebana* thing in the occupation led to all of these kind of things, you see—teaching a class, becoming the President of the Women's Club, and so on because she got involved in ikebana. Just last weekend, at the Kresge Art Center, in the garden, fundraising activity.

One of the consequences of coming here was that we had four daughters, and none of them married a Sansei for pretty obvious reasons—because we have such a small Nikkei community that they married outside the group. So, in many ways, our children's life and our grandchildren's are really quite different from what goes on in places like Los Angeles and San Francisco. But I try to keep up with what's going on over there because I take the *Rafu Shimpo* daily. And I subscribe to the *Amerasia Journal,* and I used to teach a course in human relations and so on. From the point of view of my own life and my children's life, these pictures show, there's no connection, little influence on them. One of the reasons I'm trying to write, put together data on my life is to give my grandchildren some sense of what kind of world we were raised in and what experiences we had. These are the pictures of our grandchildren.

Do you want to say anything about that? How different our life is from the West Coast?

MI: Oh, yeah. There are more Nisei and Sansei that marry Asians.

II: You know, over a half of them marry outside of the Nikkei community.

MI: Let's see. Billy married Japanese, but the rest—one married Chinese.

II: From Singapore, huh?

MI: Yeah.

II: Her daughter is a professional tennis player.

MI: She married South African.

II: Talking a little bit about children's experience because I had my Fulbright 1958, '59 in Tokyo, our children were able to go to Japan and meet with my relatives. I had an uncle who has a family in Tokyo, so some of the pictures, some chance to getting to know, at least meeting, Tokyo relatives. This is the uncle, his name is Ikeuchi. One of his sons was an architect, Ishikawajima shipping company, I think. He spent five years in Brazil with a company there. The other son is a banker, at the number two bank in Tokyo.

II: Tomi, our youngest one, was the only one that was in any way engaged in JACL activities. She was in Junior JACL, and took a couple of kids with her. There was a meeting in Salt Lake City we took her to. Didn't we go to one in San Diego? Anyway, she is not active any more. We need to encourage her to get involved again. She is the one that had the twins.

SS: *I want to go back to my question about the Asian American community in the Lansing area.*

II: Not very active out there. We have five or six Nisei families who live here. But we are not close together. We have gone our own way... for professional good.

MI: But, we have that Mid-Michigan Asian Pacific — not Asian American but Asian Pacific.

II: Are you familiar with that MAPA that they call it? I've been active in that group. Since 9/11, the city of Lansing has tried to organize a group called Unity in Community, and I've been participating in that group. It's an intent to bring different ethnic groups together. That's

about all I know. My major concern is trying to pull some literatures together on history of the Japanese Americans for my grandchildren...

MI: We are working...

SS: *How about the Detroit area?*

II: You see, we try to keep up. We are the only ones from here trying to keep up with what's going on with the Detroit Asian community. We live so far away that we can only participate in a limited extent.

MI: I think Pauline and Tom Nishi...

II: are beginning to get...

MI: He did the...

II: Yeah, he did the letters.

MI: But, I don't think any group here... Japanese American...

SS: *Now, how important is it for you to be a part of this Japanese American community?*

II: Well, the fact is that there isn't such a community here, and that's why I wish there were a community, but there isn't, so we participate in organizations like MAPA or Unity in Community. We try to participate in JACL in Detroit, but that's it. And, of course, I try to keep up with literatures, *Rafu Shimpo* and JACL.

MI: We don't have any Japanese American community here.

SS: *How do you feel about the lack of the community?*

MI: We just get involved in various activities, what there is to participate in.

II: We participate in the university's Asian Pacific Center and my former department of anthropology. There is no Japanese American community and that's sad to tell you the truth.

SS: *My last question is, what would you like to tell the future generations?*

II: Well, I think that participation in a project like this oral history [is necessary] to pass on what our view of our world was. But, also I'm interested in the question of what happened in the past and constantly revising history, and particularly interested in the post-World War II development of the Nikkei community. Actually, it is falling apart in some aspect... Japanese American historical society—one in San Francisco and we belong to San Diego historical society and we get newsletters and so on. The editor is asking me to write about my childhood experience in San Diego, but I'm a little embarrassed about that. Just recently I gave a lecture at the Lansing Community College. I used a video tape that the San Diego historical group put together and showed that to the Lansing Community College, and students wrote a report talking about my tape and gave copies of that to Japanese American Historical Society of San Diego. I try to keep...

MI: I don't know, I just feel that we participate in what we can and people treat us as individuals and not Japanese American. They don't categorize us as Japanese Americans.

II: I think they do though. I feel that I gain, in terms of my own professional career kind of things. I'm thinking, "Oh, good!" factors in selecting me in positions that I'm Japanese American that I don't think my talents or skills are up to. For example, I was the director of the Anthropology Program at the National Science Foundation and gave out millions of dollars to various kind of research. If I were not Japanese American, I had no connection with my Harvard professors, I wouldn't have been given that position. Similarly when I was the assistant dean in the International program, one part of the my appointment was due to the fact I'm Japanese American.

MI: I don't think so...

II: Well, that's my opinion.

MI: I think it's your talent.

II: Well, when I was the chairman of the Anthropology Department during the crisis, again, I don't think I would've been appointed chairman except for the fact I'm Japanese American. Affirmative action kind of thing.

MI: I think...

II: I know you have talents. That's one way, I told you at the beginning of this, a lot of things that happened in the past really influence the person in unknown ways.

I call it *unintended consequences.*

*I'm trying to... give my
grandchildren some sense of
what kind of world we were raised
in and what experiences we had.*

Iwao Ishino

Ishino Family [Ishino]

We believe this is an eye-opener to the public and have to let the students know, firsthand, since they will not learn any of this from their history books.

– Mary Kamidoi

Printed in the USA
CPSIA information can be obtained
at www.ICGtesting.com
CBHW040905290224
4751CB00002B/3